TI-84 Plus Graph[ing] Calculator For Dum[mies]

D0088789

Important Keystrokes

- [ON]: Turns the calculator on. While the calculator is on, pressing this key stops the calculator from drawing a graph, transmitting files between two calculators, evaluating an expression, and so on.
- [2nd][ON]: Turns the calculator off.
- [2nd][MODE]: Returns you to the Home screen.
- [ENTER]: Executes commands and evaluates expressions.
- [CLEAR]: Erases the last entry; erases the Home screen.
- [DEL]: Deletes the symbol under the cursor.
- [2nd][DEL]: Inserts symbols to the left of the cursor.
- [2nd]: Used to access the secondary functions (labeled in yellow above the keys).
- [ALPHA]: Used to access the green letters above the keys.
- [X,T,Θ,n]: Pastes the variable into the definition of a function.
- [2nd][ENTER]: Copies the last entry onto the Home screen.
- [2nd][(-)]: Pastes the last answer into an expression.
- [STO▸]: Assigns a value to a variable.

Special Menus

- **Angles:** Press [2nd][APPS]. (On the TI-83, press [2nd][MATRX].)
- **Catalog:** Press [2nd][0].
- **Complex:** Press [MATH][▸][▸].
- **Distribution (Chi-square, . . .):** Press [2nd][VARS].
- **Draw:** Press [2nd][PRGM].
- **Finances:** Press [APPS][ENTER]. (On the TI-83, press [2nd][x⁻¹].)
- **Link:** Press [2nd][STAT].
- **Math:** Press [MATH]. Also look in the [MATH][▸] menu.
- **Matrix:** Press [2nd][x⁻¹]. (On the TI-83, press [MATRX].)
- **Probability:** Press [MATH][▸][▸][▸].
- **Program:** Press [PRGM].
- **Statistics:** Press [STAT].
- **Test (=, ÷, >, . . .):** Press [2nd][MATH].
- **Y-Variables (Y₁, X₁ₜ, r₁, . . .):** Press [VARS][▸] and select the appropriate menu.

TI-84 Plus Graphing Calculator For Dummies®

Cheat Sheet

Zoom Commands

✔ **ZBox:** Draws a box around a portion of the graph and redraws the graph in a viewing window that has the dimensions of the box.

✔ **Zoom In:** Zooms in on the graph at the location of the cursor.

✔ **Zoom Out:** Zooms out on the graph at the location of the cursor.

✔ **ZDecimal:** Draws the graph in a $-4.7 \leq x \leq 4.7$, $-4.7 \leq y \leq 4.7$ window. When the graph is traced, the x-coordinate of the trace cursor equals an integral multiple of 0.1.

✔ **ZSquare:** Redraws the graph in a window that makes circles look like circles instead of ellipses.

✔ **ZStandard:** Draws the graph in a $-10 \leq x \leq 10$, $-10 \leq y \leq 10$ window.

✔ **ZTrig:** Draws the graph in a $-47\pi/24 \leq x \leq 47\pi/24$, $-47\pi/24 \leq y \leq 47\pi/24$ window. When the graph is traced, the x-coordinate of the trace cursor equals an integral multiple of $\pi/24$.

✔ **ZInteger:** Redraws the graph so that when it is traced, the x-coordinate of the trace cursor equals an integer.

✔ **ZoomStat:** Finds an appropriate viewing window for stat plots.

✔ **ZoomFit:** Finds an appropriate viewing window for graphing functions, parametric equations, polar equations, or sequences.

The Basics of Graphing

✔ Press MODE to set the Mode for graphing functions (**Func**), parametric equations (**Par**), polar equations (**Pol**), or sequences (**Seq**).

✔ Press Y= to enter the function in the **Y=** editor.

✔ Press 2nd ZOOM to set the Format for the graph.

✔ Press WINDOW to set the Window for the graph and then press GRAPH or press ZOOM to use a Zoom command.

Math Functions & Constants

✔ Θ: Press ALPHA 3.

✔ π: Press 2nd ^.

✔ e: Press 2nd ÷.

✔ e^x: Press 2nd LN.

✔ 10^x: Press 2nd LOG.

✔ ²: Press 2nd x^2.

For Dummies: Bestselling Book Series for Beginners

TI-84 Plus Graphing Calculator

FOR

DUMMIES®

by C. C. Edwards

WILEY

Wiley Publishing, Inc.

TI-84 Plus Graphing Calculator For Dummies®

Published by
Wiley Publishing, Inc.
111 River Street
Hoboken, NJ 07030-5774

WILEY

About the Author

C. C. Edwards has a Ph.D. in mathematics from the University of Wisconsin, Milwaukee, and is currently teaching mathematics on the undergraduate and graduate levels. She has been using technology in the classroom since before Texas Instruments came out with their first graphing calculator, and she frequently gives workshops at national and international conferences on using technology in the classroom. She has written forty activities for Texas Instrument's Explorations Web site, and she was an editor of *Eightysomething*, a newsletter formerly published by Texas Instruments. She is also the author of *TI-83 Plus Graphing Calculator For Dummies*.

Just barely five feet tall, CC, as her friends call her, has three goals in life: to be six inches taller, to have naturally curly hair, and to be independently wealthy. As yet, she is nowhere close to meeting any of these goals. When she retires, she plans to become an old lady carpenter.

Dedication

This book is dedicated to Mrs. Clark, my tenth grade geometry teacher. She taught me the beauty of mathematics in general, and of geometry in particular. But most importantly, she taught me what it means to be a mathematician. She did this by giving me a C as my first quarter grade in her course. That's the best wake-up call I've ever gotten in my academic life.

Author's Acknowledgments

I'd like to thank the folks at John Wiley & Sons who worked behind the scenes on the creation of this book. I don't come in contact with many of these people until the book is in the editing stage, which takes place after I write the acknowledgments. But from past experience I know that they do an extremely good job. Unfortunately, I can't tell you about it at this time. Their names appear in the Publisher's Acknowledgments.

The Wiley people I have been dealing with so far are the same people I worked with on the *TI-83 Plus Graphing Calculator For Dummies* book: Melody Layne, acquisitions editor, and Christopher Morris, project editor. As usual, Melody has given me many superb ideas for the book and has been a great liaison with Texas Instruments. And Chris, as before, has given me extremely good criticism. It's hard to disagree with Chris because he's usually right on target with his criticism.

I'd also like to thank the folks at Texas Instruments for helping me with several rather complicated technical dilemmas.

On the home front, I thank all of my academic colleagues, with particular thanks going to Ioana Mihaila, Bogdan Mihaila, Olcay Akman, and Fusun Akman. I also thank their children, Iulia, Cornelia, and Devin, who truly "light up my life." And I thank the other important people in my life who have not seen much of me while I was working on "the book." In particular I must, as corny as it sounds, thank my border collies, Nip and Tess, for putting up with fewer walks and less play time.

Publisher's Acknowledgments

We're proud of this book; please send us your comments through our online registration form located at www.dummies.com/register/.

Some of the people who helped bring this book to market include the following:

Acquisitions, Editorial, and Media Development

Project Editor: Christopher Morris

Acquisitions Editor: Melody Layne

Copy Editor: Jean Rogers

Technical Editor: Dr. Douglas Shaw, University of Northern Iowa

Editorial Manager: Kevin Kirschner

Permissions Editor: Laura Moss

Media Development Manager: Laura VanWinkle

Media Development Supervisor: Richard Graves

Editorial Assistant: Amanda Foxworth

Cartoons: Rich Tennant (www.the5thwave.com)

Production

Project Coordinator: Courtney MacIntyre

Layout and Graphics: Lauren Goddard, Denny Hager, Lynsey Osborn, Jacque Schneider, Julie Trippetti

Proofreaders: Andy Hollandbeck, Carl William Pierce, Dwight Ramsey, Brian H. Walls, TECHBOOKS Production Services

Indexer: TECHBOOKS Production Services

Publishing and Editorial for Technology Dummies

Richard Swadley, Vice President and Executive Group Publisher

Andy Cummings, Vice President and Publisher

Mary C. Corder, Editorial Director

Publishing for Consumer Dummies

Diane Graves Steele, Vice President and Publisher

Joyce Pepple, Acquisitions Director

Composition Services

Gerry Fahey, Vice President of Production Services

Debbie Stailey, Director of Composition Services

Contents at a Glance

Introduction *1*

Part I: Making Friends with the Calculator *7*
Chapter 1: Coping with the Basics 9
Chapter 2: Doing Basic Arithmetic 21
Chapter 3: The Math and Angle Menus 29
Chapter 4: Solving Equations 39

Part II: Doing Geometry *45*
Chapter 5: Using GeoMaster 47
Chapter 6: Constructing Geometric Figures 57
Chapter 7: Finding Measurements 81
Chapter 8: Performing Transformations 93

Part III: Graphing and Analyzing Functions *101*
Chapter 9: Graphing Functions 103
Chapter 10: Exploring Functions 117
Chapter 11: Evaluating Functions 129
Chapter 12: Graphing Transformations 139
Chapter 13: Graphing Inequalities 149

Part IV: Probability and Statistics *165*
Chapter 14: Probability 167
Chapter 15: Simulating Probabilities 171
Chapter 16: Dealing with Statistical Data 191
Chapter 17: Analyzing Statistical Data 199

*Part V: Communicating with PCs
and Other Calculators* *211*
Chapter 18: Communicating with a PC Using TI Connect™ 213
Chapter 19: Communicating Between Calculators 217

Part VI: The Part of Tens *223*
Chapter 20: Eight Topics That Didn't Make the Book 225
Chapter 21: Ten Great Applications 229
Chapter 22: Eight Common Errors 233
Chapter 23: Eleven Common Error Messages 237

Appendix A: Creating and Editing Matrices *241*

Appendix B: Using Matrices *247*

Index *253*

Table of Contents

Introduction *1*

About This Book 1

Conventions Used in This Book 2

What You're Not to Read 2

Foolish Assumptions 3

How This Book Is Organized 3

    Part I: Making Friends with the Calculator 3

    Part II: Doing Geometry 3

    Part III: Graphing and Analyzing Functions 4

    Part IV: Probability and Statistics 4

    Part V: Communicating with PCs

        and Other Calculators 4

    Part VI: The Part of Tens 4

Icons Used in This Book 4

Where to Go from Here 5

Part 1: Making Friends with the Calculator *7*

Chapter 1: Coping with the Basics 9

When to Change the Batteries 9

Turning the Calculator On and Off 10

Using the Keyboard 10

    Accessing the functions in blue 11

    Using the [ALPHA] key to write words 11

    Using the [ENTER] key 12

    Using the [X,T,Θ,n] key 12

    Using the arrow keys 12

What Is the Home Screen? 13

The Busy Indicator 13

Editing Entries 13

Using Menus 14

    Accessing a menu 14

    Scrolling a menu 15

    Selecting menu items 15

Setting the Mode 16

Using the Catalog 18

Chapter 2: Doing Basic Arithmetic 21

Entering and Evaluating Expressions 21

Important Keys 22

Order of Operations 23

Using the Previous Answer 25
Recycling the Last Entry 25
Storing Variables 26
Combining Expressions 28

Chapter 3: The Math and Angle Menus 29

The Math Menu and Submenus 29
    Using Math menu functions 30
    Inserting a Math menu function 30
    The Math MATH submenu 31
    The Math NUM submenu 33
The Angle Menu 34
    Converting degrees to radians 35
    Converting radians to degrees 36
    Converting between degrees and DMS 36
    Entering angles in DMS measure 37
    Overriding the mode of the angle 37

Chapter 4: Solving Equations 39

Using the Equation Solver 39
    Step 1. Set the mode 40
    Step 2. Enter or edit the equation to be solved 40
    Step 3. Assign values to variables 41
    Step 4. Define the solution bounds 42
    Step 5. Guess a solution 42
    Step 6. Solve the equation 43
Finding Multiple Solutions 44

Part II: Doing Geometry *45*

Chapter 5: Using GeoMaster 47

Starting GeoMaster 49
Quitting GeoMaster 50
Creating and Saving Files 51
Recalling and Deleting Files 52
Using Menus 53
Clearing the Screen 55

Chapter 6: Constructing Geometric Figures 57

Constructing Points 57
Constructing Lines, Segments, Rays, and Vectors 59
Constructing Circles 60
Constructing Triangles and Arcs 62
Constructing Polygons 63
Constructing Regular Polygons 65

Constructing Perpendicular and Parallel Lines 66
Constructing Perpendicular Bisectors 68
Constructing Angle Bisectors 68
Constructing Points of Intersection 70
Constructing a Point on an Object 71
Constructing a Midpoint 71
Moving Figures 72
Determining If Two Lines Are Parallel or Perpendicular 74
Determining If Three Points Are Collinear 76
Hiding and Deleting Objects 77
    Hiding an object 77
    Redisplaying hidden objects 78
    Deleting objects 78
Adjusting the Viewing Window 79

Chapter 7: Finding Measurements 81

Finding Length and Distance 81
Finding Area 82
    Finding the area of a polygon having
        intersecting sides 84
    Finding the area of the intersection
        of two polygons 85
Measuring an Angle 86
Performing Calculations 88
Finding Slope 89
Constructing a Vector Sum 90
Finding the Equation of a Line/Circle or
    the Coordinates of a Point 91

Chapter 8: Performing Transformations 93

Translating a Geometric Object 93
Reflecting Geometric Objects 94
Rotating Geometric Objects 95
Dilating Geometric Objects 97
Tiling the Plane 98

Part III: Graphing and Analyzing Functions 101

Chapter 9: Graphing Functions 103

Entering Functions 103
Graphing Functions 105
Graphing Several Functions 108
Is Your Graph Accurate? 110
Piecewise-Defined Functions 112
Graphing Trig Functions 113

Viewing the Function and Graph on the Same Screen 114
Saving and Recalling a Graph 115

Chapter 10: Exploring Functions 117

Using Zoom Commands 117
Tracing a Graph 121
Displaying Functions in a Table 122
Clearing a Table 126
Viewing the Table and the Graph on the Same Screen 126

Chapter 11: Evaluating Functions 129

Finding the Value of a Function 129
Finding the Zeros of a Function 131
Finding Min & Max 133
Finding Points of Intersection 134
Finding the Slope of a Curve 135
Evaluating a Definite Integral 137

Chapter 12: Graphing Transformations 139

Starting Transformation Graphing 139
Quitting Transformation Graphing 141
Entering Functions 141
Graphing Transformations 142
Creating a Slide Show 145
Graphing Transformations of Two
    or More Functions 147

Chapter 13: Graphing Inequalities 149

Starting Inequality Graphing 149
Quitting Inequality Graphing 151
Entering Functions and Inequalities 151
    Entering inequalities in the Y= editor 151
    Entering inequalities in the X= editor 153
Graphing Inequalities 154
Exploring a Graph 154
    Shading unions and intersections 155
    Finding the points of intersection 156
    Other ways to explore a graph 158
Storing Data Points 158
    Clearing the INEQX and INEQY lists 159
    Storing points in INEQX and INEQY 159
    Viewing stored data 160
Solving Linear Programming Problems 161

Part 1V: Probability and Statistics *165*

Chapter 14: Probability 167

Permutations and Combinations 167
Generating Random Numbers 168
    Generating random integers 168
    Generating random decimals 169

Chapter 15: Simulating Probabilities 171

Starting and Quitting Probability Simulation 171
Using the Probability Simulation Application 172
    Executing the commands at the bottom
        of the screen 172
    Seeding the random number generator 173
    Going back to the previous screen using
        the ESC command 174
Understanding the Settings Editor 174
    Trial Set 174
    Graph and table settings 174
    Weighted outcomes 175
Tossing Coins 176
    Simulating the tossing of coins 176
    Reading the graph and table 178
Rolling Dice 179
    Simulating the rolling of dice 180
    Reading the graph and table 181
Picking Marbles from an Urn 182
    Simulating picking marbles 182
    Reading the graph and table 184
Spinning a Spinner 185
    Simulating spinning spinners 186
    Reading the graph and table 187
Drawing Cards from a Deck 188
    Simulating drawing cards 188
    Saving the Draw Cards simulator's data 189

Chapter 16: Dealing with Statistical Data 191

Entering Data 191
Deleting and Editing Data 193
Creating User-Named Data Lists 194
Using Formulas to Enter Data 195
Saving and Recalling Data Lists 196
Sorting Data Lists 197

Chapter 17: Analyzing Statistical Data **199**

Plotting One-Variable Data 199
  Constructing a histogram 200
  Constructing a box plot 202
Plotting Two-Variable Data 203
Tracing Statistical Data Plots 204
Analyzing Statistical Data 205
  One-variable data analysis 206
  Two-variable data analysis 207
Regression Models 208

Part V: Communicating with PCs
and Other Calculators *211*

Chapter 18: Communicating with a PC
Using TI Connect™ **213**

Downloading TI Connect 213
Installing and Running TI Connect 214
Connecting Calculator and PC 214
Transferring Files 215
Upgrading the OS 216

Chapter 19: Communicating Between
Calculators **217**

Linking Calculators 217
Transferring Files 218
Transferring Files to Several Calculators 220

Part VI: The Part of Tens *223*

Chapter 20: Eight Topics That Didn't Make
the Book **225**

Topics on Wiley's Web Site 225
Topics in the TI-83 For Dummies Book 226

Chapter 21: Ten Great Applications **229**

Ten Great Applications 229
Downloading an Application 230
Installing an Application 231

Chapter 22: Eight Common Errors **233**

Using ⊟ Instead of ⊡ to Indicate That a Number
  Is Negative 233
Indicating the Order of Operations Incorrectly
  by Using Parentheses 233

Improperly Entering the Argument
for Menu Functions 234
Entering an Angle in Degrees While in Radian Mode 234
Graphing Trigonometric Functions While
in Degree Mode 234
Graphing Functions When Stat Plots Are Active 235
Graphing Stat Plots When Functions or Other
Stat Plots Are Active 235
Setting the Window Inappropriately for Graphing 235

Chapter 23: Eleven Common Error Messages 237

ARGUMENT 237
BAD GUESS 238
DATA TYPE 238
DIM MISMATCH 238
DOMAIN 238
INVALID 238
INVALID DIM 239
NO SIGN CHNG 239
SINGULAR MAT 239
SYNTAX 239
WINDOW RANGE 239

Appendix A: Creating and Editing Matrices.......241

Defining a Matrix...241
Editing a Matrix...243
Displaying Matrices 243
Augmenting Two Matrices 243
Copying One Matrix to Another...244
Deleting a Matrix from Memory 245

Appendix B: Using Matrices...............................247

Matrix Arithmetic...247
Finding the Determinant 250
Solving a System of Equations 251

Index *253*

Introduction

● ●

Do you know how to use the TI-83 Plus or TI-84 Plus family of calculators to do each of the following?

- ✔ Create and investigate geometric figures

- ✔ Graph functions, inequalities, or transformations of functions

- ✔ Create stat plots and analyze statistical data

- ✔ Simulate probability experiments like tossing coins, rolling dice, and so on

- ✔ Write calculator programs

- ✔ Transfer files between two or more calculators

- ✔ Save calculator files on your computer

- ✔ Add applications to your calculator so that it can do even more than it could when you bought it

If not, then this is the book for you. Contained within these pages are straightforward, easy-to-follow directions that tell how to do everything listed here — and much, much more.

About This Book

Although this book does not tell you how to do *everything* the calculator is capable of doing, it gets pretty close. It covers more than just the basics of using the calculator, paying special attention to warning you of the problems that you could encounter if you knew only the basics of using the calculator.

This is a reference book. It's process-driven, not application-driven. You won't be given a problem to solve and then be told how to use the calculator to solve that particular problem. Instead, you're given the steps needed to get the calculator to perform a particular task, such as constructing a histogram or perpendicular line.

Conventions Used in This Book

When I refer to "the calculator," I am referring to the TI-83 Plus and
TI-84 Plus family of calculators because the keystrokes on these
calculators are the same. When I want you to press a key on the
calculator, I use an icon for that key. For example, if I want you to
press the ENTER key, I say press [ENTER]. If I want you to press a
series of keys, such as the Stat key and then the right-arrow key, I
say (for example) press [STAT][▶]. All keys on the calculator are
pressed one at a time. On the calculator, there is no such thing as
holding down one key while you press another key.

It's tricky enough to get handy with the location of the keys on the
calculator, and even more of a challenge to remember the location
of the secondary functions, such as the blue functions on the TI-84
or the yellow functions on the TI-83 that appear above the key. So
when I want you to access one of those functions, I give you the
actual keystrokes. For example, if I want you to access the Draw
menu, I tell you to press [2nd][PRGM]. This is a simpler method than
that of the manual that came with your calculator — which would
say press [2nd][DRAW] and then make you hunt for the location of the
secondary function DRAW. The same principle holds for using key
combinations to enter specific characters; for example, I tell you to
press [ALPHA][0] to enter a space.

When I want you to use the arrow keys, but not in any specific
order, I say press [▶][◀][▲][▼] or use the arrow keys. If I want you to
use only the up- and down-arrow keys, I say press [▲][▼].

What You're Not to Read

Of course, you don't have to read anything you don't want to. The
only items in this book that really don't need to be read are the
items that follow a Technical Stuff icon. These items are designed
for the curious reader who wants to know — but doesn't really
need to know — why something happens.

Other items that you may not need to read are the paragraphs that
follow the steps in a procedure. These paragraphs are designed to
give you extra help should you need it. The steps themselves are in
bold; the explanatory paragraphs are in a normal font.

Foolish Assumptions

My nonfoolish assumption is that you know (in effect) nothing about using the calculator, or you wouldn't be reading this book. My foolish assumptions are as follows:

✔ You own, or have access to, one of the TI-83 Plus or TI-84 Plus family of calculators.

✔ If you want to transfer files from your calculator to your computer, I assume that you have a computer and know the basics of how to operate it.

✔ If you want to write programs on your calculator, I assume that you have some (albeit minor) experience in programming, but not necessarily on the calculator.

How This Book Is Organized

The parts of this book are organized by tasks that you would like to have the calculator perform.

Part I: Making Friends with the Calculator

This part describes the basics of using the calculator. It addresses such tasks as adjusting the contrast and getting the calculator to perform basic arithmetic operations. It also tells you how to deal with angles and how to solve equations.

Part II: Doing Geometry

This part tells you how to use the GeoMaster application to construct and investigate geometric figures. It tells you, among many other things, how to construct perpendicular lines or how to determine if two already constructed lines are perpendicular.

If you'd rather use the Cabri Jr. application for your geometric constructions, you can find information about this application on Wiley's Web site. The address of this Web site appears at the end of the Introduction.

Part III: Graphing and Analyzing Functions

In this part, think visual. Part III tells you how to graph and analyze functions, inequalities, and transformations of functions. It even tells you how to create a table for the graph, inequality, or transformation.

Part IV: Probability and Statistics

It's highly probable that Part IV will tell you how not only how to deal with probability and statistics, but it will also tell you how to get the calculator to simulate tossing coins, rolling dice, picking marbles from an urn, and drawing a card from a deck.

Part V: Communicating with PCs and Other Calculators

Your calculator joins the information superhighway. Part V describes how you can save calculator files on a computer and how you can transfer files from one calculator to another.

Part VI: The Part of Tens

Part VI contains a plethora of wonderful information. This part tells you about the many wonderful applications that you can put on your calculator, and it describes the most common errors and error messages that you may encounter. It also tells you about the topics that didn't fit in this book and where you can find them.

Icons Used in This Book

This book uses four icons to help you along the way. Here's what they are and what they mean:

The text following this icon tells you about shortcut and other ways of enhancing your use of the calculator.

The text following this icon tells you something you should remember because if you don't, it may cause you problems later. Usually the Remember icon highlights a reminder to enter the appropriate type of number so that you can avoid an error message.

 There is no such thing as crashing the calculator. But this icon warns you of those *few* times when you can do something wrong on the calculator and be totally baffled because the calculator is giving you confusing feedback — either no error message or a cryptic error message that doesn't really tell you the true location of the problem.

 This is the stuff you don't need to read unless you're really curious.

Where to Go from Here

This book is designed so that you do not have to read it from cover to cover. You don't even have to start reading at the beginning of a chapter. When you want to know how to get the calculator to do something, just start reading at the beginning of the appropriate section. The Index and Table of Contents should help you find whatever you're looking for. And for your first tip on where to find other information:

 See also *TI-83 Plus Graphing Calculator For Dummies,* which contains a wealth of information useful to the TI-84 user. For more about what can be found in *TI-83 Plus Graphing Calculator For Dummies,* see Chapter 20 in this book. And you can find two further topics — doing geometry using Cabri Jr. and programming the calculator — on the Wiley Web site. Check it out at www.dummies.com/go/ti84.

Part I
Making Friends with the Calculator

"IT SAYS HERE IF I SUBSCRIBE TO THIS MAGAZINE, THEY'LL SEND ME A FREE DESK-TOP CALCULATOR. DESKTOP CALCULATOR?!! WHOOAA - WHERE HAVE I BEEN?!!"

In this part . . .

*T*his part takes you once around the block with the basics of using the calculator. In addition to showing you how to use the calculator to evaluate arithmetic expressions, I discuss the elementary calculator functions — including multi-use keys, menus, modes, and the Catalog. I also cover expressions and the order of operations, storing and recalling variables, and combining expressions.

In addition, I explain how to use the numerous functions housed in the Math menu to perform tricks like converting decimals to fractions. Speaking of conversions, I also discuss how to convert angle measurement settings from degrees to radians. And if you've ever wanted a quick, powerful way to do arithmetic with complex numbers, check out the discussion of the Math CPX submenu. Finally, I show you how to solve equations using the calculator's nifty Equation Solver.

Chapter 1

Coping with the Basics

● ●

In This Chapter

▶ Turning the calculator on and off

▶ Using the keyboard

▶ Using the menus

▶ Setting the mode of the calculator

▶ Using the Catalog

● ●

*T*he TI-84 graphing calculator is loaded with many useful features. With them, you can construct and investigate geometric
figures. You can graph and investigate functions, parametric equations, polar equations, and sequences. You can use them to analyze statistical data and to manipulate matrices. You can even use
them to calculate mortgage payments.

But if you've never used a graphing calculator before, you may at
first find it a bit intimidating. After all, it contains about two dozen
menus, many of which contain three or four submenus. But it's
really not that hard to get used to using the calculator. After you
get familiar with what the calculator is capable of doing, finding
the menu that houses the command you need is quite easy. And
you have this book to help you along the way.

When to Change the Batteries

The convenience of battery power has a traditional downside: What
if the batteries run out of juice at a crucial moment, say during a
final exam? Fortunately, the calculator gives you some leeway. When
your batteries are low, the calculator displays a "Your batteries are
low" warning message. After you see this message for the first time,

the calculator should, according to the manufacturer, continue to function just fine for at least one week. There is one exception: If you attempt to download an application when the batteries are low, the calculator displays a "Batteries are low — Change is required" warning message and refuses to download the application until after you've changed the batteries. (Chapter 18 explains how to download applications.)

Because you've likely put batteries into countless toys, you should have no trouble opening the cover on the back of the calculator and popping in four AAA batteries. Above the AAA battery chamber is a panel that opens to the compartment containing the backup battery. The type of battery housed in this compartment is indicated on the lid of the panel. The manufacturer recommends that you replace this battery every three or four years. So mark your calendar!

Turning the Calculator On and Off

Press [ON] to turn the calculator on. To turn the calculator off, press [2nd], and then press [ON]. These keys are in the left column of the keyboard. The [ON] key is at the bottom of the column, and the [2nd] key is the second key from the top of this column.

To prolong the life of the batteries, the calculator automatically turns itself off after five minutes of inactivity. But don't worry — when you press [ON], all your work will appear on the calculator just as you left it before the calculator turned itself off.

In some types of light, the screen can be hard to see. To increase the contrast, press and release [2nd] and then hold down [▲] until you have the desired contrast. To decrease the contrast, press [2nd] and hold [▼].

Using the Keyboard

The row of keys under the calculator screen contains the keys you use when graphing. The next three rows, for the most part, contain editing keys, menu keys, and arrow keys. The arrow keys ([▶][◀][▲][▼]) control the movement of the cursor. The remaining rows contain, among other things, the keys you typically find on a scientific calculator.

Keys on the calculator are always pressed one at a time; they are *never* pressed simultaneously. In this book, an instruction such as [2nd][ON] indicates that you should first press [2nd] and then press [ON].

Accessing the functions in blue

Above and to the left of most keys is a secondary key function written in blue. To access that function, first press [2nd] and then press the key. For example, π is in blue above the [^] key, so to use π in an expression, press [2nd] and then press [^].

Because hunting for the function in blue can be tedious, in this book I use only the actual keystrokes. For example, I will make statements like, "π is entered into the calculator by pressing [2nd][^]." Most other books would state, "π is entered into the calculator by pressing [2nd] [π]."

When the [2nd] key is active and the calculator is waiting for you to press the next key, the blinking ■ cursor symbol is replaced with the ◻ symbol.

Using the [ALPHA] key to write words

Above and to the right of most keys is a letter written in green. To access these letters, first press [ALPHA] and then press the key. For example, because the letter O is in green above the [7] key, to enter this letter, press [ALPHA] and then press [7].

Keys to remember

The following keystrokes are invaluable:

✔ [2nd][MODE]: This is the equivalent of the Escape key on a computer. It gets you out of whatever you're doing (or have finished doing) and returns you to the Home screen. The Home screen is where the action takes place. This is where you execute commands and evaluate expressions.

✔ [ENTER]: This key is used to execute commands and to evaluate expressions. When evaluating expressions, it's the equivalent of the equal sign.

✔ [CLEAR]: This is the "erase" key. If you're entering something into the calculator and change your mind, press this key. If you want to erase the contents of the Home screen, repeatedly press this key until the Home screen is blank.

Because hunting for letters on the calculator can be tedious, I tell you the exact keystrokes needed to create them. For example, if I want you to enter the letter O, I say, "Press ALPHA 7 to enter the letter O." Most other books would say "Press ALPHA [O]" and leave it up to you to figure out where that letter is on the calculator.

You must press ALPHA before entering each letter. However, if you want to enter many letters, first press 2nd ALPHA to lock the calculator in Alpha mode. Then all you have to do is press the keys for the various letters. When you're finished, press ALPHA to take the calculator out of Alpha mode. For example, to enter the word TEST into the calculator, press 2nd ALPHA 4 SIN LN 4 and then press ALPHA to tell the calculator that you're no longer entering letters.

When the calculator is in Alpha mode, the blinking ■ cursor symbol is replaced with the ▯ symbol. This symbol indicates that the next key you press will insert the green letter above that key. To take the calculator out of Alpha mode, press ALPHA.

Using the ENTER key

The ENTER key is used to evaluate expressions and to execute commands. After you have, for example, entered an arithmetic expression (such as 5 + 4), press ENTER to evaluate that expression. In this context, the ENTER key functions as the equal sign. Entering arithmetic expressions is explained in Chapter 2.

Using the X,T,Θ,n key

X,T,Θ,n is the key you use to enter the variable in the definition of a function, a parametric equation, a polar equation, or a sequence. In Function mode, this key produces the variable **X**. In Parametric mode it produces the variable **T**; and in Polar and Sequence modes it produces the variables θ and *n*, respectively. Setting the mode is explained later in this chapter.

Using the arrow keys

The arrow keys (▶, ◀, ▲, and ▼) control the movement of the cursor. These keys are in a circular pattern in the upper-right corner of the keyboard. As expected, ▶ moves the cursor to the right, ◀ moves it to the left, and so on. When I want you to use the arrow keys — but not in any specific order — I refer to them all together, as in "Use ▶◀▲▼ to place the cursor on the entry."

What Is the Home Screen?

The Home screen is the screen that appears on the calculator when you first turn it on. This is the screen where most of the action takes place as you use the calculator — it's where you evaluate expressions and execute commands. This is also the screen you usually return to after you've completed a task such as entering a matrix in the Matrix editor or entering data in the Stat List editor.

Press [2nd][MODE] to return to the Home screen from any other screen. This combination of keystrokes, [2nd][MODE], is the equivalent of the Escape key on a computer. It always takes you back to the Home screen.

If you want to clear the contents of the Home screen, repeatedly press [CLEAR] until the Home screen is blank.

The Busy Indicator

If you see a moving vertical line in the upper-right corner of the screen, this indicates that the calculator is busy graphing a function, evaluating an expression, or executing a command.

If it's taking too long for the calculator to graph a function, evaluate an expression, or execute a command, and you want to abort the process, press [ON]. If you're then confronted with a menu that asks you to select either **Quit** or **Goto**, select **Quit** to abort the process.

Editing Entries

The calculator offers four ways to edit an entry:

~ **Deleting the entire entry:**

Use [▶][◀][▲][▼] to place the cursor anywhere in the entry and then press [CLEAR] and to delete the entry.

~ **Erasing part of an entry:**

To erase a single character, use [▶][◀][▲][▼] to place the cursor on the character you want to delete and then press [DEL] to delete that character.

✔ **Inserting characters:**

Because "typing over" is the default mode, to insert characters you must first press 2nd DEL to enter Insert mode. When you insert characters, the inserted characters are placed to the left of the cursor. For example, if you want to insert CD between B and E in the word ABEF, you would place the cursor on E to make the insertion.

To insert characters, use ▶ ◀ ▲ ▼ to place the cursor at the location of the desired insertion, press 2nd DEL, and then key in the characters you want to insert. When you're finished inserting characters, press one of the arrow keys to take the calculator out of Insert mode.

✔ **Keying over existing characters:**

"Type over" is the default mode of the calculator. So if you want to overtype existing characters, just use ▶ ◀ ▲ ▼ to put the cursor where you want to start, and then use the keyboard to enter new characters.

On the Home screen, the calculator doesn't allow you to directly edit an already-evaluated expression or an already-executed command. But you *can* recall that expression or command if it was the last entry you made in the calculator — and when it's recalled, you can edit it. To recall the last expression or command, press 2nd ENTER. This makes the calculator paste a copy of the desired expression or command on the Home screen so you can edit it.

Using Menus

Most functions and commands you use are found in the menus housed in the calculator — and just about every chapter in this book refers to them. This section is designed to give you an overview of how to find and select menu items.

Accessing a menu

Each menu has its own key or key combination. For example, to access the Math menu, press MATH; to access the Test menu, press 2nd MATH. An example of a menu appears in the first picture in Figure 1-1. This is a picture of the Math menu.

Some menus, such as the Math menu, contain submenus. This is also illustrated in the first picture in Figure 1-1. This picture shows that the submenus in the Math menu are MATH, NUM, CPX, and PRB (Math, Number, Complex, and Probability). Repeatedly press ▶ to view the items on the other submenus; repeatedly press ◀ to return to the Math MATH submenu. This is illustrated in the second and third pictures in Figure 1-1.

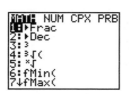

Math MATH menu

Math NUM menu

Math PRB menu

Figure 1-1: Submenus of the Math menu.

Scrolling a menu

After the number 7 in the first two pictures in Figure 1-1, a down arrow indicates that more items are available in the menu than appear on-screen. There's no down arrow after the 7 in the third picture in Figure 1-1 because that menu has exactly seven items.

To see menu items that don't appear on-screen, repeatedly press ▼. To get quickly to the bottom of a menu from the top of the menu, press ▲. Similarly, to quickly get from the bottom to the top, press ▼.

Selecting menu items

To select a menu item from a menu, key in the number (or letter) of the item or use ▼ to highlight the number (or letter) of the item and then press ENTER.

Some menus, such as the Mode menu that is pictured in Figure 1-2, require that you select an item from a list of items by highlighting that item. The list of items usually appear in a single row and the calculator requires that one item in each row be highlighted. To highlight an item, use ▶◀▲▼ to place the cursor on the item and then press ENTER to highlight the item. The selections on the Mode menu are described in the next section.

Setting the Mode

The Mode menu, which is accessed by pressing MODE, is the most important menu on the calculator; it tells the calculator how you want numbers and graphs to be displayed. The Mode menu is pictured in Figure 1-2.

Mode menu   Clock menu

Figure 1-2: The Mode and Clock menus.

One item in each row of this menu must be selected. Here are your choices:

✔ Normal, Sci, or Eng:

This setting controls how numbers are displayed on the calculator. In Normal mode, the calculator displays numbers in the usual numeric fashion that you used in elementary school — provided it can display it using no more than ten digits. If the number requires more than ten digits, the calculator displays it using scientific notation.

In Scientific (**Sci**) mode, numbers are displayed using scientific notation; and in Engineering (**Eng**) mode, numbers are displayed in engineering notation. These three modes are illustrated in Figure 1-3. In this figure, the first answer is displayed in normal notation, the second in scientific notation, and the third in engineering notation.

In scientific and engineering notation, the calculator uses **En** to denote multiplication by 10^n.

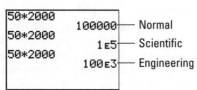

Figure 1-3: Normal, scientific, and engineering notations.

✔ **Float 0123456789:**

Select **Float** if you want the calculator to display as many digits as possible. Select **0** if you want all numbers rounded to an integer. If you're dealing with money, select **2** so that all numbers will be rounded to two decimal places. Selecting **5** rounds all numbers to five decimal places, and, well, you get the idea.

✔ **Radian or Degree:**

If you select **Radian**, all angles entered in the calculator are interpreted as being in radian measure; all angular answers given by the calculator will also be in radian measure. Similarly, if you select **Degree**, any angle you enter must be in degree measure, and any angular answer given by the calculator is also in degree measure.

✔ **Func, Par, Pol, or Seq:**

This setting tells the calculator what type of functions you plan to graph. Select **Func** to graph plain old vanilla functions, $y = f(x)$. Select **Par** to graph parametric equations; **Pol** to graph polar equations; and **Seq** to graph sequences. (Sequences are also called *iterative equations*.)

✔ **Connected or Dot:**

In **Dot** mode, the calculator produces a graph by plotting only the points it calculates. In **Connected** mode, the calculator joins consecutively plotted points with a line.

My recommendation is to select the **Connected** mode because each of the graphing options (**Func**, **Par**, **Pol**, and **Seq**) allows you to select a graphing style, one of which is the dot style.

✔ **Sequential or Simul:**

In **Sequential** mode, the calculator completes the graph of one function before it graphs the next function. In Simultaneous (**Simul**) mode, the calculator graphs all functions at the same time. It does so by plotting the values of all functions for one value of the independent variable, and then plotting the values of all functions for the next value of the independent variable.

Simul mode is useful if you want to see whether two functions intersect at the same value of the independent variable. You have to watch the functions as they are graphed in order to *see* if this happens.

✔ **Real, a + b*i*, or re^θ*i*:**

If you're dealing with only real numbers, select the **Real** mode. If you're dealing with complex numbers, select **a + b*i*** if you want the complex numbers displayed in rectangular form. If you want complex numbers displayed in polar form, select the **re^θ*i*** mode.

✔ **Full, Horiz, or G-T:**

The **Full** screen mode displays the screen as you see it when you turn the calculator on. The other screen modes are split-screen modes. The **Horiz** mode is for when you want to display a graph and the Y= editor or the Home screen at the same time. Use the **G-T** mode when you want to display a graph and a table at the same time. (The split-screen modes are explained in detail in Chapters 9 and 10.)

✔ **Set Clock:**

This is where you set the clock on the TI-84 Plus family of calculators. To do this, use the arrow keys to place the cursor on the **SET CLOCK** option and press x̄. You see the second picture in Figure 1-2. You use the arrow keys to move from item to item. To select items in the first, fifth, and eighth rows, place the cursor on the desired item and press x̄ to highlight that item. To enter numbers in the other options, edit the existing number or press x̄ and use the keypad to enter a new number. When you are finished setting the clock, save your settings by placing the cursor on **SAVE** and pressing x̄.

If you're planning on graphing trigonometric functions, put the calculator in Radian mode. Reason: Most trig functions are graphed for $-2\pi \le x \le 2\pi$. That is approximately $-6.28 \le x \le 6.28$. That's not a bad value for the limits on the *x*-axis. But if you graph in Degree mode, you would need $-360 \le x \le 360$ for the limits on the *x*-axis. This is doable . . . but trust me, it's easier to graph in Radian mode.

If your calculator is in Radian mode and you want to enter an angle in degrees, Chapter 3 tells you how to do so without resetting the mode.

Using the Catalog

The calculator's Catalog houses every command and function used by the calculator. However, it's easier to use the keyboard and the menus to access these commands and functions than it is to use the Catalog. There are several exceptions; for example, the hyperbolic functions are found only in the Catalog. If you have to use the Catalog, here's how to do it:

1. **If necessary, use** ▸◂▴▾ **to place the cursor at the location where you want to insert a command or function found in the Catalog.**

   The command or function is usually inserted on the Home screen, or in the Y= editor when you're defining a function you plan to graph.

2. **Press** 2nd 0 **to enter the Catalog.**

   This is illustrated in the first picture in Figure 1-4.

3. **Enter the first letter in the name of the command or function.**

   Notice that the calculator is already in Alpha mode, as is indicated by the Ⓐ in the upper-right part of the screen. To enter the letter, all you have to do is press the key corresponding to that letter. For example, if you're using the Catalog to access the hyperbolic function tanh, press ④ because the letter **T** is written in green above this key. This is illustrated in the second picture in Figure 1-4.

4. **Repeatedly press** ▾ **to move the indicator to the desired command or function.**

5. **Press** ENTER **to select the command or function.**

   This is illustrated in the third picture in Figure 1-4. After pressing ENTER, the command or function is inserted at the cursor location.

Press 2nd 0   Enter first letter   Select item

Figure 1-4: Steps for using the Catalog.

Chapter 2

Doing Basic Arithmetic

• •

In This Chapter

▶ Entering and evaluating arithmetic expressions

▶ Obeying the order of operations

▶ Storing and recalling variables

▶ Combining expressions

▶ Writing small programs

• •

*W*hen you use the calculator to evaluate an arithmetic expression such as $5^{10} + 4^6$, the format in which the calculator displays the answer depends on how you have set the mode of the calculator. Do you want answers displayed in scientific notation? Do you want all numbers rounded to two decimal places?

Setting the *mode* of the calculator affords you the opportunity to tell the calculator how you want these, and other questions, answered. (Setting the mode is explained in Chapter 1.) When you're doing basic, real-number arithmetic, the mode is usually set as it appears in Figure 1-2 of Chapter 1.

Entering and Evaluating Expressions

Arithmetic expressions are evaluated on the Home screen. The Home screen is the screen you see when you turn the calculator on. If the Home screen is not already displayed on the calculator, press [2nd][MODE] to display it. If you want to clear the contents of the Home screen, repeatedly press [CLEAR] until the screen is empty.

Arithmetic expressions are entered in the calculator the same way you would write them on paper if you were restricted to using the division sign (/) for fractional notation. This restriction sometimes requires parentheses around the numerator or the denominator, as illustrated in the first two calculations in Figure 2-1.

There is a major difference between the subtraction ⊟ key and the ⊡ negation key. They are not the same, nor are they interchangeable. Use the ⊟ key to indicate subtraction; use the ⊡ key before a number to identify that number as negative. If you improperly use ⊡ to indicate a subtraction problem, or if you improperly use ⊟ to indicate that a number is negative, you get the ERR: SYNTAX error message. The use of these two symbols is illustrated in the last calculation in Figure 2-1.

When entering numbers, do not use commas. For example, the number 1,000,000 is entered in the calculator as 1000000.

After entering the expression, press ENTER to evaluate it. The calculator displays the answer on the right side of the next line, as shown in Figure 2-1.

```
5+3/2
            6.5
(5+3)/2
              4
-3--4
              1
```

Figure 2-1: Evaluating arithmetic expressions.

Important Keys

Starting with the fifth row of the calculator, you find the functions commonly used on a scientific calculator. Here's what they are and how you use them:

- **π and *e*:**

   The transcendental numbers π and *e* are respectively located in the fifth and sixth rows of the last column of the keyboard. To enter π in the calculator, press 2nd^; to enter *e*, press 2nd÷, as shown in the first line of Figure 2-2.

- **The trigonometric and inverse trigonometric functions:**

   The trigonometric and inverse trigonometric functions are located in the fifth row of the keyboard. These functions require that the argument of the function be enclosed in parentheses. To remind you of this, the calculator provides the first parenthesis for you (as in the first line of Figure 2-2).

✔ **The square-root and exponential functions:**

The square-root function, 10^x function, and e^x function are respectively located in the sixth, seventh, and eighth rows of the first column on the keyboard. Each of these functions requires that its argument be enclosed in parentheses. To remind you of this, the calculator provides the first parenthesis for you (as in the third line of Figure 2-2).

✔ **The inverse and square functions:**

The inverse and square functions are respectively located in the fifth and sixth rows of the left column on the calculator. To enter the multiplicative inverse of a number, enter the number and then press $\boxed{x^{-1}}$. Similarly, to square a number, enter the number and then press $\boxed{x^2}$. The third line of Figure 2-2 shows this operation.

```
sin⁻¹(cos(π))
          86.85840735
√(3²+4²)
                    5
-3²
                   -9
```

Figure 2-2: Examples of arithmetic expressions.

If you want to evaluate an arithmetic expression and you need a function other than those just listed, you'll most likely find that function in the Math menu (described in detail in the next chapter). The hyperbolic functions are an exception; those you find in the calculator's Catalog. (Chapter 1 discusses the Catalog and how to access the hyperbolic functions.)

Order of Operations

The order in which the calculator performs operations is the standard order that we are all used to. Spelled out in detail, here is the order in which the calculator performs operations:

1. **The calculator simplifies all expressions surrounded by parentheses.**

2. **The calculator evaluates all functions that are followed by the argument.**

   These functions supply the first parenthesis in the pair of parentheses that must surround the argument. An example is sin x. When you press $\boxed{\text{SIN}}$ to access this function, the calculator inserts **sin(** on-screen. You then enter the argument and press $\boxed{)}$.

3. **The calculator evaluates all functions entered after the argument.**

   An example of such a function is the square function. You enter the argument and then press $\boxed{x^2}$ to square it.

   Evaluating -3^2 may not give you the expected answer. We think of -3 as being a single, negative number. So when we square it, we expect to get $+9$. But the calculator gets -9 (as indicated in the fifth line of Figure 2-2). This happens because the normal way to enter -3 into the calculator is by pressing $\boxed{(-)}\boxed{3}$ — and pressing the $\boxed{(-)}$ key is equivalent to multiplying by -1. Thus, in this context, $-3^2 = -1 * 3^2 = -1 * 9 = -9$. To avoid this potentially hazardous problem, always surround negative numbers with parentheses *before* raising them to a power.

4. **The calculator evaluates powers entered using the $\boxed{\wedge}$ key and roots entered using the $^x\sqrt{}$ function.**

   The $^x\sqrt{}$ function is found in the Math menu which is explained in Chapter 3. You can also enter various roots by using fractional exponents — for example, the cube root of 8 can be entered as 8^(1/3).

5. **The calculator evaluates all multiplication and division problems as it encounters them, proceeding from left to right.**

6. **The calculator evaluates all addition and subtraction problems as it encounters them, proceeding from left to right.**

Well, okay, what does the phrase "x plus 1 divided by x minus 2" actually *mean* when you say it aloud? Well, that depends on how you say it. Said without pausing, it means $(x + 1)/(x - 2)$. Said with a subtle pause after the "plus" and another before the "minus," it means $x + (1/x) - 2$. The calculator can't hear speech inflection, so make good use of those parentheses when you're "talking" to the calculator.

Using the Previous Answer

You can use the previous answer in the next arithmetic expression you want to evaluate. If that answer is to appear at the beginning of the arithmetic expression, first key in the operation that is to appear after the answer. The calculator displays **Ans** followed by the operation. Then key in the rest of the arithmetic expression and press ENTER to evaluate it, as illustrated in Figure 2-3.

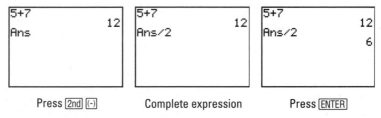

| Press [2nd] [(-)] | Complete expression | Press [ENTER] |

Figure 2-3: Steps for starting an expression with the last answer.

If you want to embed the last answer in the next arithmetic expression, key in the beginning of the expression to the point where you want to insert the previous answer. Then press [2nd][(-)] to key in the last answer. Finally, key in the rest of the expression and press ENTER to evaluate it, as shown in Figure 2-4.

| Start expression | Press [2nd] [(-)] | Complete expression |

Figure 2-4: Steps for embedding the last answer in an expression.

Recycling the Last Entry

If you want to reuse the last command, function, or expression entered in the calculator — but with different instructions, arguments, or variables — you can simply recall that command, function, or expression and then edit it. To do so, follow these steps:

1. **Enter the command, function, or expression on the Home screen and then press ENTER to execute command or evaluate the function.**

   This is illustrated in the first picture in Figure 2-5.

2. **Press 2nd ENTER to paste a copy of that command or function on the home screen.**

   This procedure is shown in the second picture in Figure 2-5.

3. **Edit the command, function, or expression and then press ENTER to reevaluate it.**

   The third picture in Figure 2-5 shows this procedure. Editing is explained in Chapter 1.

Original expression   Press 2nd ENTER   Edit expression

Figure 2-5: Steps for recycling a command, function, or expression.

Storing Variables

If you plan to use the same number many times when evaluating arithmetic expressions, consider storing that number in a variable. To do so, follow these steps:

1. **If necessary, press 2nd MODE to enter the Home screen.**

2. **Enter the number you want to store in a variable.**

   You can store the number as an arithmetic expression. This is illustrated in the first picture in Figure 2-6. After you complete the steps for storing the number, the calculator evaluates that expression.

3. **Press STO▸.**

   The result of this action is shown in the first picture in Figure 2-6.

4. **Press ALPHA and then press the key corresponding to the letter of the variable in which you want to store the number.**

The second picture in Figure 2-6 shows this process. The letters used for storing variables are the letters of the alphabet and the Greek letter θ.

5. Press ENTER **to store the value.**

This is illustrated in the third picture in Figure 2-6.

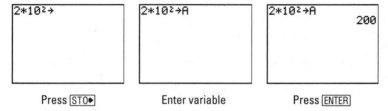

Press STO▸   Enter variable   Press ENTER

Figure 2-6: Steps for storing a number in a variable.

The number you store in a variable remains stored in that variable until you *or the calculator* stores a new number in that variable. Because the calculator uses the letters X, T, and θ when graphing functions, parametric equations, and polar equations, it is possible that the calculator will change the value stored in these variables when the calculator is in graphing mode. For example, if you store a number in the variable X and then ask the calculator to find the zero of the graphed function X^2, the calculator will replace the number stored in X with 0, the zero of X^2. So avoid storing values in these three variables if you want that value to remain stored in that variable after you have graphed functions, parametric equations, or polar equations.

After you have stored a number in a variable, you can insert that number into an arithmetic expression. To do so, place the cursor where you want the number to appear, press ALPHA, and then press the key corresponding to the letter of the variable in which the number is stored. Figure 2-7 shows how.

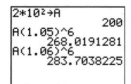

Figure 2-7: Inserting a stored variable into an expression.

Combining Expressions

You can *combine* (link) several expressions or commands into one expression by using a colon to separate the expressions or commands. The colon is entered into the calculator by pressing ALPHA .

Combining expressions is a really handy way to write mini-programs, as detailed in the "Writing a mini-program" sidebar.

Writing a mini-program

This figure depicts a program that calculates n^2 when n is a positive integer. The first line of the program initiates the program by storing the value 1 in n and calculating its square. (Storing a number in a variable and combining expressions are explained elsewhere in this chapter.)

The next line on the left shows the real guts of the program. It increments n by 1 and then calculates the square of the new value of n. Of course, the calculator doesn't do these calculations until after you press ENTER. But the really neat thing about this is that the calculator will continue to execute this same command each time you press ENTER. Because n is incremented by 1 each time you press ENTER, you get the values of n^2 when n is a positive integer.

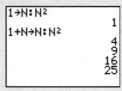

Chapter 3

The Math and Angle Menus

In This Chapter

▶ Inserting a Math menu function into an expression

▶ Converting between degrees and radians

▶ Entering angles in degrees, minutes, and seconds

▶ Converting between degrees and degrees, minutes, and seconds

▶ Entering angles in degrees, minutes, and seconds

▶ Overriding the angle mode of the calculator

*A*re you hunting for the absolute value function? Look no far-ther — it's in the Math menu. Do you want to convert a deci-mal to a fraction? You can find the function that does this in the Math menu. In general, any math function that cannot be directly accessed using the keyboard is housed in the Math menu. Similarly, any function that deals with angles is housed in the Angle menu. This chapter tells you how to access and use those functions.

The Math Menu and Submenus

Press MATH to access the Math menu. This menu contains four sub-menus: MATH, NUM, CPX, and PRB. Use the ▶◀ keys to get from one submenu to the next, and back again.

The Math MATH submenu contains the general mathematical func-tions such as the cubed root function. It also contains the calcula-tor's Equation Solver that, as you would expect, is used to solve equations. The Equation Solver is explained in Chapter 4. The Math NUM submenu contains the functions usually associated with num-bers, such as the least common multiple function. A detailed expla-nation of the functions in these two menus is given later in this chapter.

The Math CPX submenu contains functions normally used with complex numbers. This submenu is explained in detail in the next chapter. The Math PRB submenu contains the probability and random-number functions. (Probability is explained in Chapter 14.)

Using Math menu functions

Most functions housed in the Math menu require that the argument be entered after entering the function. Such functions are easily recognizable by the parenthesis following the name of the function; the cube-root function, $^3\sqrt{(}$, is an example.

With one exception, functions in the Math menu that have no parenthesis at the end of their names require that the argument be entered before the function is entered. The cube function is an example of such a function. (The exception is the xth root function, $^x\sqrt{}$. This function requires that the root be entered first, then the $^x\sqrt{}$ function, and then the argument.)

Inserting a Math menu function

Math menu functions are usually inserted into arithmetic expressions entered on the Home screen, or into definitions of functions in the Y= editor. Pressing [2nd][MODE] puts you in the Home screen, and pressing [Y=] puts you in the Y= editor. The Y= editor is used to define functions you want to graph. This editor is explained in detail in Chapter 9. To insert a Math menu function into an expression, follow these steps:

1. **If necessary, use [▸][◂][▴][▾] to place the cursor where you want to insert the function.**

   Inserting a Math menu item in an arithmetic expression that is entered on the Home screen is illustrated in Figure 3-1. This figure shows how to insert the cube function in order to evaluate $\sqrt{(2^3 + 17)}$.

2. **Press [MATH].**

3. **Use [▸] to select the appropriate submenu of the Math menu.**

4. **Enter the number of the function or use [▾] to highlight the number of the function and then press [ENTER].**

5. **If necessary, complete the expression.**

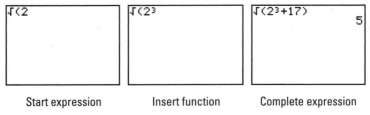

| Start expression | Insert function | Complete expression |

Figure 3-1: Steps for inserting a Math menu function in an expression.

The Math MATH submenu

Press MATH to access the Math MATH submenu. This submenu contains general mathematical functions you can insert into an expression. The following sections explain the items housed in this submenu, except for the **Solver** function at the bottom of the Math MATH submenu. This latter function, used to solve equations, is discussed in Chapter 4.

Converting between decimals and fractions

The **Frac** function always converts a finite decimal to a fraction. Sometimes this function can convert an infinite repeating decimal to a fraction. When it can't, it lets you know by redisplaying the decimal. Be sure to enter the decimal before inserting the **Frac** function, as shown in the first two lines of the first picture in Figure 3-2.

The **Dec** function converts a fraction to a decimal. Enter the fraction before you insert the **Dec** function. An example is shown in the first picture in Figure 3-2.

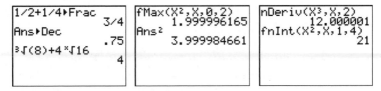

Figure 3-2: Using the functions in the Math MATH submenu.

Cubing and taking cube roots

The cube function, ³, cubes the value that precedes the function (as illustrated in Figure 3-1). The cube-root function, ³√, finds the cube root of a value that follows the function. This value must be enclosed in parentheses; the calculator supplies the opening parenthesis; you must supply the closing parenthesis. The first picture in Figure 3-2 shows an example of using the cube-root function.

Taking the xth root

The xth root function, $\sqrt[x]{\ }$, finds the xth root of the value that follows the function. To use this function, first enter the root x, then insert the $\sqrt[x]{\ }$ function, and then enter the argument. This is illustrated in the first picture in Figure 3-2. In this example, the calculator is evaluating the fourth root of 16.

Finding the location of maximum and minimum values

The **fMin** and **fMax** functions approximate *where* the minimum or maximum value of a function occurs in a specified interval. *They do not compute the minimum or maximum value of the function;* they just give you the x-coordinate of the minimum or maximum point. Chapter 11 tells you how to get the calculator to compute minimum and maximum values of a function.

The **fMin** and **fMax** functions are standalone functions in the sense that they cannot be used in an expression. To use these functions, insert the appropriate function, **fMin** or **fMax,** at the beginning of a new line on the Home screen. Then enter the definition of the function whose minimum or maximum you want to locate. Press ⊡ and enter the variable used in the definition of the function you just entered. Press ⊡ and enter the lower limit of the specified interval. Then press ⊡, enter the upper limit, and press ⊡. Finally, press ENTER to *approximate* the location of the minimum or maximum in the specified interval. This is illustrated in the second picture in Figure 3-2. In this picture the calculator is *approximating* the location of the maximum value of the function x^2 in the interval $0 \le x \le 2$.

Doing numerical differentiation and integration

The calculator cannot perform symbolic differentiation and integration. For example, it cannot tell you that the derivative of x^2 is $2x$, nor can it evaluate an indefinite integral. But the **nDeriv** function will approximate the derivative (slope) of a function at a specified value of the variable, and the **fnInt** function will approximate a definite integral.

Insert the **nDeriv** function, enter the function whose derivative you want to find, and then press ⊡. Enter the variable used in the definition of the function you just entered and press ⊡. Then enter the value at which the derivative is to be taken, and press ⒥. Finally, press ENTER to *approximate* the derivative. This is illustrated in the third picture in Figure 3-2.

To use the **fnInt** function, insert **fnInt**, and then enter the function you are integrating. Press ⒥ and enter the variable used in the definition of the function you just entered. Press ⒥ and enter the lower limit of the definite integral. Press ⒥, enter the upper limit, and press ⒥. Finally, press ENTER to *approximate* the definite integral. This is illustrated in the third picture in Figure 3-2.

The calculator may give you an error message or a false answer if **nDeriv** is used to find the derivative at a nondifferentiable point or if **fnInt** is used to evaluate an improper integral.

The Math NUM submenu

Press MATH▶ to access the Math NUM submenu. (Inserting a Math menu function into an expression is explained earlier in this chapter.) The following sections explain the items housed in this submenu.

Finding the absolute value

The **abs** function evaluates the absolute value of the number or arithmetic expression that follows the function. This number or expression must be enclosed in parentheses. The calculator supplies the first parenthesis; you must supply the last parenthesis. An example of using the **abs** function is illustrated in the first picture in Figure 3-3.

```
abs(6*3-5*4)            int(-π)
               2                      -4
round(π+e,2)            max({4,π,e})
               5.86                    4
iPart(π+e)              lcm(lcm(2,6),8)
               5                      24
```

Figure 3-3: Using the functions in the Math NUM submenu.

Rounding numbers

The **round** function rounds a number or arithmetic expression to a specified number of decimal places. The number or expression to be rounded and the specified number of decimal places are placed after the function separated by a comma and surrounded by parentheses. The calculator supplies the opening parenthesis; you must supply the closing parenthesis. An example of using the **round** function is the first picture in Figure 3-3.

Finding the integer and fractional parts of a value

The **iPart** and **fPart** functions (respectively) find the integer and fractional parts of the number, or the arithmetic expression that follows the function. This number or expression must be enclosed in parentheses. The calculator supplies the opening parenthesis; you must supply the closing parenthesis. An example of using the **iPart** function is the first picture in Figure 3-3.

Using the greatest-integer function

The **int** function finds the largest integer that is less than or equal to the number or arithmetic expression that follows the function. This number or expression must be enclosed in parentheses. The calculator supplies the opening parenthesis; you must supply the closing parenthesis. An example of using the **int** function is the second picture in Figure 3-3.

Finding minimum and maximum values in a list of numbers

The **min** and **max** functions find (respectively) the minimum and maximum values in the list of numbers that follows the function. Braces must surround the list, and commas must separate the elements in the list. You can access the braces on the calculator by pressing [2nd][(] and [2nd][)]. The list must be enclosed in parentheses. The calculator supplies the opening parenthesis; you must supply the closing parenthesis. An example of using the **max** function is the second picture in Figure 3-3.

When using the **min** or **max** function to find the minimum or maximum of a two-element list, you can omit the braces that surround the list. For example, **min**(2, 4) returns the value 2.

Finding least common multiple and greatest common divisor

The **lcm** and **gcd** functions find (respectively) the least common multiple and the greatest common divisor of the two numbers that follow the function. These two numbers must be separated by a comma and surrounded by parentheses. The calculator supplies the opening parenthesis; you must supply the closing parenthesis. An example of using the **lcm** function is the second picture in Figure 3-3.

The Angle Menu

The functions housed in the Angle menu allow you to convert between degrees and radians or convert between rectangular and polar coordinates. They also allow you to convert between degrees and DMS (degrees, minutes, and seconds). You can also override the angle setting in the Mode menu of the calculator when you use these functions. For example, if the calculator is in Radian mode and you want to enter an angle measure in degrees, there is a function in the Angle menu that allows you to do so. (Setting the mode is explained in Chapter 1.)

Converting degrees to radians

To convert degrees to radians, follow these steps:

1. **Put the calculator in Radian mode.**

   Setting the mode is explained in Chapter 1.

2. **If necessary, press [2nd][MODE] to access the Home screen.**

3. **Enter the number of degrees.**

4. **Press [2nd][APPS][1] to paste in the ° function.**

5. **Press [ENTER] to convert the degree measure to radians.**

   This is illustrated at the top of the first picture in Figure 3-4.

```
30°
        .5235987756
Ans/π
        .1666666667
Ans▶Frac
                1/6
```
```
(π/18)ʳ
                10
(π/27)ʳ
        6.666666667
Ans▶DMS
            6°40'0"
```

Figure 3-4: Converting between degrees and radians.

If you're a purist (like me) who likes to see radian measures expressed as a fractional multiple of π whenever possible, continuing with the following steps accomplishes this goal if it's mathematically possible.

6. **Press [÷][2nd][^][ENTER] to divide the radian measure by π.**

   This is illustrated in the third line in the first picture in Figure 3-4.

7. **Press [MATH][1][ENTER] to convert the result to a fraction, if possible.**

   This is illustrated at the bottom of the first picture in Figure 3-4, where 30° is equal to π/6 radians. If the calculator can't convert the decimal obtained in Step 6 to a fraction, it says so by returning the decimal in Step 7.

Converting radians to degrees

To convert radians to degrees:

1. **Put the calculator in Degree mode.**

   Setting the mode is explained in Chapter 1.

2. **If necessary, press [2nd][MODE] to access the Home screen.**

3. **Enter the radian measure.**

   If the radian measure is entered as an arithmetic expression, surround that expression with parentheses. This is illustrated at the top of the second picture in Figure 3-4.

4. **Press [2nd][APPS][3] to paste in the *r* function.**

5. **Press [ENTER] to convert the radian measure to degrees.**

   This is illustrated in the second picture in Figure 3-4.

Converting between degrees and DMS

To convert degrees to DMS (degrees, minutes, and seconds), follow these steps:

1. **Put the calculator in Degree mode.**

   Setting the mode is explained in Chapter 1.

2. **If necessary, press [2nd][MODE] to access the Home screen.**

3. **Enter the degree measure.**

4. **Press [2nd][APPS][4][ENTER] to convert the degrees to DMS.**

   This is illustrated at the bottom of the second picture in Figure 3-4, and also at the top of Figure 3-5.

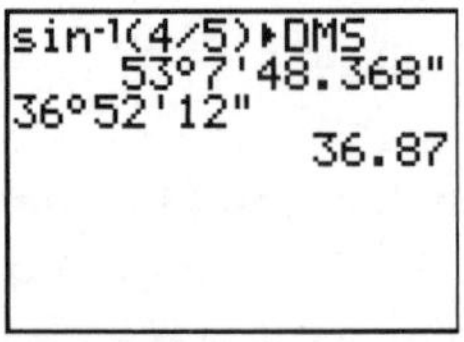

```
sin⁻¹(4/5)▸DMS
          53°7'48.368"
36°52'12"
              36.87
```

Figure 3-5: Converting between degrees and DMS.

To convert DMS to degrees, follow these steps:

1. **Follow the above Steps 1 and 2.**

2. **Enter the DMS measure.**

   The next section tells you how to insert the symbols for degrees, minutes, and seconds.

3. **Press** ENTER **to convert the DMS entry to degrees.**

   This is illustrated at the bottom of Figure 3-5.

Entering angles in DMS measure

To enter an angle in DMS measure:

1. **Enter the number of degrees and press** 2nd APPS 1 **to insert the degree symbol.**

2. **Enter the number of minutes and press** 2nd APPS 2 **to insert the symbol for minutes.**

3. **Enter the number of seconds and press** ALPHA + **to insert the symbol for seconds.**

   This is illustrated at the bottom of Figure 3-5.

Overriding the mode of the angle

If the calculator is in Radian mode but you want to enter an angle in degrees, enter the number of degrees and then press 2nd APPS 1 to insert in the ° degree symbol. If you want to enter an angle in DMS measure while the calculator is in Radian mode, the previous section tells you how to do so. (Setting the mode is explained in Chapter 1.)

If the calculator is in Degree mode and you want to enter an angle in radian measure, enter the number of radians and then press 2nd APPS 3 to insert in the radian-measure symbol. If the radian measure is entered as an arithmetical expression, such as $\pi/4$, be sure to surround it with parentheses before you insert the radian-measure symbol.

Chapter 4

Solving Equations

• •

In This Chapter

▶ Entering, editing, and solving equations in the Equation Solver

▶ Assigning values to the variables in the equation

▶ Defining the interval containing the solution

▶ Guessing the value of the solution

▶ Finding multiple solutions

• •

*T*he Equation Solver solves an equation for one variable given the values of the other variables in the equation. The Solver is capable of dealing only with real numbers and is capable of finding only real-number solutions.

Using the Equation Solver

The following lists the basic steps for using the Equation Solver. Each of these steps is explained in detail following this list. If you have never used the Equation Solver before, I suggest that you read the detailed explanations for each step because the Equation Solver is a bit tricky. After you have had experience using the Solver, you can refer back to this list, if necessary, to refresh your memory on its use.

1. **If necessary, set the Mode for real-number arithmetic.**

2. **Enter a new equation (or edit the existing equation) in the Equation Solver.**

3. **Assign values to all variables except the variable you're solving for.**

4. **Enter the bounds for the interval that contains the solution.**

5. **Enter a guess for the solution.**

6. **Press** ALPHA ENTER **to solve the equation.**

Step 1. Set the mode

Because the Equation Solver is equipped to deal only with real numbers, press MODE and highlight all entries on the left. (To see what I mean, refer to Figure 1-2 in Chapter 1.)

Step 2. Enter or edit the equation to be solved

To enter a new equation in the Equation Solver, follow these steps:

1. **Press** MATH 0 **to access the Equation Solver from the Math menu.**

   When the Equation Solver appears, it looks like one of the pictures in Figure 4-1. The first picture shows the Equation Solver when no equation is stored in the Solver; the second picture depicts the Solver and the equation currently stored in it.

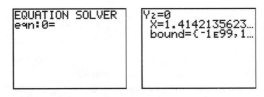

Without an equation   With an equation

Figure 4-1: The Equation Solver.

2. **If your Equation Solver already contains an equation, repeatedly press** ▲ **until the screen titled EQUATION SOLVER appears.**

   This is illustrated in the first picture in Figure 4-2.

3. **If you need to, press** CLEAR **to erase any equation in the Solver.**

Press ▲   Enter equation   Press [ENTER]

Figure 4-2: Steps for entering a new equation in the Equation Solver.

4. Enter the equation you want to solve.

The equation you enter must be set equal to zero and can contain only real numbers. For example, if you want to solve the area equation A = L*W, enter it as 0 = A – L*W or as 0 = L*W – A (as illustrated in the second picture in Figure 4-2).

You can also use a function that you've entered in the Y= editor in the definition of your equation. For example, if Y_1 = X – 1 in the Y= editor, you can enter $1/Y_1$ – 1 in the Equation Solver to solve the equation $1/(x – 1)$ – 1 = 0. To insert such a function into the equation, press [VARS]▶[1] to access the Function menu, and then press the number of the function you want to enter (as in the first picture in Figure 4-2). The Y= editor is explained in Chapter 9.

5. Press [ENTER] to enter the equation in the solver.

To edit an equation that is already entered in the Equation Solver, follow these steps:

1. Follow the above Steps 1 and 2.

2. Edit the equation and press [ENTER] when you're finished.

Step 3. Assign values to variables

After you have entered an equation in the Equation Solver, the values assigned to the variables in your equation are the values that are currently stored in those variables in your calculator. This is illustrated in the last picture in Figure 4-2. You must assign an accurate value to all variables except the variable you're solving for. These values must be real numbers or arithmetic expressions that simplify to real numbers.

To assign a value to a variable, use ▶◀▲▼ to place the cursor on the number currently assigned to that variable and then key in the new value. As you start to key in the new value, the old value is erased. Press ENTER when you're finished entering the new value (as illustrated in the first picture of Figure 4-3, where values are assigned to variables **A** and **W**).

Step 4. Define the solution bounds

The **bound** variable at the bottom of the screen, as illustrated in the first picture in Figure 4-3, is where you enter the bounds of the interval containing the solution you're seeking. The default setting for this interval is $[-10^{99}, 10^{99}]$, as is indicated by **bound** = {-1E99, 1E99}. 1E99 is 10^{99} in scientific notation. The ellipsis at the end of the line containing this variable indicate that you have to repeatedly press ▶ to see the rest of the line.

This default setting is more than sufficient for equations that have a unique solution. So if your equation has a unique solution, you don't have to do anything with the value in the **bound** variable.

When the equation you're solving has multiple solutions, it's sometimes necessary to redefine the **bound** variable. Finding multiple solutions is discussed in the last section of this chapter.

To redefine the **bound** variable:

1. **Use ▶◀▲▼ to place the cursor anywhere in the line containing the bound variable.**

2. **Press CLEAR to erase the current entry.**

3. **Press 2nd (to insert the left brace.**

4. **Enter the lower bound, press , , enter the upper bound, and then press 2nd) to insert the right brace.**

5. **Press ENTER to store the new setting in the bound variable.**

Step 5. Guess a solution

Guess at a solution by assigning a value to the variable you're solving for. Any value in the interval defined by the **bound** variable will do. If your guess is close to the solution, the calculator quickly solves the equation; if it's not, it may take the calculator a while to solve the equation. (Assigning a value to a variable in the Equation Solver is explained earlier in this chapter.)

If your equation has more than one solution, the calculator will find the one closest to your guess. The section at the end of this chapter tells you how to find the other solutions.

If the variable you're solving for is assigned a value (guess) that isn't in the interval defined by the **bound** variable, then you get the ERR: BAD GUESS error message.

Step 6. Solve the equation

To solve an equation, follow these steps:

1. **Use** ▶◀▲▼ **to place the cursor anywhere in the line that contains the variable you're solving for.**

   This procedure is shown in the second picture in Figure 4-3.

2. **Press** ALPHA ENTER **to solve the equation.**

   The third picture of Figure 4-3 shows this procedure; the square indicator shown next to the **L** indicates that **L** is the variable just solved for. The **left – rt** value that appears at the bottom of this picture evaluates the two sides of the equation (using the values assigned to the variables) and displays the difference — that is, the accuracy of this solution. A **left – rt** value of zero indicates an exact solution. Figure 4-4 shows a solution that is off by the very small number $-1 * 10^{-11}$.

If you get the ERR: NO SIGN CHNG error message when you attempt to solve an equation using the Equation Solver, then the equation has no real solutions in the interval defined by the **bound** variable.

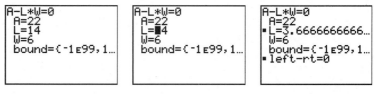

Define variables	Guess solution	Press ALPHA ENTER

Figure 4-3: Steps for solving an equation in the Equation Solver.

Finding Multiple Solutions

To find other solutions to an equation, first find one solution to the equation by following Steps 1 through 6 in the first section of this chapter. This is illustrated in the first picture in Figure 4-4.

Then enter a new guess for the solution you're seeking, or, in the **bound** variable, enter the bounds of an interval that possibly contains a different solution. In the second picture in Figure 4-4 a new guess for the solution is entered.

After making a new guess or after redefining the **bound** variable, follow the steps in the previous section to find another solution to the equation. The third picture in Figure 4-4 shows this procedure.

| Find 1st solution | Enter new guess | Press ALPHA ENTER |

Figure 4-4: Steps for finding multiple solutions to an equation.

Part II
Doing Geometry

Beyond Euclidean and Cartesian geometry, there is Ed Dubrowski geometry which proves that the volume of a sphere changes in proportion to the amount of food at an All-U-Can-Eat buffet.

©RICHTENNANT

In this part . . .

*P*ut down that compass and ruler — in this part, I show you how to get the calculator to make accurate geometric constructions. I even show you how to get the calculator to rotate, translate, reflect, and dilate those constructions.

Hey, the calculator can even find lengths, areas, and the degree measure of angles. So trust me, this part of the book shows that you really don't need that compass and ruler.

Chapter 5

Using GeoMaster

● ●

In This Chapter

▶ Starting and quitting GeoMaster

▶ Creating, saving, recalling, and deleting files

▶ Using menus

▶ Clearing the screen

● ●

*1*f you've ever used a dynamic geometry computer software package such as the Geometer's Sketchpad or Cabri Geometry II Plus, then you appreciate its ability to not only accurately construct geometric figures, but to also perform translations, rotations, dilations, and reflections. These software packages can even take measurements, create tessellations, and much, much more. If you haven't used such software packages, wouldn't you like to?

Because the TI-84 comes equipped with two geometry applications, Cabri Jr. and GeoMaster, you can now do your geometric investigations on the calculator. Granted, the calculator screen is rather small for some investigations, but other than that, these two calculator applications do almost everything that the computer software packages do.

In this and the following three chapters, I explain how to use the GeoMaster application. A four-chapter explanation of how to use the Cabri Jr. application can be downloaded from the Dummies Books Web site. The URL for this site is in the Introduction of this book. To help you decide which application is best for you, consider the following differences between Cabri Jr. (version 1.03) and GeoMaster (version 1.10).

Some Cabri Jr. features not found in GeoMaster are

- ✔ Cabri Jr. has an Undo tool; GeoMaster does not. However, they both allow you to delete a selected construction.

- ✔ Cabri Jr. allows you to display constructions as dotted or solid lines; GeoMaster uses only solid lines.

- ✔ Cabri Jr. has an Animate tool and a Locus tool; GeoMaster does not. Such tools allow you to show, for example, how the definition of a conic section is used to construct the conic section.

- ✔ The Cabri Jr.'s Calculate tool can add, subtract, multiply, divide, and find square roots. GeoMaster's Calculate tool can only add and subtract.

- ✔ When you quit Cabri Jr. without saving your work, the next time you start the application your work appears as you left it. When you quit GeoMaster, your unsaved work vanishes.

- ✔ Cabri Jr. can talk to (share files with) the Cabri Geometry II Plus computer software and to the Cabri Jr. applications found on the TI-89, TI-92 Plus, and Voyage 200 calculators. GeoMaster is not on speaking terms with anything.

Some GeoMaster features not found in Cabri Jr. are

- ✔ GeoMaster has a tool for constructing any type of polygon, while Cabri Jr. has tools for constructing only triangles and quadrilaterals. In both applications, one can, of course, construct a polygon by stringing together consecutive line segments.

- ✔ GeoMaster has a tool for constructing regular polygons; Cabri Jr. does not.

- ✔ GeoMaster allows you to construct points by entering their coordinates; Cabri Jr. does not.

- ✔ GeoMaster has three tools not found in Cabri Jr. that answer the questions: Are two lines parallel? Are two lines perpendicular? Are three points collinear?

- ✔ As you move the cursor in GeoMaster, the coordinates of its location are displayed at the bottom of the screen. This feature is not available in Cabri Jr., although Cabri Jr. tells you the coordinates of a point after it is constructed. GeoMaster also allows you to adjust the size of the viewing window the same way you do when graphing functions, as explained in Chapter 9.

- GeoMaster can construct and add vectors; Cabri Jr. cannot.
- GeoMaster can construct arcs of a circle; Cabri Jr. cannot.
- GeoMaster has a tool that stores measured data (lengths, areas, and angle measures) in a list; Cabri Jr. does not. When the data is in a list, it can be accessed from the home screen, where you can perform more calculations on these measures than you can with Cabri Jr.

When you start the geometry application of your choice, you see the version number on the screen, as illustrated in the first picture in Figure 5-1 for the GeoMaster application. If that number is larger than 1.03 for Cabri Jr. or 1.10 for GeoMaster, the versions in existence at the time this book was written, then the differences listed above may no longer exist. If the version number is not larger, check out Texas Instruments' Web site to see if there is a more recent version for you to download. Chapter 21 tells you how to do this.

Starting GeoMaster

To start GeoMaster, press [APPS][ALPHA][TAN], if necessary use [▼] to move the cursor to the GeoMaster application, and press [ENTER] to select the application. You are confronted with one of the three screens in Figure 5-1.

GeoMaster screen — GeoMaster is running — Another application is running

Figure 5-1: What you see when you select the GeoMaster application.

If no other applications are running, you see the first screen in Figure 5-1. Just press any key to enter the GeoMaster application. If GeoMaster is already running, after you press [APPS], you see the second screen in Figure 5-1. Press [2] to re-enter the application. The third screen in Figure 5-1 tells you that another application is currently running. Press [2] to exit that application, and then press any key to enter GeoMaster. After you enter GeoMaster, you are confronted with one of the two screens in Figure 5-2.

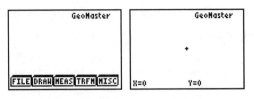

With menus   Without menus

Figure 5-2: What you see when you enter or re-enter GeoMaster.

When you enter the GeoMaster application, you usually see the first screen in Figure 5-2. But if you re-enter GeoMaster while it is still running, you see the screen as you left it but without the menus at the bottom of the screen, as in the second screen in Figure 5-2. To reinstate the Menu headings at the bottom of the screen, press [GRAPH] or [ALPHA].

If you press a menu key such as [MODE], [STAT], [MATH], or [VARS] while GeoMaster is running, you are sent to that menu while GeoMaster continues to run in the background. The same thing happens when you press [Y=], [WINDOW], or [ZOOM] when the Menu bar is not at the bottom of the GeoMaster screen. To re-enter the GeoMaster application, just press [GRAPH] or [APPS][2].

Quitting GeoMaster

You can use either a clean way or a dirty way of quitting the GeoMaster application. The clean way truly terminates GeoMaster, *without saving your work;* the dirty way leaves GeoMaster running in the background. When you re-start GeoMaster after a dirty exit, your work will be the way you left it — provided you don't run any other applications in the interim.

Before performing a clean exit from GeoMaster, you may want to save your work since this type of exit eradicates anything that you have not saved. How to save your work is explained in the next section. A clean exit is achieved by using the **Quit** command in GeoMaster's **FILE** menu ([Y=][6][1]).

A dirty exit, which leaves GeoMaster running in the background, is achieved by pressing [2nd][MODE] or any other key combination that sends you elsewhere — such as [MODE] which sends you to the Mode menu. After performing a dirty exit, you re-enter GeoMaster by pressing [GRAPH] or [APPS][2]. To reinstate the menu headings at the bottom of the screen, press [GRAPH] or [ALPHA].

When you start GeoMaster, the application removes the highlights from all equal signs in the Y= editor so that no function will be graphed when you press the [GRAPH] key to, for example, display GeoMaster's menu bar. It also resets the viewing window. When you exit GeoMaster, the application leaves all the equal signs in the Y= editor not highlighted and does not return the viewing window to its previous settings. For more information on the Y= editor and the viewing window, refer to Chapter 9.

Creating and Saving Files

You can create a file in two ways. If the GeoMaster screen is empty, just start creating your geometric figures. If the GeoMaster screen is not empty, select **New File** from GeoMaster's File menu by pressing [Y=][1] if the Menu bar is visible or [GRAPH][Y=][1] if it is not. You will be asked if you want to save your previous work. If you select **Yes**, the calculator is automatically put in Alpha mode so that you can enter a filename. Press [ENTER] after entering the filename. (Entering filenames is explained in Step 3 in the following list.) After selecting **Yes** and entering a filename or after selecting **No**, you are confronted with a blank GeoMaster screen, on which you can start creating geometric figures. Creating Geometric figures is explained in Chapter 6.

To save your work, follow these steps:

1. **Select Save File from GeoMaster's File menu.**

   To do this, press [Y=][3] if the Menu bar is visible; press [GRAPH][Y=][3] if it is not. After selecting **Save File**, you see a screen similar to the first picture in Figure 5-3.

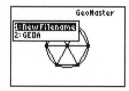
Press [Y=] [3]

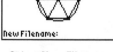
Select **New Filename**

Enter a name

Figure 5-3: The steps for saving a GeoMaster file.

2. **Select an existing filename or create a new filename.**

If you select an existing filename, such as GEOA in the first picture in Figure 5-3, the contents of that file will be replaced with your new work. If you select **New Filename**, you see a screen similar to the second picture in Figure 5-3.

GeoMaster does not allow you to save a blank screen.

3. **If you selected New Filename, give your file a name and then press [ENTER].**

The name of your file can consist of one to eight characters, which must be letters, numbers, or the Greek letter θ. The first character in the name must be a letter or θ.

The 🄰 in the upper-right corner of the screen indicates that the calculator is in Alpha mode. So when you press a key you will be entering the green letter above the key. To enter a number, press [ALPHA] to take the calculator out of Alpha mode and then enter the number. To enter a letter after entering a number, you must press [ALPHA] to put the calculator back in alpha mode. This is illustrated in the third picture in Figure 5-3.

Press [ENTER] to save the file under its new name. As the file is being saved, you see a moving vertical line in the upper-right corner of the screen. This indicates that the calculator is busy saving your file.

If you save a GeoMaster file under the name of an existing GeoMaster file, the original file will be replaced by the new file. The calculator will give you no warning message that this is going to happen.

Recalling and Deleting Files

To recall a GeoMaster file previously saved in memory, select **Open File** from GeoMaster's **FILE** menu by pressing [Y=][2] if the Menu bar is visible or [GRAPH][Y=][2] if it is not. Then press the number of the file you want to recall.

To delete a GeoMaster file from the memory of the calculator, follow these steps:

1. **Press [2nd][+][2] to enter the Memory manager.**

It may take a few seconds for the Memory manager to appear.

2. **Repeatedly use ⊡ until the cursor is to the left of AppVars, and then press ⌊ENTER⌋.**

3. **Repeatedly use ⊡⊡ until the cursor is to the left of the file you want to delete and press ⌊DEL⌋.**

4. **Press ⌊2⌋ if you really want to delete the file; press ⌊1⌋ if you chicken out about deleting the file from memory.**

Using Menus

When you enter GeoMaster, the Menu bar appears at the bottom of the screen. If you are re-entering the application after it has been running in the background, press ⌊GRAPH⌋ or ⌊ALPHA⌋ to make the Menu bar appear.

The five menus on GeoMaster's Menu bar are

- ✓ **FILE:** This menu contains the commands that allow you to create, save, and recall files. How to do this is explained in the sections, "Creating and Saving Files" and "Recalling and Deleting Files," earlier in this chapter. The menu also contains the command that allows you to clear the screen and quit the GeoMaster application.

- ✓ **DRAW:** The tools housed in this menu allow help you draw geometric figures. How to use these tools is explained in Chapter 6.

- ✓ **MEAS:** This menu contains the commands that allow you to take measurements (length, distance, angle, area, and so on) Using these commands is explained in Chapter 7.

- ✓ **TRFM:** If you want to transform objects by translating, reflecting, rotating, and/or dilating them, the tools needed to perform these tasks are found in this menu. How to use these tools is explained in Chapter 8.

- ✓ **MISC:** This menu contains some really great commands that answer the questions: Are these points collinear? Are these lines parallel or perpendicular? It also houses the commands for hiding objects in your construction. How to use these commands is explained in Chapter 6.

If you are cruising through GeoMaster's menus and decide not to make a selection, press ⌊CLEAR⌋ to get out of the menus and back to the GeoMaster screen.

To select a menu, press the key under the menu. That is, press Y= to enter the **FILE** menu, WINDOW to enter the **DRAW** menu, ZOOM to enter the **MEAS** menu, TRACE to enter the **TRFM** menu, and GRAPH to enter the **MISC** menu. A down arrow after the number of the last item in a menu screen or an up arrow after the number of the first menu item on the screen indicates that there are more items in the menu than can be displayed on the screen. This is illustrated in the two pictures in Figure 5-4. Use ▼|▲ to view these items.

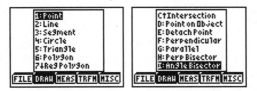

More items are below   More items are above

Figure 5-4: A menu containing more items than can fit on one screen.

GRAPH and CLEAR are your friends

Can't find GeoMaster's Menu bar?

    Press GRAPH and it instantly appears.

Did you accidentally exit GeoMaster?

    Press GRAPH and it appears as you left it.

Want to get rid of the Menu bar?

    Press CLEAR and it vanishes.

Want to stop using a Menu item?

    Press CLEAR and the item is deactivated.

Want to get out of the Menu bar without selecting an item?

    Press CLEAR and you're out.

Change your mind about creating a new file?

    Press CLEAR and no new file will be created.

In a nutshell, GRAPH gets you back into GeoMaster while it is running in the background and displays the menu bar while it is running in the foreground. CLEAR stops whatever it was you were doing or it makes the Menu bar disappear.

To activate a menu item, use ▼▲ to move the cursor to the
desired item and press ⌈ENTER⌋. Using the commands housed in
these menus is explained in the next three chapters.

If you press ▲ when the cursor is at the top of the menu, as in the
first picture in Figure 5-4, the cursor jumps to the last menu item,
as illustrated in the second picture in Figure 5-4. If you press ▼
when the cursor is at the bottom of a menu, the cursor jumps to
the top of the menu.

Clearing the Screen

The **Clear All** command in GeoMaster's **FILE** menu erases all
objects on the screen. It is equivalent to starting a new file without
saving your work. But be warned, GeoMaster does not have an
undo feature. So if you clear the screen, what was on the screen is
gone for good. To select **Clear All** from the **FILE** menu, press ⌈Y=⌋⌈5⌋
if the Menu bar is visible or ⌈GRAPH⌋⌈Y=⌋⌈5⌋ if it is not.

Chapter 6

Constructing Geometric Figures

In This Chapter

▶ Constructing geometric figures

▶ Finding midpoints, points of intersection, and angle bisectors

▶ Determining if two lines are parallel or perpendicular

▶ Determining if three points are collinear

▶ Hiding, deleting, and moving objects

▶ Adjusting GeoMaster's viewing window

*T*he GeoMaster **DRAW** menu contains a plethora of tools that enable you to do mundane things such as construct lines, segments, triangles, polygons, and circles. The **DRAW** menu also contains tools that enable you to do really neat things such as bisecting angles, constructing perpendicular and parallel lines, locating midpoints, and finding the points of intersection of geometric objects. And the **MISC** menu contains commands that will get the calculator to tell you if two lines are parallel or perpendicular, or if three points are collinear. This chapter tells you how to use these commands.

Constructing Points

This section explains how to construct a freestanding point, that is, a point that is not intended to be part of another object such as a point on a line or a point on the circumference of a circle. Constructing a point that is part of an existing object is explained later in this chapter.

You can tell the calculator where you want to construct a point in two ways: Use the arrow keys to identify the location of the point, or tell the calculator the coordinates of the point. Both ways are described in the following steps. To construct a freestanding point, follow these steps:

1. **Press** GRAPH WINDOW 1 **to select the Point tool from the DRAW menu.**

   "Point" appears in the upper-right corner of the screen.

2. **Use the arrow keys to move the cursor to the location where you want to construct the point and press** ENTER.

   As you move the cursor, the coordinates of its location appear at the bottom of the screen. The point is constructed at the location of the cursor.

   After pressing ENTER in this step, you can precisely locate the point by giving the calculator the coordinates of that point. You can also label the point. The "Precisely locating and labeling points" sidebar in this chapter tells you how to do this.

3. **Press** ENTER **or move the cursor away from the object.**

   This is a crucial step. If it is not followed, then the last point you constructed may vanish when you ask GeoMaster to perform another operation.

After constructing one point, the **Point** tool remains active until you deactivate it. So if you want to construct more points, just repeat Steps 2 and 3. When you're finished using the **Point** tool, deactivate it by pressing CLEAR or by selecting another menu item.

Precisely locating and labeling points

You can enter the coordinates of the location of the point after pressing ENTER to approximately establish the location of the point. But be warned, the numbers you enter for these coordinates can contain no more than one decimal place. If you enter a number with two or more decimal places for the *x*-coordinate, the calculator will not allow you to enter the *y*-coordinate. To enter the coordinates of the point after pressing ENTER to approximately locate the point, use the number keys to enter the single-decimal-place *x*-coordinate of the point and press ENTER. Then use the number keys to enter the *y*-coordinate of the point and press ENTER. The point is constructed at the specified coordinates.

Points can be labeled immediately after they are constructed. For example, if you are constructing a segment, after pressing ENTER to establish the first point defining that segment, you can label it before continuing with the construction of the segment. To do this, after pressing ENTER to establish the point, press ALPHA to label it with one letter, or press 2nd ALPHA to label it with more than one letter. Enter the label and continue with your construction.

Constructing Lines, Segments, Rays, and Vectors

Because two points determine a line, segment, ray, or vector, the directions for creating these objects are pretty much the same. To construct such objects, follow these steps:

1. **Select the appropriate tool from the DRAW menu.**

   To do this, press WINDOW if the Menu bar is visible at the bottom of the screen or GRAPH WINDOW if it is not. Use ⊡ to move the cursor to the tool you wish to use and press ENTER to select that tool. The tool you selected appears in the upper-right corner of the screen. The first picture in Figure 6-1 illustrates that the **Ray** tool was selected from the **DRAW** menu.

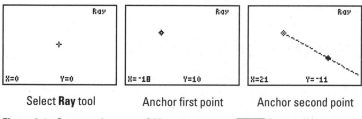

Select **Ray** tool   Anchor first point   Anchor second point

Figure 6-1: Constructing a ray. (When done, press ENTER.)

2. **Use the arrow keys to move the cursor to the location of the first point that determines your line, segment, ray, or vector. Press ENTER to establish this point.**

   As you move the cursor, its coordinates are displayed at the bottom of the screen and the anchored point appears in the shape of a diamond, as illustrated in the second picture in Figure 6-1.

   After pressing ENTER in this step, you can precisely locate the point by giving the calculator the coordinates of that point. You can also label the point. The "Precisely locating and labeling points" sidebar in this chapter tells you how to do this.

3. **Use the arrow keys to move the cursor to the location of the second point that determines the object and press ENTER to anchor that point.**

The third picture in Figure 6-1 illustrates this step when constructing a ray. Notice that the ray appears as a dashed line. This indicates that the ray, although it appears on the screen, has not yet been housed in the memory of the calculator.

4. **Press ENTER or move the cursor away from the object.**

This is a crucial step. If it is not followed, then the last object you created may vanish when you ask GeoMaster to perform another operation. After doing this step, the figure that appeared as a dashed line after performing Step 3 appears as a solid line. This indicates that your construction is now housed in the memory of the calculator.

After constructing a line segment, ray, or vector, the GeoMaster tool you were using remains active until you deactivate it. So if you want to construct more objects of the same kind, just repeat Steps 2 through 4. When you are finished using the tool, you deactivate it by pressing CLEAR or by selecting another menu item.

Constructing Circles

A circle is determined by its center and its radius. To construct a circle, follow these steps:

1. **Select the Circle tool from the DRAW menu.**

To do this, press GRAPH WINDOW 4. "Circle" in the upper-right corner of the first picture in Figure 6-2 illustrates that the **Circle** tool is active.

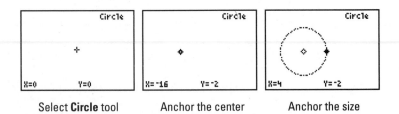

Select **Circle** tool   Anchor the center   Anchor the size

Figure 6-2: Constructing a circle.

2. **Use the arrow keys to move the cursor to the location on the screen where you want to place the center of the circle. Press ENTER to anchor this point.**

As you move the cursor, its coordinates are displayed at the bottom of the screen and the center of the circle appears in the shape of a diamond, as illustrated in the second picture in Figure 6-2.

After pressing ENTER in this step, you can precisely locate the center by giving the calculator the coordinates of that point. You can also label the center. The "Precisely locating and labeling points" sidebar in this chapter tells you how to do this.

3. **Use the arrow keys to expand the circle to the desired size and press ENTER to anchor the size of the circle.**

   The third picture in Figure 6-2 illustrates this step. The circle appears as dashed lines, indicating that the construction is not yet complete.

After pressing ENTER in this step, you can precisely locate the point on the circumference by giving the calculator the coordinates of that point. You can also label this. The "Precisely locating and labeling points" sidebar in this chapter tells you how to do this.

4. **Press ENTER or move the cursor away from the object.**

This is a crucial step. If it is not followed, then the last circle you created may vanish when you ask GeoMaster to perform another operation. After doing this step, the circle which appeared as a dashed circle after performing Step 3 appears as a solid circle. This indicates that your construction is now housed in the memory of the calculator.

After constructing your first circle, the **Circle** tool remains active until you deactivate it. So if you want to construct more circles, just follow Steps 2 through 4. When you are finished using this tool, you deactivate it by pressing CLEAR or by selecting another menu item.

Did you make a mistake?

If you make a mistake immediately after completing a construction (or part of a construction), press CLEAR to erase the construction, and then start over. This will erase the whole construction made by the active tool appearing in the upper-right corner of the screen. But that tool remains active, so you can start over with the same construction. If you need to erase a previously constructed object, the "Hiding and Deleting Objects" section, later in this chapter, tells you how to do this.

After a circle has been constructed, you can move its location on the screen by moving the circumference of the circle, and you can change the size of its radius by moving the point on the circumference of the circle. Moving points and objects is explained later in this chapter.

Constructing Triangles and Arcs

A triangle and an arc are determined by three points, so their construction is pretty much the same. To construct a triangle or an arc, follow these steps:

1. **Select the appropriate tool from the DRAW menu.**

   To do this, press [WINDOW] if the Menu bar is visible at the bottom of the screen or [GRAPH][WINDOW] if it is not. Use [▼] to move the cursor to the tool you want to use and press [ENTER] to select that tool. The tool you selected appears in the upper-right corner of the screen. The first picture in Figure 6-3 illustrates that the **Arc** tool was selected from the **DRAW** menu.

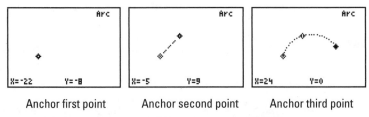

Anchor first point   Anchor second point   Anchor third point

Figure 6-3: Constructing an arc. (When done, press [ENTER].)

2. **Use the arrow keys to move the cursor to the location on the screen where you want to construct the first point of the triangle or arc. Press [ENTER] to construct this point.**

   As you move the cursor, its coordinates are displayed at the bottom of the screen and the anchored point appears in the shape of a diamond, as illustrated in the first picture in Figure 6-3.

   After pressing [ENTER] in this step, you can precisely locate the point by giving the calculator the coordinates of that point. You can also label the point. The "Precisely locating and labeling points" sidebar in this chapter tells you how to do this.

3. **Use the arrow keys to move the cursor to the location on the screen where you wish to construct the second point defining the triangle or arc. Press [ENTER] to anchor this point.**

   The second picture in Figure 6-3 illustrates this step when constructing an arc.

4. **Use the arrow keys to move the cursor to the location on the screen where you wish to construct the third point defining the triangle or arc. Press [ENTER] to anchor this point.**

   The third picture in Figure 6-3 illustrates this step when constructing an arc. The arc appears as dashed lines indicating that the construction is not yet complete.

5. **Press [ENTER] or move the cursor away from the object.**

   This is a crucial step. If it is not followed, then the last object you created may vanish when you ask GeoMaster to perform another operation. After doing this step, the figure which appeared as a dashed lines or arcs after performing Step 4 appear as a solid lines or arcs. This indicates that your construction is now housed in the memory of the calculator.

After constructing a triangle or arc, the GeoMaster tool you were using remains active until you deactivate it. So if you want to construct more objects of the same kind, just follow Steps 2 through 5. When you are finished using that tool, you deactivate it by pressing [CLEAR] or by selecting another menu item.

After a triangle or an arc has been constructed, you can move its location on the screen by moving one of the segments defining the triangle or arc, or you can change its shape by moving the points defining the object. Moving points and objects is explained later in this chapter.

Constructing Polygons

If you want to create a regular polygon, the next section tells you how to do it. To create an (irregular) polygon, follow these steps:

1. **Press [GRAPH][WINDOW][6] to select the Polygon tool from the DRAW menu.**

   "Polygon" in the upper-right corner of the screen indicates that the **Polygon** tool is active.

2. **Use the arrow keys to move the cursor to the location on the screen where you want to construct the first point defining your polygon. Press ENTER to anchor this point.**

   As you move the cursor, its coordinates are displayed at the bottom of the screen, and the anchored point appears in the shape of a diamond, as illustrated in the first picture in Figure 6-4.

   After pressing ENTER in this step, you can precisely locate the point by giving the calculator the coordinates of that point. You can also label the point. The "Precisely locating and labeling points" sidebar in this chapter tells you how to do this.

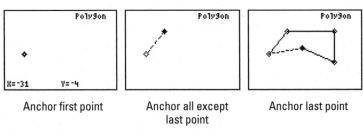

| Anchor first point | Anchor all except last point | Anchor last point |

Figure 6-4: Constructing a polygon.

3. **Use the arrow keys to move the cursor to the location on the screen where you wish to construct the second point defining the polygon. Press ENTER to anchor this point.**

   The second picture in Figure 6-4 illustrates this step. Notice that the dashed line between these points indicates that the polygon is not yet constructed.

4. **Use the arrow keys to construct the remaining points that define the polygon. Press ENTER to anchor each point.**

   The third picture in Figure 6-4 illustrates this step. Notice that the line joining the first and last points you constructed is a dashed line. This indicates that the construction of the polygon is not yet complete.

5. **Press ENTER and move the cursor away from the object.**

   All sides of the polygon appear as solid lines indicating the construction of the polygon is complete.

After constructing a polygon, the **Polygon** tool remains active until you deactivate it. So if you want to construct more polygons, just follow Steps 2 through 5. When you are finished using this tool, you deactivate it by pressing CLEAR or by selecting another menu item.

Constructing Regular Polygons

A regular polygon is determined by its center and the number of its sides. To construct a regular polygon, follow these steps:

1. **Press** GRAPH WINDOW 7 **to select the Reg Polygon tool from the DRAW menu.**

   "Reg Polygon" in the upper-right corner of the screen indicates that the **Reg Polygon** tool is active.

2. **Use the arrow keys to move the cursor to the location on the screen where you want to place the center of the regular polygon. Press** ENTER **to anchor this point.**

   As you move the cursor, its coordinates are displayed at the bottom of the screen.

   After pressing ENTER in this step, you can precisely locate the center by giving the calculator the coordinates of that point. You can also label the point. The "Precisely locating and labeling points" sidebar in this chapter tells you how to do this.

3. **Press** ▶ **to display the number of sides of the polygon. The default number of sides is 6. Press** − **to decrease the number of sides of the polygon, or press** + **to increase the number of sides.** *Do not* **press** ENTER **when your polygon has the desired number of sides or you will be unable to rotate or adjust the size of the polygon.**

   This is illustrated in the first picture in Figure 6-5 for the construction of a pentagon. GeoMaster can construct polygons having a minimum of 3 sides and a maximum of 12 sides.

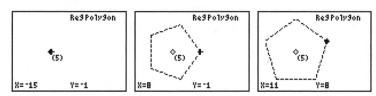

Anchor center and size   Adjust size   Rotate and adjust size

Figure 6-5: Constructing a regular polygon.

4. **Repeatedly press ◄ and/or ► to adjust the size of your polygon and repeatedly press ▲ and/ or ▼ to rotate the polygon. Press ENTER *only when* the polygon is to your liking.**

   Pressing ► increases its size and ◄ decreases its size. This is illustrated in the second picture of Figure 6-5. Pressing ▲ rotates the polygon in the counterclockwise direction and ▼ rotates it in the clockwise direction. Continue using these arrow keys, in any order, until the polygon is exactly the way you want it. Press ENTER when you are done. This is illustrated in the third picture in Figure 6-5.

5. **Press ENTER or move the cursor away from the polygon.**

   This is a crucial step. If it is not followed, then the last polygon you created may vanish when you ask GeoMaster to perform another operation. After doing this step, the polygon which appeared as dashed lines after performing Step 4 appears as solid lines. This indicates that your construction is now housed in the memory of the calculator.

After constructing your first regular polygon, the **Reg Polygon** tool remains active until you deactivate it. So if you want to construct more regular polygons, just repeat Steps 2 though 5. When you are finished using this tool, you deactivate it by pressing CLEAR or by selecting another menu item.

If you want to label the vertices defining your regular polygon, the "Labeling objects" sidebar in this chapter tells you how to do this.

Constructing Perpendicular and Parallel Lines

The next section tells you how to construct a perpendicular bisector. This section tells you how to construct perpendicular or parallel lines. To construct such lines, you have to start with an already constructed line, segment, ray, vector, or side of a polygon or triangle. Earlier sections in this chapter explain how to construct these objects. To construct a line that is perpendicular or parallel to an already constructed line, segment, ray, vector, or side of a triangle or polygon, follow these steps:

1. Select the appropriate tool from the DRAW menu.

To do this, press WINDOW if the Menu bar is visible at the bottom of the screen or GRAPH WINDOW if it is not. Use ▾ to move the cursor to the tool you wish to use and press ENTER to select that tool. The tool you select appears in the upper-right corner of the screen. The first picture in Figure 6-6 illustrates that the **Perpendicular** tool was selected from the **DRAW** menu.

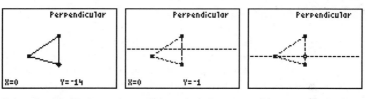

Select **Perpendicular** tool   Select given line   Move perpendicular

Figure 6-6: Constructing a perpendicular line. (When done, press ENTER .)

2. Use the arrow keys to move the cursor to the already constructed line, segment, ray, vector, or side of a triangle or polygon, and then press ENTER .

A perpendicular or parallel line appears, as illustrated in the second picture in Figure 6-6. In the next step, this line is moved to the location of your choice.

3. Use the arrow keys to move the cursor to the location on the screen where you want to construct the perpendicular or parallel line. Press ENTER to anchor this location.

The third picture in Figure 6-6 illustrates this step when constructing a perpendicular line. Notice that the coordinates of the cursor location appear at the bottom of the screen and that your figure is drawn in dashed lines, indicating that the construction is not yet complete.

4. Press ENTER or move the cursor away from the object.

This is a crucial step. If it is not followed, then the last object you created may vanish when you ask GeoMaster to perform another operation. After doing this step, the figure which appeared as a dashed line after performing Step 3 appears as a solid line. This indicates that your construction is now housed in the memory of the calculator.

After constructing a parallel or perpendicular line, the GeoMaster tool you were using remains active until you deactivate it. So if you want to construct more objects of the same kind, just repeat Steps 2 though 4. When you are finished using that tool, you deactivate it by pressing CLEAR or by selecting another menu item.

Constructing Perpendicular Bisectors

In GeoMaster, a perpendicular bisector can be constructed to an already existing line, segment, ray, vector, or side of a polygon or triangle. Constructing these objects is explained earlier in this chapter. To construct a perpendicular bisector, follow these steps:

1. **Select the Perp Bisector tool from the DRAW menu.**

   To do this, press WINDOW if the Menu bar is visible at the bottom of the screen or GRAPH WINDOW if it is not. Press ▲ to move the cursor to the bottom of the menu, press ▲ again to move the cursor to the **Perp Bisector** tool, and press ENTER. The tool you selected appears in the upper-right corner of the screen.

2. **Use the arrow keys to move the cursor to the already constructed line and press ENTER.**

   The perpendicular bisector appears as a solid line. This indicates that you are finished with the construction.

After constructing a perpendicular bisector, the **Perp Bisector** tool remains active until you deactivate it. So if you want to construct more perpendicular bisectors, just repeat Step 2. When you are finished using the tool, you deactivate it by pressing CLEAR or by selecting another menu item.

Constructing Angle Bisectors

For GeoMaster to recognize the existence of an angle, that angle must contain three defining points — the vertex and a point on each side of the angle. Also, GeoMaster recognizes a point only if it appears on the screen as a small square, such as the three points defining the triangle in Figure 6-6. If the angle you want to bisect does not contain the small squares representing the three points defining the angle, then GeoMaster cannot bisect it. But all is not lost. The next section tells you how to establish the point of intersection of two lines, and the section after that tells you how to place a point on a line. After you have constructed the three points defining your angle, GeoMaster can bisect it.

To construct the bisector of an already constructed angle containing three defining points, follow these steps:

1. **Select the Angle Bisector tool from the DRAW menu.**

   To do this, press [WINDOW] if the Menu bar is visible at the bottom of the screen or [GRAPH][WINDOW] if it is not. Press [▲] to move the cursor to **Angle Bisector**, the last menu item, and press [ENTER]. The tool you selected appears in the upper-right corner of the screen.

2. **Use the arrow keys to move the cursor to an existing point on one side of the angle and press [ENTER] to anchor that point.**

   GeoMaster uses a small square to indicate that a point exists. If you don't see a small square on the side of the angle, the first paragraph in this section tells you what to do about the situation.

3. **Use the arrow keys to move the cursor to the vertex of the angle and press [ENTER] to anchor the vertex.**

   The vertex must always be the second point that defines the angle.

4. **Use the arrow keys to move the cursor to an existing point on the other side of the angle and press [ENTER] to anchor that point.**

   The angle bisector appears as a solid line, indicating that your construction is complete.

After constructing an angle bisector, the **Angle Bisector** tool remains active until you deactivate it. So if you want to construct more angle bisectors, just repeat Steps 2 through 4. When you are finished using the tool, you deactivate it by pressing [CLEAR] or by selecting another menu item.

Constructing Points of Intersection

GeoMaster can construct the points of intersection of any pair of the following types of objects: lines, segments, rays, vectors, sides of polygons, circles, and arcs. If there is more than one point of intersection, GeoMaster will find all of these points.

To construct points of intersection, follow these steps:

1. **Select the Intersection tool from the DRAW menu.**

   To do this, press [WINDOW] if the Menu bar is visible at the bottom of the screen or [GRAPH][WINDOW] if it is not. Repeatedly press ▼ to highlight the **Intersection** tool and press [ENTER]. The tool you selected appears in the upper-right corner of the screen.

2. **Use the arrow keys to move the cursor to one of the objects in the intersecting pair of objects and press [ENTER].**

   After pressing [ENTER], the object just selected appears as a dashed figure.

3. **Use the arrow keys to move the cursor to the other object in the intersecting pair and press [ENTER].**

   The point or points of intersection appear on the screen and the **Intersection** tool remains active. You can construct more points of intersections by following Steps 2 and 3. When you are finished using this tool, you deactivate it by pressing [CLEAR] or by selecting another menu item.

When you press [ENTER] to select an object and GeoMaster isn't sure which object you want, it gives you a list of objects from which you choose one by pressing the number of the object. This is illustrated in Figure 6-7.

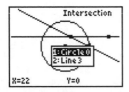

Figure 6-7: What you see when GeoMaster doesn't know what you want.

If you want to label the point of intersection you just constructed, the "Labeling objects" sidebar in this chapter tells you how to do this.

Constructing a Point on an Object

The first section in this chapter explains how to construct a free-standing point; this section explains how to construct a point so that it is part of an existing object. To construct a point on an object, first select the **Point on Object** tool from the **DRAW** menu (press GRAPH WINDOW, repeatedly press ▾ to highlight the **Point on Object** tool, and press ENTER). Then use the arrow keys to move the cursor to the location on the object where you wish to place a point and press ENTER. The point is constructed at the location of the cursor and the **Point on Object** tool remains active so that you can construct more points on the same object or another object. When you are finished constructing points on objects, press CLEAR to deactivate the **Point on Object** tool or select another menu item.

The **Detach Point** tool in the **DRAW** menu is used to detach a point that was constructed using the **Point on Object** tool. The detached point remains on the screen, but GeoMaster no longer considers it to be associated with the object to which it was previously attached. So if you move or transform the object, though the object changes, the point will not change its location. When the **Detach Point** tool is active, you detach a point by placing the cursor on the point and pressing ENTER.

 If you want to label the point you just constructed, the "Labeling objects" sidebar in this chapter tells you how to do this.

Constructing a Midpoint

GeoMaster can construct the midpoint of an already constructed segment or the midpoint between two existing points. The segment can be the side of a triangle or polygon. GeoMaster recognizes only those points that appear on the screen as small squares.

To construct a midpoint, first select the **Midpoint** tool from the **DRAW** menu (press GRAPH WINDOW, repeatedly press ▾ to highlight the **Midpoint** tool, and press ENTER). If you are constructing the midpoint of a segment, use the arrow keys to place the cursor on the segment and press ENTER to construct the midpoint. If you are constructing the midpoint between two points, move the cursor to the first point and press ENTER. Then move the cursor to the second point and press ENTER to have GeoMaster construct the midpoint.

After constructing the first midpoint, the **Midpoint** tool remains active so that you can construct more midpoints. When you are finished constructing midpoints, press CLEAR to deactivate the **Midpoint** tool or select another menu item.

If you want to label the midpoint you just constructed, the "Labeling objects" sidebar in this chapter tells you how to do this.

Moving Figures

When you move an object, all other objects associated with that object will also undergo a change. Figure 6-8 provides a surprising example. The circle and line in the first picture of this figure are associated objects because the center of the circle is also one of the points defining the line. So if you move *only* the line, as illustrated in the second picture of Figure 6-8, the center of the circle moves with the line because it is on the line. But the point on the circumference of the circle remains fixed because it is not on the line. Because the center and point on the circumference determine the radius of the circle, the size of the circle changes when only the line is moved.

And if you move *only* the circle, as illustrated in the third picture in Figure 6-8, the slope of the line changes because one of the points defining the line (the point that is also the center of the circle) moves with the circle but the other point stays fixed. Now if you move *both* the circle and the line, then the size of the circle and the slope of the line remain the same. This is illustrated in the third picture in Figure 6-9.

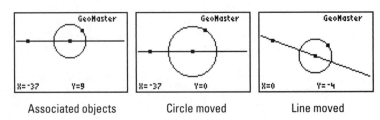

Associated objects   Circle moved   Line moved

Figure 6-8: Moving associated objects.

Labeling objects

I personally prefer to avoid labeling objects. Labels take time to create, crowd the screen, are rarely placed where you want them, and after you have gone to the trouble of moving them to a desirable location, they move out of place when you move or transform the object they label. But let's face it — there are times when you just have to label those points and objects so that you can refer to them by name. Figure 6-11 is a good example of a figure requiring labels.

To label an already constructed object, first press [GRAPH][GRAPH][2] to select the **Label** tool from the **MISC** menu. Then move the cursor to the point or object you want to label and press [ENTER] to select that object. [A] appears in the upper-right corner, indicating that the calculator is in Alpha mode so that you can enter letters. *Without moving the cursor,* enter the label for the object and press [ENTER] when you are finished. After creating one label, you can move the cursor to another object, press [ENTER], give that object a label, and press [ENTER] to anchor the label. When you are finished creating labels, deactivate the **Label** tool by pressing [CLEAR] or by selecting another menu item.

The label can contain up to eight characters consisting of letters and numbers. (Writing words in Alpha mode is explained in Chapter 1.) After you have created a label, you can move that label to a more desirable location. Moving objects, such as labels, is explained elsewhere in this chapter.

To reshape a polygon or triangle, move one or more of its vertices. To change the size of a circle, move a point on the circumference of that circle or move the center of the circle.

To move one or more objects, follow these steps:

1. Press [CLEAR] to deactivate all GeoMaster tools.

When no tools are active, you see "GeoMaster" in the upper-right corner of the screen, as illustrated in the first picture in Figure 6-8.

2. Use the arrow keys to move the cursor to the first object you want to move and press [ENTER].

The object you selected is displayed as dashed lines. This is illustrated in the first picture in Figure 6-9, where the circle is one of the objects that to be moved.

3. **If you are moving more than one object, move the cursor to the second object and press** 2nd ENTER. **Select other objects in the same manner — move the cursor to the object and press** 2nd ENTER.

The additional objects you select appear as dashed lines. This is illustrated in the second picture in Figure 6-9, where the line was selected as the other object to be moved.

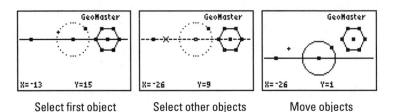

Select first object   Select other objects   Move objects

Figure 6-9: Moving one or more objects.

4. **When you are finished selecting objects to be moved, press** ENTER **while the cursor is on one of the selected objects.**

The cursor appears in the shape of a times sign, as illustrated in the second picture in Figure 6-9.

5. **Use the arrow keys to move the selected objects and press** ENTER **to anchor the new location.**

The cursor changes to the shape a small plus sign.

6. **Move the cursor to a blank spot on the screen and press** ENTER.

The objects appear as solid lines, as illustrated in the third picture in Figure 6-9.

Determining If Two Lines Are Parallel or Perpendicular

It is often the case that when you construct lines, two lines may look parallel or perpendicular, when in fact they aren't. The first picture in Figure 6-10 provides an example. Two lines in this picture appear to be parallel, and thus perpendicular to the third line, but they are not. How do I know this? I asked GeoMaster!

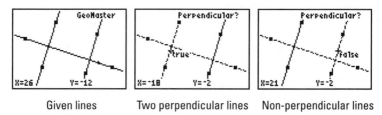

Given lines   Two perpendicular lines   Non-perpendicular lines

Figure 6-10: Determining if lines are perpendicular.

To get GeoMaster to determine if two lines are perpendicular or parallel, follow these steps:

1. **Select the Perpendicular? or Parallel? tool from the MISC menu.**

   To do this, press GRAPH GRAPH, use the arrow keys to move the cursor to the appropriate tool, and press ENTER. The tool you selected appears in the upper-right corner of the screen, as is illustrated in the second picture in Figure 6-10 where the **Perpendicular?** tool is active.

2. **Use the arrow keys to move the cursor to the first line and press ENTER. Move the cursor to the second line and press ENTER. The conclusion as to whether or not the lines are parallel or perpendicular appears on the screen.**

   The two selected lines appear as dashed lines, as illustrated in the second picture in Figure 6-10. The word "true" appearing on the screen in this picture indicates that the lines are indeed perpendicular.

3. **If you want to use the same tool to test another pair of lines, press CLEAR and then repeat Step 2.**

   This is illustrated in the third picture in Figure 6-10. The word "false" appearing on the screen indicates that the lines are not perpendicular.

4. **When you are finished using the Perpendicular? or Parallel? tool, deactivate it by pressing CLEAR *two times* or by selecting another menu item.**

Determining If Three Points Are Collinear

Three points are collinear if they are on the same line. It is sometimes difficult to determine if three points are collinear by just looking at the screen. For example, points D, B, and E in the first picture in Figure 6-11 are collinear, but the points A, B, and C are not. How do I know this? I asked GeoMaster!

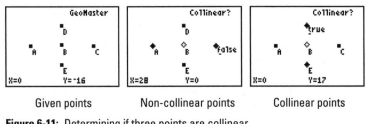

Given points   Non-collinear points   Collinear points

Figure 6-11: Determining if three points are collinear.

To determine if three points are collinear, follow these steps:

1. **Select the Collinear? tool from the MISC menu.**

   To do this, press GRAPH GRAPH, use the arrow keys to move the cursor to the **Collinear?** tool, and press ENTER. The tool you selected appears in the upper-right corner of the screen, as is illustrated in the second picture in Figure 6-11.

2. **Use the arrow keys to move the cursor to the first point and press ENTER. Move the cursor to the second point and press ENTER. Then move the cursor to the third point and press ENTER. The conclusion as to whether or not the points are collinear appears on the screen.**

   The selected points appear as diamonds, as illustrated in the second picture in Figure 6-11 where the points A, B, and C are selected. The word "false" appearing on the screen in this picture indicates that the points are not collinear.

3. **If you want to determine if three other points are collinear, press CLEAR and then repeat Step 2.**

   This is illustrated in the third picture in Figure 6-11. The word "true" appearing on the screen indicates that the points D, B, and E are collinear.

4. **When you are finished using the Collinear? tool, deactivate it by pressing** $\boxed{\text{CLEAR}}$ *two times* **or by selecting another menu item.**

Hiding and Deleting Objects

There is a big difference between hiding and deleting an object. If you hide an object, you can, if you so choose, bring it back in view at a later time. But if you delete an object, it is gone for good.

Hiding an object

The first picture in Figure 6-12 provides an example of when you may want to hide an object. Because GeoMaster has no tool that instantly creates a tangent to a circle, the tangents in this picture were created by first constructing radii, and then constructing lines perpendicular to these radii. (Constructing such objects is explained earlier in this chapter.) If all you really want to see is the circle and tangents, you can hide the radii, as illustrated in the third picture in Figure 6-12. If you were to delete the radii, the tangents would also be deleted because they were constructed perpendicular to the radii, and are thus dependent on the existence of the radii.

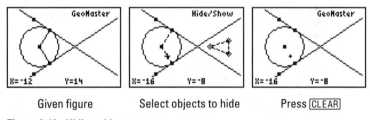

| Given figure | Select objects to hide | Press $\boxed{\text{CLEAR}}$ |

Figure 6-12: Hiding objects.

To hide one or more objects, follow these steps:

1. **Press** $\boxed{\text{GRAPH}}\boxed{\text{GRAPH}}\boxed{\blacktriangle}\boxed{\blacktriangle}\boxed{\blacktriangle}\boxed{\text{ENTER}}$ **to select the Hide/Show tool from the MISC menu.**

   The name **Hide/Show** appears in the upper-right corner of the screen and any previously hidden objects appear on the screen as dashed lines. This is illustrated in the second picture in Figure 6-12, where the triangle is a previously hidden object. For now, ignore any previously hidden objects. They will be hidden again in Step 3.

2. **Use the arrow keys to move the cursor to the first object you want to hide and press** ENTER**. Move the cursor to the second object you want to hide and press** ENTER**. Continue selecting objects to hide by placing the cursor on the object and pressing** ENTER**.**

   The selected objects appear as dashed lines, as illustrated in the second picture in Figure 6-12, where the radii are selected.

3. **Press** CLEAR **to hide the objects selected in Step 2 and to again hide any previously hidden objects.**

   This is illustrated in the third picture in Figure 6-12, where the selected radii and the previously hidden triangle are all hidden.

Redisplaying hidden objects

To redisplay hidden objects, press GRAPH GRAPH ▲ ▲ ▲ ENTER to select the Hide/Show tool from the MISC menu. All previously hidden objects appear on the screen. For each object that you no longer want to hide, place the cursor on that object and press ENTER. Then press CLEAR. The objects that you did not select to bring out of hiding are again hidden, and the objects you did select to show remain on the screen.

Deleting objects

GeoMaster has no undo feature. So if you delete an object, it's gone for good. Also, if you delete an object, then all other objects whose construction is dependent on the deleted object will also be deleted. For example, the tangents in the first picture in Figure 6-12 were constructed perpendicular to the radii of the circle. If you were to delete the radii, the tangents would also vanish because their existence is dependent on the existence of the radii.

To delete an object, press CLEAR to ensure that no tools are active. Use the arrow keys to move the cursor to the object and press ENTER to select that object. The object appears as a dashed line. Press DEL to delete the object.

Adjusting the Viewing Window

GeoMaster uses a default window in which $-47 \leq x \leq 47$ and $-31 \leq y$ ≤ 31. You can change this window by pressing CLEAR WINDOW and redefining the settings in the Window editor. You can also change the window by pressing CLEAR ZOOM and selecting one of the pre-defined Zoom features. The Window editor and the Zoom features are explained in Chapters 9 and 10. To return GeoMaster to its default window, press CLEAR ZOOM 8 to select **ZoomCenter** from the **Zoom** menu.

Chapter 7

Finding Measurements

· ·

In This Chapter

▶ Evaluating length and area

▶ Measuring an angle

▶ Constructing the sum of two vectors

▶ Determining the coordinates of a point or the slope of a line

▶ Finding the equation of a line or a circle

· ·

*G*eoMaster's **MEAS** menu houses the tools you use to find the length of a segment, degree measure of an angle, or area of a circle, triangle, or polygon. It also contains a tool that allows you to add and subtract like measurements. It even has a tool that determines the equation of a line or a circle. This chapter explains how to use these and other tools.

Finding Length and Distance

The **Distance/Length** tool in the **MEAS** menu is used to find the distance between two points, the length of a segment or vector, the circumference of a circle, or the perimeter of a polygon. To use this tool, follow these steps:

1. **Press** GRAPH ZOOM ENTER **to select the Distance/Length tool from the MEAS menu.**

   The name of the tool appears in the upper-right corner of the screen, as illustrated in the first picture of Figure 7-1.

2. **Select the object you want to measure.**

   If you are measuring the distance between two points, use the arrow keys to move the cursor to the first point and press ENTER to select it. Then move the cursor to the second and press ENTER. The distance between the points appears on the screen, as illustrated in the first picture in Figure 7-1.

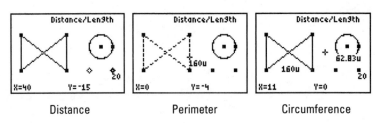

Distance   Perimeter   Circumference

Figure 7-1: Using the **Distance/Length** tool.

If you are measuring the length of a segment or vector, the circumference of a circle, or the perimeter of a polygon, use the arrow keys to move the cursor to that object and press ENTER to select the object. The object is displayed using dashed lines and the requested measure appears on the screen. This is illustrated in the second picture in Figure 7-1, where GeoMaster found the perimeter of the polygon.

If you don't like GeoMaster's placement of the length or distance, before performing the next step, you can use the arrow keys to relocate it. This is illustrated in the third picture in Figure 7-1 where the measurement of the perimeter of the polygon is relocated. The measurements of the other two objects in this picture remain where GeoMaster placed them.

3. **Press** ENTER **to anchor the placement of the measurement.**

4. **To measure another object, repeat Steps 2 and 3.**

   This is illustrated in the third picture of Figure 7-1, where all three objects on the screen have been measured.

5. **When you are finished taking measurements, press** ENTER **again or move the cursor away from the last object. To deactivate the Distance/Length tool, press** ENTER **or select another menu item.**

   After pressing ENTER, all objects are displayed using solid lines, as illustrated in the third picture in Figure 7-1.

Finding Area

GeoMaster can find the area of any circle, triangle, or *simple* polygon constructed using the **Circle**, **Triangle**, **Polygon**, or **RegPolygon** tool in the **DRAW** menu. (Using these tools is explained in Chapter 6.)

A polygon is *simple* if its sides intersect only at the vertices of the polygon. For example, the polygon ABCD in Figure 7-3 is not simple, whereas all regular polygons, such as the hexagon in Figure 7-4, are simple.

In addition, GeoMaster is also not capable of directly finding the area of a polygon formed by the intersection of two other polygons, such as the quadrilateral in Figure 7-4 formed by the intersection of the hexagon and triangle. But all is not lost. The following subsections tell you how to find the area of a polygon that is not simple and the area of a polygon formed by the intersection of two other polygons.

To find the area of a circle, triangle, or simple polygon constructed using the tools in the **DRAW** menu, follow these steps:

   1. **Press** GRAPH ZOOM 2 **to select the Area tool.**

      The name of the tool appears in the upper-right corner of the screen, as illustrated in Figure 7-2.

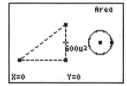 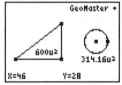

Area of triangle   Area of circle

Figure 7-2: Finding the area of a triangle and a circle.

   2. **Use the Arrow keys to move the cursor to the object whose area you want to find, and then press** ENTER **to select that object.**

      The object is displayed using dashed lines and the requested area appears on the screen. This is illustrated in the first picture in Figure 7-2 for the area of the triangle.

      If you don't like GeoMaster's placement of the area, before performing the next step, you can use the arrow keys to relocate it. This is illustrated in the second picture of Figure 7-2 for the location of the area of the triangle.

   3. **Press** ENTER **to anchor the placement of the area measurement.**

4. **To find the area of another object, repeat Steps 2 and 3.**

5. **When you are finished finding areas, press** ENTER **again or move the cursor away from the last object. To deactivate the Area tool, press** ENTER **or select another menu item.**

After pressing ENTER, all objects are displayed using solid lines, as illustrated in the second picture in Figure 7-2.

Finding the area of a polygon having intersecting sides

To find the area of a polygon having intersecting sides, such as polygon ABCD in Figure 7-3, break the polygon down into simple polygons (polygons whose sides intersect only at vertices) and then add up the areas of the simple polygons.

Sounds simple, but it's not. To get GeoMaster to find the area of the smaller polygons, those polygons have to be constructed using the **Polygon** tool in the **DRAW** menu. But to construct a polygon using the **Polygon** tool, GeoMaster needs to know all the vertices of the polygon. So you must first find the point of intersection of the intersecting sides of the original polygon.

Again: Sounds simple, but it's not. Unfortunately, GeoMaster's **Intersection** tool can't find the intersection of sides of polygons. So here's what you can do to find the area of a polygon having intersecting sides:

1. **Press** GRAPH WINDOW 3 **to select the Segment tool from the DRAW menu. Construct segments over the sides of the intersecting sides of the polygon.**

Using the **Segment** tool is explained in Chapter 6. In the polygon in Figure 7-3, I constructed the segments AD and BC.

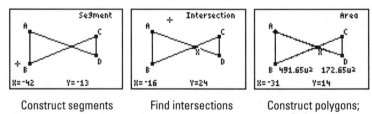

Construct segments   Find intersections   Construct polygons;
                                                 find areas

Figure 7-3: Finding the area of a polygon having intersecting sides.

2. **Press** GRAPH WINDOW ALPHA PRGM **to select the Intersection tool from the DRAW menu and use this tool to find the point of intersection of the segments constructed in Step 2.**

   Using the **Intersection** tool is explained in Chapter 6. If GeoMaster asks you which segment you want to select, choose the one with the highest number because this is the number of the most recently constructed segment. The second picture in Figure 7-3 shows that I labeled the point of intersection. You don't have to do this, but you can if you want to. (Labeling is explained in Chapter 6.)

3. **Press** GRAPH WINDOW 6 **to select the Polygon tool from the DRAW menu and use this tool to construct the smaller polygons contained in the polygon having intersecting sides.**

   Using the **Polygon** tool is explained in Chapter 6. In the second picture in Figure 7-3, I used the polygon tool to construct the triangles ABX and CDX.

4. **Press** GRAPH ZOOM 2 **to select the Area tool from the MEAS menu. Find the areas of the smaller polygons. Add these areas to find the area of the original polygon.**

   The steps in the previous section tell you how to find the area of a polygon. The third picture in Figure 7-3 shows the areas of the smaller triangles contained in the original polygon. The "Performing Calculations" section, later in this chapter, tells you how to add these areas.

Finding the area of the intersection of two polygons

GeoMaster can't find the area of a polygon formed by the intersection of two other polygons because GeoMaster doesn't know that it's there. For example, in the first picture in Figure 7-4, GeoMaster doesn't recognize the existence of the quadrilateral formed by the intersection of the hexagon and triangle because GeoMaster didn't construct that quadrilateral.

To get GeoMaster to find the area of the intersection, you must use GeoMaster to define the polygon formed by this intersection. To do this, you first find the points of intersection of the sides of the original two polygons. And then you use these points to get GeoMaster to define the polygon formed by the intersection. But this is not as easy as it seems because GeoMaster is not capable of finding the points of intersection of two polygons.

However, the steps in the previous subsection on how to find the area of a polygon having intersecting sides can also be followed to find the area of the intersection of two polygons. These steps are briefly listed in the following list. For a more detailed explanation, see the steps in the previous subsection.

1. **Use the Segment tool ([GRAPH][WINDOW][3]) to construct segments over the intersecting sides of the polygons.**

   In the first picture in Figure 7-4, I used the **Segment** tool to construct segments AB, AC, PQ, and QR.

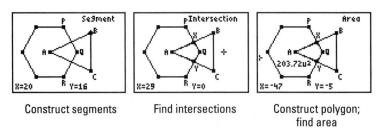

Construct segments   Find intersections   Construct polygon; find area

Figure 7-4: Finding the area of the intersection of two polygons.

2. **Use the Intersection tool ([GRAPH][WINDOW][ALPHA][PRGM]) to find the points of intersection of the segments constructed in Step 1.**

   In the second picture of Figure 7-4, I used the **Intersection** tool construct the points of intersection X and Y.

3. **Use the Polynomial tool ([GRAPH][WINDOW][6]) to construct the polygon formed by the intersection of the original polygons.**

   In the third picture of Figure 7-4, I used the **Polygon** tool to construct polygon AXQY.

4. **Use the Area tool ([GRAPH][ZOOM][2]) to find the area of the polygon formed by the intersection of the original polygons.**

   This is illustrated in the third picture in Figure 7-4.

Measuring an Angle

For GeoMaster to recognize the existence of an angle, that angle must contain three defining points: the vertex and a point on each side of the angle. Also, GeoMaster recognizes a point only if it appears on the screen as a small square, such as the four points defining the polygon in Figure 7-1. If the angle you want to measure does not contain the small squares representing these three defining points, then GeoMaster cannot measure it. But all is not lost. The previous chapter tells you how to establish the point of intersection of two lines and how to place a point on a line. After you have constructed the three points defining your angle, GeoMaster can find its measure.

GeoMaster measures all angles in degrees — even if the Mode is set to radian measure. Chapter 3 tells you how to convert degrees to radians. This chapter also tells you how to convert degree measures to degrees, minutes and seconds.

To find the degree measure of an already constructed angle containing three defining points, follow these steps:

1. **Press** GRAPH ZOOM 3 **to select the Angle tool from the MEAS menu.**

   The tool you selected appears in the upper-right corner of the screen.

2. **Use the arrow keys to move the cursor to an existing point on one side of the angle and press** ENTER **to anchor that point.**

   GeoMaster uses a small square to indicate that a point exists. If you don't see a small square on the side of the angle, the first paragraph in this section tells you what to do about the situation.

3. **Use the Arrow keys to move the cursor to the vertex of the angle and press** ENTER **to anchor the vertex.**

   The vertex must always be the second point that defines the angle.

4. **Use the Arrow keys to move the cursor to an existing point on the other side of the angle and press** ENTER **to anchor that point.**

   The degree measure of the angle appears near the location of the cursor.

5. **Use the arrow keys to move the angle measure to the location of your choice and press** ENTER **to anchor that location.**

After measuring an angle, the **Angle** tool remains active until you deactivate it. So if you want to measure more angles, repeat Steps 2 through 5. When you are finished using the tool, deactivate it by pressing CLEAR or by selecting another menu item.

Performing Calculations

GeoMaster is capable of adding and subtracting like measures that GeoMaster found using the **Distance/Length**, **Area**, or **Angle** tools in the **MEAS** menu. By *like measures,* I mean it can, for example, add two area measures; it cannot add unlike measures such as an area measure and an angle measure. GeoMaster cannot multiply, divide, or square a number. So if you want to use GeoMaster to verify the Pythagorean Theorem, you're out of luck.

To add or subtract like measures found by the **Distance/Length**, **Area**, or **Angle** tool, follow these steps:

1. **Press** GRAPH ZOOM 4 **to select the Calculate tool from the MEAS menu.**

   The tool you selected appears in the upper-right corner of the screen, as illustrated in the first picture in Figure 7-5.

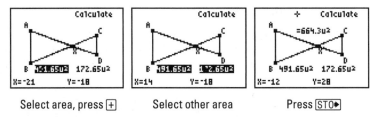

Select area, press +   Select other area   Press STO►

Figure 7-5: Finding the sum of two area measurements.

2. **Use the arrow keys to move the cursor to the first measurement and press** ENTER **to select that measure.**

   Place the cursor at the beginning of a measurement to select it. After you press ENTER, the measurement is highlighted. This is illustrated in the first picture in Figure 7-5.

3. **Press** + **if you want to add another measurement to the measure selected in Step 2; press** − **if you want to subtract.**

4. **Use the arrow keys to move the cursor to the next measurement in your addition or subtraction problem and press** ENTER.

   This is illustrated in the second picture in Figure 7-5.

5. **Repeat Steps 3 and 4 to add and/or subtract more measurements.**

   GeoMaster allows you to add and/or subtract up to a maximum of six measurements.

6. **Press STO▶ to find the answer to the addition and/or subtraction of measurements.**

   This step is not necessary if you added and/or subtracted six measurements. In this case, GeoMaster automatically calculates the answer.

   The calculated answer, preceded by an equal sign, appears on the screen near the location of the cursor.

7. **Use the arrow keys to move the answer to a better location and press ENTER to anchor that location. Press ENTER again or move the cursor.**

   This is illustrated in the third picture in Figure 7-5.

After adding or subtracting measurements, the **Calculate** tool remains active until you deactivate it. So if you want to add or subtract more measures, repeat Steps 2 through 7. When you are finished using the tool, deactivate it by pressing CLEAR or by selecting another menu item.

The **Calculate** tool will not allow you to use a calculated answer in an addition and/or subtraction problem involving measurements. A calculated answer is preceded by an equal sign.

Finding Slope

The **Slope** tool in the **MEAS** menu can be used to find the slope of a line, segment, ray, vector, or side of a polygon. To find the slope, follow these steps:

1. **Press GRAPH ZOOM 5 to select the Slope tool from the MEAS menu.**

2. **Use the arrow keys to move the cursor to the line, segment, ray, vector, or side of a polygon and press ENTER.**

   The slope appears at the location of the cursor.

3. **Use the arrow keys to move the slope to a better location and press ENTER to anchor that location. Press ENTER again or move the cursor.**

The **Slope** tool remains active until you deactivate it. So if you want to find the slope of another line or segment, repeat Steps 2 and 3. When you are finished using the tool, deactivate it by pressing CLEAR or by selecting another menu item.

Constructing a Vector Sum

To construct the sum of two vectors, follow these steps:

1. **Press** GRAPH ZOOM 6 **to select the Vector Sum tool from the MEAS menu.**

2. **Use the arrow keys to move the cursor to the first vector in the sum and press** ENTER.

   The selected vector appears as a dashed vector, as illustrated in the first picture in Figure 7-6.

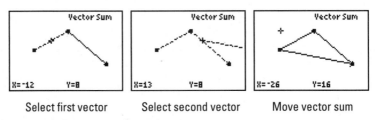

| Select first vector | Select second vector | Move vector sum |

Figure 7-6: Constructing the sum of two vectors.

3. **Use the arrow keys to move the cursor to the second vector in the sum and press** ENTER.

   The vector sum is constructed at the location of the cursor, as illustrated in the second picture in Figure 7-6.

4. **Use the arrow keys to move the vector sum to a better location and press** ENTER **to anchor that location. Press** ENTER **again or move the cursor.**

   This is illustrated in the third picture in Figure 7-6.

The **Vector Sum** tool remains active until you deactivate it. So if you want to construct the sum of more vectors, repeat Steps 2 through 4. When you are finished using the tool, deactivate it by pressing CLEAR or by selecting another menu item.

Finding the Equation of a Line/Circle or the Coordinates of a Point

The **Eqns/Coords** tool in the **MEAS** menu can be used to find the equation of a line, the equation of a circle, or the coordinates of an already constructed point. It will not find the equation of a segment, ray, vector, or side of a polygon. To find the equation of a line or a circle, or to find the coordinates of a point, follow these steps:

1. Press GRAPH ZOOM 7 to select the Eqns/Coords tool from the MEAS menu.

2. Use the arrow keys to move the cursor to the object whose equation or coordinates you want to find and press ENTER.

   The equation or coordinates appear at the location of the cursor.

3. Use the arrow keys to move the equation or coordinates to a better location and press ENTER to anchor that location. Press ENTER again or move the cursor.

The **Eqns/Coords** tool remains active until you deactivate it. So if you want to find the equation of other lines or circles, or the coordinates of other points, repeat Steps 2 and 3. When you are finished using the tool, deactivate it by pressing CLEAR or by selecting another menu item.

Chapter 8

Performing Transformations

• •

In This Chapter

▶ Translating, reflecting, rotating, and dilating figures

▶ Creating tessellations

• •

*G*eoMaster has all the tools you need to transform your geometric constructions by translating, reflecting, rotating, or dilating them. It even has a tool that lets you tessellate (tile) the plane with a geometric figure. This chapter tells you how to use these tools.

Translating a Geometric Object

When you translate a geometric object, you move it in a given direction for a given distance. A vector is used to tell GeoMaster the direction in which to move the object. The length of the vector tells GeoMaster how far to move the object.

To translate an already constructed geometric object, follow these steps:

1. **Press** GRAPH WINDOW 9 **to select the Vector tool from the DRAW menu and use it to construct the vector that defines the translation.**

   Using the **Vector** tool is explained in Chapter 6. The first picture in Figure 8-1 shows the vector by which the already constructed triangle is to be translated.

2. **Press** GRAPH TRACE 1 **to select the Translation tool from the TRFM menu.**

3. **Use the arrow keys to move the cursor to the object you want to translate and press** ENTER.

   GeoMaster can translate only one object at a time. The object to be translated appears as a dashed figure. This is illustrated in the second picture in Figure 8-1, where the triangle is the object that will be translated.

4. **Use the arrow keys to move the cursor to the vector and press** ENTER.

The translation of the original object appears along with the original object, as illustrated in the third picture in Figure 8-1.

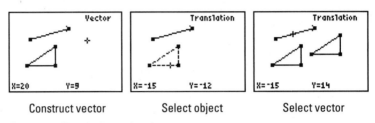

| Construct vector | Select object | Select vector |

Figure 8-1: Translating a triangle.

The **Translation** tool remains active until you deactivate it. So if you want to translate another object by the same vector, repeat Steps 3 and 4. When you are finished using the tool, deactivate it by pressing CLEAR or by selecting another menu item.

After translating objects, if you move the vector, the translated objects will move to the location defined by the new vector. If you delete the vector, the translated object is also deleted. Moving and deleting objects is explained in Chapter 6.

Reflecting Geometric Objects

When a geometric object is reflected in a line, that line acts like a mirror — hence the term *reflection* — so the mirror image of the original object appears on the other side of the line. GeoMaster allows objects to be reflected in a line, segment, ray, or vector.

To reflect an already constructed geometric object, follow these steps:

1. **Construct the line of reflection.**

The line of reflection may be a line, segment, ray, or vector. Constructing such objects is explained in Chapter 6. The first picture in Figure 8-2 shows that the already constructed hexagon is to be reflected in a vector.

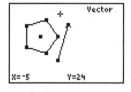 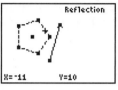 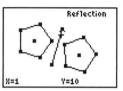

Construct reflection line   Select object   Select reflection line

Figure 8-2: Reflecting a pentagon.

_____

    2. **Press** GRAPH TRACE 2 **to select the Reflection tool from the TRFM menu.**

    3. **Use the arrow keys to move the cursor to the object you want to reflect and press** ENTER.

      GeoMaster can reflect only one object at a time. The object to be reflected appears as a dashed figure. This is illustrated in the second picture in Figure 8-2, where the pentagon is the object to be reflected.

    4. **Use the arrow keys to move the cursor to the line of reflection and press** ENTER.

      The reflection of the original object appears along with the original object, as illustrated in the third picture in Figure 8-2.

The **Reflection** tool remains active until you deactivate it. So if you want to reflect another object, repeat Steps 3 and 4. When you are finished using the tool, deactivate it by pressing CLEAR or by selecting another menu item.

 After reflecting objects, if you move the line of reflection, the reflected objects will move to the location defined by the line of reflection. If you delete the line, the reflected object is also deleted. Moving and deleting objects is explained in Chapter 6.

Rotating Geometric Objects

When a geometric object is rotated, it is rotated about a given point through a given angle. To rotate an already constructed geometric object, follow these steps:

    1. **Construct the point of rotation.**

      Constructing points is explained in Chapter 6. The point about which rotation occurs can be one of the points on the already constructed object. The first picture in Figure 8-3 shows that the already constructed triangle is to be rotated about the point.

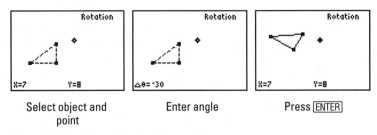

Select object and   Enter angle   Press ENTER
point

Figure 8-3: Rotating a triangle about a point.

2. **Press** GRAPH TRACE 3 **to select the Rotation tool from the TRFM menu.**

3. **Use the arrow keys to move the cursor to the object you want to rotate and press** ENTER.

   GeoMaster can rotate only one object at a time. The object to be rotated appears as a dashed figure.

4. **Use the arrow keys to move the cursor to the point of rotation and press** ENTER.

   This is illustrated in the first picture in Figure 8-3.

5. **Use the keypad to enter the degree measure of the angle of rotation.**

   As you begin to enter the angle, "$\Delta\theta =$" appears in the lower-left corner of the screen, and the calculator places your angle measure after this symbol. You can enter your angle as a negative number to rotate in the clockwise direction or as a positive number to rotate in the counterclockwise direction. The second picture in Figure 8-3 illustrates that the triangle is about to be rotated 30 degrees in the clockwise direction.

   Instead of entering the measure of the angle of rotation, you can repeatedly press ＋ and/or － to rotate the object about the point. Each time you press ＋, the object is rotated 5 degrees in the counterclockwise direction; － rotates it 5 degrees clockwise.

6. **Press** ENTER.

   The original placement of the object vanishes, and the rotation of the object appears on the screen, as illustrated in the third picture in Figure 8-3.

The **Rotation** tool remains active until you deactivate it. So if you want to rotate another object, repeat Steps 3 through 6. When you are finished using the tool, deactivate it by pressing CLEAR or by selecting another menu item.

Dilating Geometric Objects

The **Dilation** tool in the in the **TRFM** menu is used to increase or decrease the size of an object by a factor of k. When $0 < k < 1$, the object decreases in size, and when $k > 1$, it increases in size. For example, if $k = 0.5$, the dilated object is half its original size, and if $k = 2$, the dilated object doubles in size. Guess what it does when $k = 1$? That's right: The object doesn't change at all.

The dilation of an object also takes place with respect to a fixed point appropriately called the *dilation point.* If that point is at the center of the object, such as the center of a circle, the object increases or decreases in size and the center of the object remains fixed. But when the dilation point is not in the center of the object, not only does the object increase or decrease in size, but it also moves away from the dilation point when $k > 1$ or closer when $0 < k < 1$. The distance that the dilated object moves is determined by k. For example, if $k = 2$, the dilated object doubles in size and is twice as far away for the dilation point.

To dilate an already constructed geometric object, follow these steps:

1. **Construct the dilation point.**

   Constructing points is explained in Chapter 6. The dilation point can be one of the points on the already constructed object. The first picture in Figure 8-4 shows that the already constructed pentagon is to be dilated with respect to a point outside the pentagon.

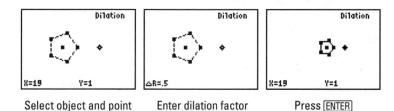

Select object and point   Enter dilation factor   Press ENTER

Figure 8-4: Dilating a pentagon with respect to a point.

2. **Press** GRAPH TRACE 4 **to select the Dilation tool from the**
   TRFM menu.

3. **Use the arrow keys to move the cursor to the object you**
   want to dilate and press ENTER.

   GeoMaster can dilate only one object at a time. The object
   to be dilated appears as a dashed figure.

4. **Use the arrow keys to move the cursor to the dilation**
   point and press ENTER.

   This is illustrated in the first picture in Figure 8-4.

5. **Use the keypad to enter the dilation factor** *k*.

   As you begin to enter the dilation factor, "$\Delta R =$" appears in
   the lower-left corner of the screen, and the calculator
   places your entry after this symbol. The second picture in
   Figure 8-4 illustrates that the pentagon is about to be
   reduced to half its size and moved halfway closer to the
   dilation point.

   Instead of entering the dilation factor, you can repeatedly
   press + and/or − to dilate the object about the dilation
   point. Each time you press +, the object is increased in
   size by a factor of 1.1; − decreased its size by a factor of 0.9.

6. **Press** ENTER.

   The original placement of the object vanishes and the dilation of the object appears on the screen, as illustrated in
   the third picture in Figure 8-4.

The **dilation** tool remains active until you deactivate it. So if you
want to dilate another object, repeat Steps 3 through 6. When you
are finished using the tool, deactivate it by pressing CLEAR or by
selecting another menu item.

Tiling the Plane

The **Symmetry** tool in the **TRFM** menu can be used to tessellate
(tile) the plane with a geometric figure by rotating that object 180
degrees about a specified point. Unlike the **Rotation** tool, the
Symmetry tool displays both the original and rotated object. To
tessellate the plane with an already constructed polygon, follow
these steps:

1. **Press** GRAPH TRACE 5 **to select the Symmetry tool from the TRFM menu.**

2. **Use the arrow keys to move the cursor to the object you want to tessellate and press** ENTER.

   The object to be rotated appears as a dashed figure, as illustrated in the first picture in Figure 8-5.

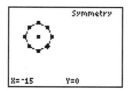 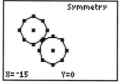 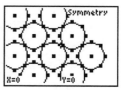

Select object and point   Press ENTER   Repeat process

Figure 8-5: Tessellating the plane with an octagon.

3. **Use the arrow keys to move the cursor to the point of rotation and press** ENTER.

   The point of rotation is usually any vertex of the polygon. After you press ENTER, the rotated figure appears, as illustrated in the second picture in Figure 8-5.

4. **Repeat Step 3 until the plane is tiled.**

   This is illustrated in the third picture in Figure 8-5.

When you are finished tiling the plane, deactivate the **Symmetry** tool by pressing CLEAR or by selecting another menu item.

Part III
Graphing and Analyzing Functions

The 5th Wave   By Rich Tennant

"WHAT EXACTLY ARE YOU TRYING TO SAY?"

In this part . . .

*T*his part looks at graphing a function and analyzing it by tracing the graph or by creating a table of functional values. You get pointers on how to find values associated with the graph, such as minimum and maximum points, points of intersection, and the slope of the curve. And you are shown how to graph inequalities and transformations of functions.

Chapter 9

Graphing Functions

. . . .

In This Chapter

▶ Entering functions into the calculator

▶ Graphing functions

▶ Recognizing whether the graph is accurate

▶ Graphing piecewise-defined and trigonometric functions

▶ Viewing the graph and the function on the same screen

▶ Saving and recalling a graph and its settings in a Graph Database

. . . .

The calculator has a variety of features that help you painlessly graph a function. The first step is to enter the function into the calculator. Then to graph the function, you set the viewing window and press GRAPH. Or (better yet) you can use one of several Zoom commands to get the calculator to set the viewing window for you. Finally, after you have graphed the function, you can use Zoom commands to change the look of the graph. For example, you can zoom in or zoom out on a graph the same way that a zoom lens on a camera lets you zoom in or out on the subject of the picture you're about to take.

Entering Functions

Before you can graph a function, you must enter it into the calculator. The calculator can handle up to ten functions at once, Y_1 through Y_9 and Y_0. To enter functions in the calculator, perform the following steps:

1. **Press MODE and put the calculator in Function mode, as shown in Figure 9-1.**

   To highlight an item in the Mode menu, use the ▶ ◀ ▲ ▼ keys to place the cursor on the item, and then press ENTER.

Highlight **Func** in the fourth line to put the calculator in Function mode. (For more about the other items on the Mode menu, refer to Chapter 1.)

Figure 9-1: Setting Function mode.

2. **Press [Y=] to access the Y= editor.**

3. **Enter the definitions of your functions.**

   To erase an entry that appears after **Y**$_n$, use the [▶][◀][▲][▼] keys to place the cursor to the right of the equal sign and press [CLEAR]. Then enter your definition for the new function and press [ENTER].

When you're defining functions, the only symbol the calculator allows for the independent variable is the letter X. Press [X,T,Θ,n] to enter this letter in the definition of your function. In Figure 9-2, this key was used to enter the functions Y_1, Y_2, Y_4, Y_5, and Y_6.

As a timesaver, when entering functions in the Y= editor, you can reference another function in its definition. (Figure 9-2, for example, shows function Y_3 defined as $-Y_2$.) To paste a function name in the function you're entering in the Y= editor, follow these steps:

1. **Press [VARS][▶] to access the Y-Variables menu.**

2. **Press [1] to access the Function menu.**

3. **Press the number key for the name of the function you want to paste in the definition.**

Figure 9-2: Examples of entering functions.

Graphing Functions

Here's where your calculator draws pretty pictures. After you have entered the functions into the calculator, as described in the previous section, you can use the following steps to graph the functions:

1. **Turn off any Stat Plots that you don't want to appear in the graph of your functions.**

   The first line in the Y= editor tells you the graphing status of the Stat Plots. (Stat Plots are discussed in Chapter 17.) If **Plot1**, **Plot2**, or **Plot3** is highlighted, then that Stat Plot will be graphed along with the graph of your functions. If it's not highlighted, it won't be graphed. In Figure 9-2, **Plot1** will be graphed along with the functions.

   To turn off a highlighted Stat Plot in the Y= editor, use the ▶◀▲▼ keys to place the cursor on the highlighted Stat Plot and then press ENTER. The same process is used to highlight the Stat Plot again in order to graph it at a later time.

   When you're graphing functions, Stat Plots can cause problems if they're turned on when you don't really want them to be graphed. The most common symptom of this problem is the ERR: INVALID DIM error message — which by itself gives you almost no insight into what's causing the problem. So if you aren't planning to graph a Stat Plot along with your functions, make sure all Stat Plots are turned off.

2. **Press 2nd ZOOM to access the Format menu.**

3. **Set the format for the graph by using the ▶◀▲▼ keys to place the cursor on the desired format, and then press ENTER to highlight it.**

   In the Format menu, each line of the menu will have one item highlighted. An explanation of each menu selection follows:

   - **RectGC and PolarGC:** This gives you a choice between having the coordinates of the location of the cursor displayed in (x, y) rectangular form or in (r, θ) polar form. Select **RectGC** for rectangular form or **PolarGC** for polar form.

   - **CoordOn and CoordOff:** This tells the calculator whether you want to see the coordinates of the cursor location displayed at the bottom of the screen as you move the cursor. Select **CoordOn** if you want to see these coordinates; select **CoordOff** if you don't.

- **GridOff and GridOn:** If you select **GridOn**, grid points appear in the graph at the intersections of the tick marks on the *x*- and *y*-axes (as illustrated in Figure 9-3). If you select **GridOff**, no grid points appear in the graph.

- **AxesOn and AxesOff:** If you want to see the *x*- and *y*-axes on your graph, select **AxesOn**. If you don't want to see them, select **AxesOff**.

- **LabelOff and LabelOn:** If you want the *x*- and *y*-axes to be labeled, select **LabelOn** (as in Figure 9-3). Because the location of the labels isn't ideal, selecting **LabelOff** is usually a wise choice.

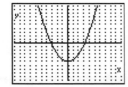

Figure 9-3: A graph with grid points and labeled axes.

- **ExprOn and ExprOff:** If you select **ExprOn**, when you're tracing the graph of a function, the definition of that function appears in the upper left of the screen. If you select **ExprOff** and **CoordOn**, then only the number of the function appears when you trace the function. If you select **ExprOff** and **CoordOff**, then nothing at all appears on the screen to indicate which function you're tracing.

4. Press [WINDOW] to access the Window editor.

5. After each of the window variables, enter a numerical value that is appropriate for the functions you're graphing. Press [ENTER] after entering each number.

Figure 9-4 shows the Window editor when the calculator is in Function mode. The items in this menu determine the viewing window for your graph — in particular, how the *x*- and *y*-axes look on the screen. The following gives an explanation of the variables you must set in this editor:

- **Xmin and Xmax:** These are, respectively, the smallest and largest values of *x* in view on the *x*-axis.

If you don't know what values your graph will need for **Xmin** and **Xmax**, press ZOOM 6 to invoke the **ZStandard** command. This command automatically graphs your functions in the Standard viewing window; the settings for this window appear in Figure 9-4. You can then, if necessary, use the other Zoom commands (described in Chapter 10) to get a better picture of your graph.

```
WINDOW
 Xmin=-10
 Xmax=10
 Xscl=1
 Ymin=-10
 Ymax=10
 Yscl=1
 Xres=1
```

Figure 9-4: Window editor in Function mode.

- **Xscl:** This is the distance between tick marks on the x-axis. (Go easy on the tick marks; using too many makes the axis look like a railroad track. Twenty or fewer tick marks makes for a nice looking axis.)

- **Ymin and Ymax:** These are, respectively, the smallest and largest values of y that will be placed on the y-axis.

If you have assigned values to **Xmin** and **Xmax** but don't know what values to assign to **Ymin** and **Ymax**, press ZOOM 0 to invoke the **ZoomFit** command. This command uses the **Xmin** and **Xmax** settings to determine the appropriate settings for **Ymin** and **Ymax**, and then automatically draws the graph. It does not change the **Yscl** setting. (You must return to the Window editor, if necessary, to adjust this setting yourself.)

- **Yscl:** This is the distance between tick marks on the y-axis. (As with the x-axis, too many tick marks make the axis look like a railroad track. Fifteen or fewer tick marks is a nice number for the y-axis.)

- **Xres:** This setting determines the resolution of the graph. It can be set to any of the integers 1 through 8. When **Xres** is set equal to 1, the calculator evaluates the function at each of the 94 pixels on the x-axis and graphs the result. If **Xres** is set equal to 8, the function is evaluated and graphed at every eighth pixel.

Xres is usually set equal to 1. If you're graphing a lot of functions, it may take the calculator a while to graph them at this resolution, but if you change **Xres** to a higher number, you may not get an accurate graph.

If it's taking a long time for the calculator to graph your functions, and this causes you to regret setting **Xres** equal to 1, press [ON] to terminate the graphing process. You can then go back to the Window editor and adjust the **Xres** setting to a higher number.

6. **Press [GRAPH] to graph the functions.**

Graphing Several Functions

If you're graphing several functions at once, it's not easy to determine which graph each function is responsible for. To help clear this up, the calculator allows you to identify the graphs of functions by setting a different graph style for each function. To do this, follow these steps:

1. **Press [Y=] to access the Y= editor.**

2. Use the [▶][◀][▲][▼] keys to place the cursor on the icon appearing at the far left of the definition of the function.

3. **Repeatedly press [ENTER] until you get the desired graph style.**

   You have seven styles to choose from: ＼ (Line), ＼ (Thick Line), ＼ (shading above the curve), ▙ (shading below the curve), ⊹ (Path), ◊ (Animate), and ⋰ (Dotted Line). Each time you press [ENTER], you get a different style.

   • **Line, Thick Line, and Dotted Line styles:** In Figure 9-2, Y_1 is set to the default line style. Y_2 and Y_3 are set to Thick Line style; and Y_6 is set to Dotted Line style. Figure 9-5 illustrates these styles.

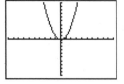 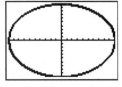 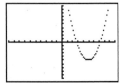

Line   Thick Line   Dotted Line

Figure 9-5: Line style, Thick Line style, and Dotted Line style.

- **Shading above and below the curve styles:** In Figure 9-2, Y_4 is set to the shading above the curve style and Y_5 is set to the shading below the curve style. The calculator has four shading patterns: vertical lines, horizontal lines, negatively sloping diagonal lines, and positively sloping diagonal lines. You don't get to select the shading pattern. If you're graphing only one function in this style, the calculator uses the vertical line pattern. If you're graphing two functions, the first is graphed in the vertical line pattern and the second in the horizontal line pattern. If you graph three functions in this style, the third appears in the negatively sloping diagonal lines pattern, and so on (as illustrated in Figure 9-6).

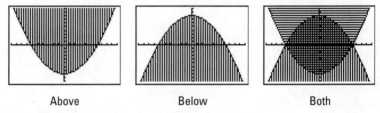

Above   Below   Both

Figure 9-6: Shading above the curve, shading below the curve, and two shaded functions.

- **Path and Animated styles:** The Path style, denoted by the ⫶ icon, uses a circle to indicate a point as it's being graphed (as illustrated in Figure 9-7). When the graph is complete, the circle disappears and leaves the graph in Line style.

  The animate style, denoted by the ⫶ icon, also uses a circle to indicate a point as it's being graphed, but when the graph is complete, no graph appears on the screen. For example, if this style is used, graphing $y = -x^2 + 9$ looks like a movie of the path of a ball thrown in the air.

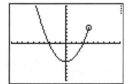

Figure 9-7: Path style.

If you don't want the calculator to graph a function in the Y=
editor, remove the highlight from the equal sign in that function. To
graph it at a later time, highlight the equal sign again. This is done
in the Y= editor by using the ▶◀▲▼ keys to place the cursor on
the equal sign in the definition of the function and then pressing
ENTER to toggle the equal sign between highlighted and not highlighted. In the example in Figure 9-2, the calculator won't graph
functions Y_2 through Y_6.

Is Your Graph Accurate?

The calculator can do only what you tell it to do — which doesn't
always produce an accurate graph. The three main causes of inac-
curate graphs, and their solutions, are the following:

✓ **The graph is distorted by the size of the screen.**

Because the calculator screen isn't square, circles don't look
like circles unless the viewing window is properly set. How do
you properly set the viewing window? No problem! Just graph
the function as described earlier in this chapter, and then
press ZOOM 5 to invoke the **ZSquare** command. **ZSquare** readjusts the window settings for you and graphs the function
again in a viewing window in which circles look like circles.
Figure 9-8 illustrates this. (The circle being drawn in each of
these figures is the circle defined by Y_2 and Y_3, as shown in
Figure 9-2.)

✓ **The viewing window is too small or too big.**

If you don't know what the graph should look like, then after
graphing it you should zoom out to see more of the graph or
zoom in to see a smaller portion of the graph. To do this,
press ZOOM 3 to zoom out, or press ZOOM 2 to zoom in.

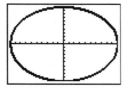 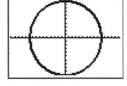

ZStandard   ZSquare

Figure 9-8: A circle graphed using **ZStandard** and then using **ZSquare**.

Then use the ▶◀▲▼ keys to move the cursor to the point from which you want to zoom out or in, and press ENTER. It's just like using a camera. The point you want to move the cursor to is the focal point.

After zooming in or out, you may have to adjust the window settings, as described earlier in this chapter.

As an example, Figure 9-9 shows the progression of graphing Y_1 in Figure 9-2. It was first graphed in the Standard viewing window. Then it was zoomed out from the point (0, 10). And finally, the window settings were adjusted to get a better picture of the graph.

✔ **Vertical asymptotes may not be recognizable.**

In all graph styles except Animate and Dotted Line, the calculator graphs one point, and then the next point, and connects those two points with a line segment. This sometimes causes vertical asymptotes to appear on the graph. The last graph in Figure 9-9 illustrates an example of when a vertical asymptote is present. Don't mistake this almost-vertical line for a part of the graph. It's not; it's just a vertical asymptote.

In a different viewing window, the vertical asymptote may not even appear. This happens when the calculator graphs one point, but the next point is undefined because the x value of that point is exactly at the location of the vertical asymptote. Figure 9-10 gives an example of re-graphing the last graph shown in Figure 9-9, using a viewing window in which the vertical asymptote does not appear.

If you want to ensure that vertical asymptotes don't appear on your graph, graph the function in the Dotted Line style described in the previous section. For an explanation of how you can draw a vertical asymptote on a graph, see Chapter 12 in the book *TI-83 Plus Graphing Calculator For Dummies*.

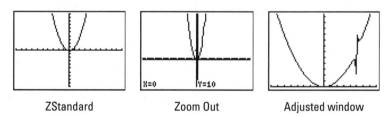

ZStandard   Zoom Out   Adjusted window

Figure 9-9: A graph using **ZStandard**, then **Zoom Out**, and then an adjusted viewing window.

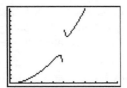

Figure 9-10: A viewing window in which no vertical asymptotes appear.

Piecewise-Defined Functions

When graphing a piecewise-defined function, some people cop out and simply graph each of the separate functions that appear in it. But this does not result in an accurate graph. To accurately graph the following piecewise-defined function, perform the following steps:

$$y = \begin{cases} y_1, & x < a \\ y_2, & a \le x \le b\text{~} \\ y_3, & x > b \end{cases}$$

1. **Enter the functions Y_1, Y_2, and Y_3 in the Y= editor.**

    Entering functions in the Y= editor is explained earlier in the chapter. Examples of three such functions appear in Figure 9-11.

2. **Turn off Y_1, Y_2, and Y_3 by removing the highlight from their equal signs.**

    This is done in the Y= editor by using the ▶◀▲▼ keys to place the cursor on the equal sign in the definition of the function and then pressing ENTER to toggle the equal sign between highlighted and not highlighted. The calculator graphs a function only when its equal sign is highlighted. An example of this appears in Figure 9-11.

3. **Enter the piecewise-defined function in Y_4 as $(Y_1)(x < a) + (Y_2)(a \le x)(x \le b) + (Y_3)(x > b)$.**

    The function must be entered as it appears above, complete with parentheses. $(Y_1)(x < a)$ tells the calculator to graph the function Y_1 for $x < a$ and $(Y_2)(a \le x)(x \le b)$ tells it to graph Y_2 for $a \le x \le b$.

- **To enter Y₁, Y₂, and Y₃:** Press VARS ▶ 1 and then press the number of the function you want to use in the definition.

- **To enter the inequalities:** Press 2nd MATH to access the Test menu, and then press the number of the inequality you want to use in the definition. For example, to enter the less-than (<) symbol, press 2nd MATH 5.

An example of entering this function appears in Figure 9-11.

4. **Press ENTER.**

5. **Graph the piecewise-defined function.**

An earlier section of this chapter explains how to graph functions. An example graph of a piecewise-defined function appears in Figure 9-11.

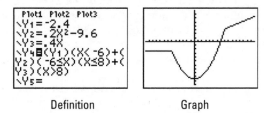

| Definition | Graph |

Figure 9-11: Defining and graphing a piecewise-defined function.

If one or more of the functions in your piecewise-defined function is a trigonometric function, make sure the calculator is in Radian and not Degree mode. Otherwise, your piecewise-defined function may look like a step function instead of the graph you were expecting. The next section tells you how to change the mode and how to graph trigonometric functions.

Graphing Trig Functions

The calculator has built-in features especially designed for graphing trigonometric functions. They produce graphs that look like graphs you see in text books; and when you trace these graphs, the x-coordinate of the tracing point is always given as a fractional multiple of π. To use these features when graphing trigonometric functions, follow these steps:

1. **Put the calculator in Function and Radian mode.**

   Press MODE. In the third line, highlight **Radian**, and in the fourth highlight **Func**. (To highlight an item in the Mode menu, use the ▶◀▲▼ keys to place the cursor on the item, and then press ENTER.)

2. **Enter your trigonometric functions into the Y= editor.**

   Entering functions in the Y= editor is explained earlier in the chapter.

3. **Press ZOOM7 to graph the function.**

   ZOOM7 invokes the **ZTrig** command that graphs the function in a viewing window in which $-47\pi/24 \leq x \leq 47\pi/24$ and $-4 \leq y \leq 4$. It also sets the tick marks on the x-axis to multiples of $\pi/2$.

   When you trace a function graphed in a **ZTrig** window, the x-coordinate of the trace cursor will be a multiple of $\pi/24$, although the x-coordinate displayed at the bottom of the screen will be a decimal approximation of this value. (Tracing is explained in the next chapter.)

If you want to graph trigonometric functions in Degree mode, to get at least one period of a sine or cosine function, you must set **Xmin** to 0 and **Xmax** to 2π. This is why I say that it is a lot easier to graph trig functions in Radian mode. Setting the mode to degrees or radians is explained in Step 1.

Viewing the Function and Graph on the Same Screen

If you're planning to play around with the definition of a function you're graphing, it's quite handy to have both the Y= editor and the graph on the same screen. That way you can edit the definition of your function and see the effect your editing has on your graph. To do so, follow these steps:

1. **Put the calculator in Horizontal mode.**

   Press MODE and highlight **Horiz** in the last line of the menu, as illustrated in Figure 9-12. To highlight an item in the Mode menu, use the ▶◀▲▼ keys to place the cursor on the item, and then press ENTER.

2. **Press** Y=.

   The Graph window appears at the top of the screen and the Y= editor at the bottom of the screen.

3. **Enter or edit a function in the Y= editor.**

   Entering functions in the Y= editor is explained earlier in this chapter. Editing expressions is explained in Chapter 1.

4. **Graph the function.**

   Graphing functions is explained earlier in this chapter.

To edit or enter a function, press Y=. To see the resulting graph, press GRAPH.

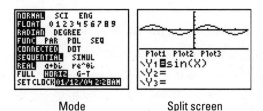

| Mode | Split screen |

Figure 9-12: Function and graph on the same screen.

Saving and Recalling a Graph

If you want to save your graph as a Graph Database, when you recall the graph at a later time, the graph remains interactive. This means that you can, for example, trace the graph and resize the viewing window because a Graph Database also saves the Graph Mode, Window, Format, and Y= editor settings. It does not, however, save the split-screen settings (**Horiz** and **G-T**) entered in the last line of the Mode menu. This section explains how to save, delete, and recall a graph in a Graph Database.

To save a Graph Database, perform the following steps:

1. **Press** 2nd PRGM ▶ ▶ **to access the Draw Store menu.**

2. **Press** 3 **to store your graph as a Graph Database.**

3. **Enter an integer 0 through 9.**

   The calculator can store up to 10 Graph Databases. If, for example, you enter the number **5**, your Graph Database is stored in the calculator as **GDB5**.

If you save your Graph Database as **GDB5** without realizing that you had previously stored another Graph Database as **GDB5**, the calculator — without warning or asking your permission — erases the old **GDB5** and replaces it with the new **GDB5**. To see a list of the Graph Databases already stored in your calculator, press 2nd+29.

If you already have ten Graph Databases stored in your calculator and don't want to sacrifice any of them, consider saving some of them on your PC. Chapter 18 describes how to do this.

   4. **Press** ENTER.

To delete a Graph Database from your calculator, perform the following steps:

   1. **Press 2nd+ to access the Memory menu.**

   2. **Press 2 to access the Mem Mgt/Del menu.**

   3. **Press 9 to access the GBD files stored in the calculator.**

   4. **If necessary, repeatedly press ⏷ to move the indicator to the GBD you want to delete.**

   5. **Press** DEL.

   If there is more than one Graph Database stored in your calculator, you are asked whether or not you really want to delete this item. Press 2 if you want it deleted, or press 1 if you have changed your mind about deleting it.

   6. **Press 2nd MODE to exit this menu and return to the home screen.**

To recall a saved Graph Database, perform the following steps:

   1. **Press 2nd PRGM ▸ ▸ to access the Draw Store menu.**

   2. **Press 4 to recall your Graph Database.**

   3. **Enter the number of your stored Graph Database.**

   4. **Press** ENTER.

When you recall a Graph Database, the Mode, Window, Format, and Y= editor settings in your calculator change to those saved in the Graph Database. If you don't want to lose the settings you have in the calculator, save them in another Graph Database before recalling your saved Graph Database. (Saving a Graph Database is described earlier in this section.)

Chapter 10

Exploring Functions

. . . .

In This Chapter

▶ Using Zoom commands

▶ Tracing the graph of a function

▶ Constructing tables of functional values

▶ Creating and clearing user-defined tables

▶ Viewing graphs and tables on the same screen

. . . .

*T*he calculator has three very useful features that help you explore the graph of a function: zooming, tracing, and creating tables of functional values. Zooming allows you to quickly adjust the viewing window for the graph so that you can get a better idea of the nature of the graph. Tracing shows you the coordinates of the points that make up the graph. And creating a table — well, I'm sure you already know what that shows you. This chapter explains how to use each of these features.

Using Zoom Commands

After you've graphed your functions (as described in Chapter 9), you can use Zoom commands to adjust the view of your graph. Press ZOOM to see the ten Zoom commands that you can use. The following list explains the Zoom commands and how to use them:

✔ **Zoom commands that help you to initially graph or regraph your function in a preset viewing window:**

• **ZStandard:** This command graphs your function in a preset viewing window where $-10 \le x \le 10$ and $-10 \le y \le 10$. You access it by pressing ZOOM 6.

This is a nice Zoom command to use when you haven't the slightest idea what size viewing window to use for your function. After graphing the function using **ZStandard**, you can, if necessary, use the **Zoom In** and **Zoom Out** commands to get a better idea of the nature of the graph. Using **Zoom In** and **Zoom Out** are described later in this section.

- **ZDecimal:** This command graphs your function in a preset viewing window where $-4.7 \leq x \leq 4.7$ and $-3.1 \leq y \leq 3.1$. It is accessed by pressing ZOOM 4.

  When you trace a function graphed in a **ZDecimal** window, the x-coordinate of the trace cursor will be a multiple of 0.1. Tracing is explained in the next section.

- **ZTrig:** This command, which is most useful when graphing trigonometric functions, graphs your function in a preset viewing window where $-47\pi/24 \leq x \leq 47\pi/24$ and $-4 \leq y \leq 4$. It also sets the tick marks on the x-axis to multiples of $\pi/2$. You access **ZTrig** by pressing ZOOM 7.

  When you trace a function graphed in a **ZTrig** window, the x-coordinate of the trace cursor will be a multiple of $\pi/24$. Tracing is explained in the next section.

To use the zoom commands described above, enter your function into the calculator (as described in Chapter 9), press ZOOM, and then press the key for the number of the command. The graph automatically appears.

✔ **Zoom commands that help you find an appropriate viewing window for the graph of your functions:**

- **ZoomFit:** This is my favorite Zoom command. If you know how you want to set the x-axis, **ZoomFit** automatically figures out the appropriate settings for the y-axis.

  To use **ZoomFit**, press WINDOW and enter the values you want for **Xmin**, **Xmax**, and **Xscl**. Then press ZOOM 0 to get **ZoomFit** to figure out the y-settings and graph your function. **ZoomFit** does not figure out an appropriate setting for **Yscl**, so you may want to go back to the Window editor and adjust this value. The Window editor is discussed in Chapter 9.

- **ZoomStat:** If you're graphing functions, this command is useless. But if you're graphing Stat Plots (as explained in Chapter 17), this command finds the appropriate viewing window for your plots. See Chapter 17 for information on how this works.

✔ **Zoom commands that readjust the viewing window of an already-graphed function:**

- **ZSquare:** Because the calculator screen isn't perfectly square, graphed circles won't look like real circles unless the viewing window is properly set. **ZSquare** readjusts the existing Window settings for you and then regraphs the function in a viewing window in which circles look like circles.

  To use **ZSquare**, graph the function as described in Chapter 9, and then press ZOOM 5. The graph automatically appears.

- **ZInteger:** This command is quite useful when you want the trace cursor to trace your functions using integer values of the *x*-coordinate, such as when graphing a function that defines a sequence. (Tracing is explained in the next section.) **ZInteger** readjusts the existing Window settings and regraphs the function in a viewing window in which the trace cursor displays integer values for the *x*-coordinate.

  To use **ZInteger**, graph the function as described in Chapter 9, and then press ZOOM 8. Use the ▶ ◀ ▲ ▼ keys to move the cursor to the spot on the screen that will become the center of the new screen. Then press ENTER. The graph is redrawn centered at the cursor location.

✔ **Zoom commands that zoom in or zoom out from an already graphed function:**

- **Zoom In and Zoom Out:** After the graph is drawn (as described in Chapter 9), these commands allow you to zoom in on a portion of the graph or to zoom out from the graph. They work very much like a zoom lens on a camera.

  Press ZOOM 2 to zoom in or press ZOOM 3 to zoom out. Then use the ▶ ◀ ▲ ▼ keys to move the cursor to the spot on the screen from which you want to zoom in or zoom out. Then press ENTER. The graph is redrawn centered at the cursor location.

  You can press ENTER again to zoom in closer or to zoom out one more time. Press CLEAR when you're finished zooming in or zooming out. You may have to adjust the window settings, as described earlier in the Chapter 9.

• **ZBox:** This command allows you to define a new viewing window for a portion of your graph by enclosing it in a box, as illustrated in Figure 10-1. The box becomes the new viewing window.

To construct the box, press ZOOM 1 and use the ▶ ◀ ▲ ▼ keys to move the cursor to the spot where you want one corner of the box to be located. Press ENTER to anchor that corner of the box. Then use the ▶ ◀ ▲ ▼ keys to construct the rest of the box. When you press these keys, the calculator draws the sides of the box. Press ENTER when you're finished drawing the box. The graph is then redrawn in the window defined by your box (as shown in Figure 10-1).

When you use **ZBox**, if you don't like the size of the box you get, you can use any of the ▶ ◀ ▲ ▼ keys to resize the box. If you don't like the location of the corner you anchored, press CLEAR and start over.

When you use **ZBox**, ENTER is pressed only two times. The first time you press it is to anchor a corner of the zoom box. The next time you press ENTER is when you're finished drawing the box, and you're ready to have the calculator redraw the graph.

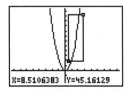

    The box   Redrawn graph

Figure 10-1: Constructing the Zoom Box and redrawing the graph.

Undoing a zoom

If you used a Zoom command to redraw a graph and then want to undo what that command did to the graph, follow these steps:

1. **Press ZOOM ▶ to access the Zoom Memory menu.**

2. **Press 1 to select ZPrevious.**

The graph is redrawn as it appeared in the previous viewing window.

Tracing a Graph

After you have graphed your function, as described in the previous chapter, you can press TRACE and then use ▶ and ◀ to more closely investigate the function.

If you use only the ▶◀▲▼ keys instead of TRACE to locate a point on a graph, all you will get is an *approximation* of the location of that point. You rarely get an actual point on the graph. So always use TRACE to identify points on a graph.

The following list describes what you see, or don't see, as you trace a graph:

- ✔ **The definition of the function:** The function you're tracing is displayed at the top of the screen, provided the calculator is in **ExprOn** format, as discussed in Chapter 9. If the Format menu is set to **ExprOff** and **CoordOn**, then the Y= editor number of the function appears at the top right of the screen. If the Format menu is set to **ExprOff** and **CoordOff**, then tracing the graph is useless because all you see is a cursor moving on the graph. The calculator won't tell you which function you're tracing, nor will it tell you the coordinates of the cursor location. (The Format menu and Y= editor are described in Chapter 9.)

  If you've graphed more than one function and you would like to trace a different function, press ▲. Each time you press this key, the cursor jumps to another function. Eventually it jumps back to the original function.

- ✔ **The values of *x* and *y*:** At the bottom of the screen, you see the values of the *x*- and *y*-coordinates that define the cursor location, provided the calculator is in **CoordOn** format (as discussed in Chapter 9). In the **PolarGC** format, the coordinates of this point display in polar form.

  When you press TRACE, the cursor is placed on the graph at the point having an *x*-coordinate that is approximately midway between **Xmin** and **Xmax**. If the *y*-coordinate of the cursor location isn't between **Ymin** and **Ymax**, then the cursor does not appear on the screen. The sidebar, "Panning in Function mode," tells you how to correct this situation.

  Each time you press ▶, the cursor moves right to the next plotted point on the graph, and the coordinates of that point are displayed at the bottom of the screen. If you press ◀, the cursor moves left to the previously plotted point. And if you press ▲ to trace a different function, the tracing of that function starts at the point on the graph that has the *x*-coordinate displayed on-screen before you pressed this key.

Panning in Function mode

When you're tracing a function and the cursor hits the top or bottom of the screen, you will still see the coordinates of the cursor location displayed at the bottom of the screen but you won't see the cursor itself on the screen because the viewing window is too small. Press ENTER to get the calculator to adjust the viewing window to a viewing window that is centered about the cursor location. If the function you were tracing isn't displayed at the top of the screen, repeatedly press ▲ until it is. The trace cursor then appears in the middle of the screen and you can use ▶ and ◀ to continue tracing the graph.

When you're tracing a function and the cursor hits the left or right side of the screen, the calculator automatically pans left or right. It also appropriately adjusts the values assigned to **Xmin** and **Xmax** in the Window editor, but it does not change the values of **Ymin** and **Ymax**. So you may not see the cursor on the screen. If this happens, follow the directions in the previous paragraph to see both the function and the cursor on the screen.

Press CLEAR to terminate tracing the graph. This also removes the name of the function and the coordinates of the cursor from the screen.

 When you're using TRACE, if you want to start tracing your function at a specific value of the independent variable x, just key in that value and press ENTER when you're finished. (The value you assign to x must be between **Xmin** and **Xmax**; if it's not, you get an error message.) After you press ENTER, the trace cursor moves to the point on the graph having the x-coordinate you just entered. If that point isn't on the portion of the graph appearing on the screen, the sidebar, "Panning in Function mode," tells you how to get the cursor and the graph in the same viewing window.

 If the name of the function and the values of x and y are interfering with your view of the graph when you use TRACE, increase the height of the screen by pressing WINDOW, and then decrease the value of **Ymin** and increase the value of **Ymax**.

Displaying Functions in a Table

After you've entered the functions in the Y= editor (as described in Chapter 9), you can have the calculator create a table of functional values. To create a table, perform the following steps:

1. Highlight the equal sign of those functions in the Y= editor that you want to appear in the table.

Only those functions in the Y= editor that are defined with a highlighted equal sign appear in the table. To highlight or remove the highlight from an equal sign, press Y=, use the ▶◀▲▼ keys to place the cursor on the equal sign in the definition of the function, and then press ENTER to toggle the equal sign between highlighted and not highlighted.

2. Press 2nd WINDOW to access the Table Setup editor (shown in Figure 10-2).

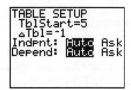

Figure 10-2: The Table Setup editor.

3. Enter a number in TblStart, and then press ENTER.

TblStart is the first value of the independent variable *x* to appear in the table. In Figure 10-2, **TblStart** is assigned the value 5.

To enter the number you have chosen for **TblStart**, place the cursor on the number appearing after the equal sign, press the number keys to enter your new number, and then press ENTER.

4. Enter a number in ΔTbl, and then press ENTER.

ΔTbl gives the increment for the independent variable *x*. In Figure 10-2, **ΔTbl** is assigned the value –1.

To enter the number you have chosen for **ΔTbl**, place the cursor on the number appearing after the equal sign, press the number keys to enter your new number, and then press ENTER.

5. Set the mode for Indpnt and Depend.

To change the mode of either **Indpnt** or **Depend**, use the ▶◀▲▼ keys to place the cursor on the desired mode, either **Auto** or **Ask**, and then press ENTER.

To have the calculator automatically generate the table for you, put both **Indpnt** and **Depend** in **Auto** mode. The table in Figure 10-3 was constructed in this fashion.

X	Y₁	Y₂
5	ERROR	8.6603
4	15	9.1652
3	8.5	9.5394
2	3.6667	9.798
1	.75	9.9499
0	-.2	10
-1	.83333	9.9499

X=5

Figure 10-3: A table automatically generated by the calculator.

If you want to create a user-defined table in which you specify which values of the independent variable x appear in the table — and then have the calculator figure out the corresponding values of the functions — put **Indpnt** in **Ask** mode and **Depend** in **Auto** mode. (How you construct the table is explained in Step 6.) The table in Figure 10-4 was constructed in this fashion.

For a user-defined table, you don't have to assign values to **TblStart** and **ΔTbl** in the Table Setup editor.

The other combinations of mode settings for **Indpnt** and **Depend** are not all that useful, unless you want to play a quick round of "Guess the y-coordinate."

X	Y₁	Y₂
5	ERROR	8.6603
4.5	18.25	8.9303
5.5	32.25	8.3516
-7	48.917	7.1414

X=

Figure 10-4: A user-generated table.

6. **Press [2nd][GRAPH] to display the table.**

When you display the table, what you see on the screen depends on the modes you set for **Indpnt** and **Depend** in Step 5. And what you can do with the table also depends on these modes. Here's what you see and what you can do:

- **An automatically generated table:**

 If **Indpnt** and **Depend** are both in **Auto** mode, then when you press [2nd][GRAPH], the table is automatically

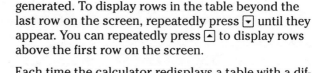

generated. To display rows in the table beyond the last row on the screen, repeatedly press ⊡ until they appear. You can repeatedly press ⊡ to display rows above the first row on the screen.

Each time the calculator redisplays a table with a different set of rows, it also automatically resets **TblStart** to the value of x that appears in the first row of the newly displayed table. To return the table to its original state, press 2nd WINDOW to access the Table Setup editor, and then change the value that the calculator assigned to **TblStart**.

If you're constructing a table for more than two functions, only the first two functions appear on the screen. To see the other functions, repeatedly press ▸ until they appear. This causes one or more of the initial functions to disappear. To see them again, repeatedly press ◂ until they appear.

- **A user-generated table:**

  If you put **Indpnt** in **Ask** mode and **Depend** in **Auto** mode so that you can generate your own table, then when you display the table, it should be empty. If it's not empty, clear the table (as described in the next section).

  In an empty table, key in the first value of the independent variable x that you want to appear in the table, and then press ENTER. The corresponding y-values of the functions in the table automatically appear. Key in the next value of x you want in the table and press ENTER, and so on. The values of x that you place in the first column of the table don't have to be in any specific order, nor do they have to be between the **Xmin** and **Xmax** settings in the Window editor.

The word ERROR appearing in a table doesn't indicate that the creator of the table has done something wrong. It indicates that either the function is undefined or the corresponding value of x is not a real-valued number. This is illustrated in Figures 10-3 and 10-4.

While displaying the table of functional values, you can edit the definition of a function without going back to the Y= editor. To do this, use the ▸◂⊡⊡ keys to place the cursor on the column heading for that function and then press ENTER. Edit the definition of the function (editing expressions is explained in Chapter 1) and press ENTER when you're finished. The calculator automatically updates the table and the definition of the function in the Y= editor.

Clearing a Table

Not all tables are created alike. An automatically generated table, for example, cannot be cleared. To change the contents of such a table, you have to change the values assigned to **TblStart** and **ΔTbl** in the Table Setup editor. After you have created a user-defined table, however, you can perform the following steps to clear its contents:

1. **Press** 2nd WINDOW **to access the Table Setup editor, and then set Indpnt to Auto.**

2. **Press** 2nd GRAPH **to display an automatically generated table.**

3. **Press** 2nd WINDOW **and set Indpnt back to Ask.**

4. **Press** 2nd GRAPH **to display an empty table.**

Viewing the Table and the Graph on the Same Screen

After you have graphed your functions and created a table of functional values, you can view the graph and the table on the same screen. To do so, follow these steps:

1. **Press** MODE.

2. **Put the calculator in G-T screen mode.**

   To do so, use the ▶◀▲▼ keys to place the cursor on **G-T** in the lower-right corner of the Mode menu, and then press ENTER to highlight it. This is illustrated in Figure 10-5.

Figure 10-5: Setting the mode for viewing a graph and a table.

3. Press GRAPH.

After you press GRAPH, the graph and the table appear on the same screen (as shown in Figure 10-6).

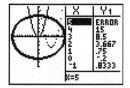

Figure 10-6: A Graph-Table split screen.

If you press any key used in graphing functions, such as ZOOM or TRACE, the cursor becomes active on the graph side of the screen. To return the cursor to the table, press 2nd GRAPH.

If you press TRACE and then use the ▶◀▲▼ keys to trace the graph, the value of the independent variable *x* corresponding to the cursor location on the graph is highlighted in the table and the column for the function you're tracing appears next to it. If necessary, the calculator updates the table so you can see that row in the table (as in Figure 10-7).

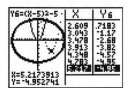

Figure 10-7: Using TRACE in Graph-Table mode.

To view the graph or the table in full screen mode, you can use these steps:

1. Press MODE.

2. Put the calculator in Full screen mode.

To do so, use the ▶◀▲▼ keys to place the cursor on **Full** in the bottom left hand corner of the Mode menu and press ENTER to highlight it.

3. Press GRAPH to see the graph, or press 2nd GRAPH to see the table.

Chapter 11

Evaluating Functions

. . . .

In This Chapter

▶ Finding the value of a function

▶ Finding the zeros (*x*-intercepts) of a function

▶ Finding the maximum and minimum values of a function

▶ Finding the point of intersection of two functions

▶ Finding the slope of a tangent to the graph of a function

▶ Finding the value of the definite integral of a function

. . . .

*A*fter graphing a function (as described in Chapter 9), you can use the options on the Calculate menu to find the value of the function at a specified value of *x*, to find the zeros (*x*-intercepts) of the function, and to find the maximum and minimum values of the function. You can even find the derivative of the function at a specified value of *x*, or you can evaluate a definite integral of the function. This, in turn, enables you to find the slope of the tangent to the graph of the function at a specified value of *x* or to find the area between the graph and the *x*-axis. Moreover, if you have graphed two functions, there is an option on the Calculate menu that finds the coordinates of these two functions' points of intersection.

The rest of this chapter tells you how to use the Calculate menu to find these values. But be warned: The calculator is not perfect. In most cases, using the options on the Calculate menu yields only an approximation of the true value (albeit a very *good* approximation).

Finding the Value of a Function

When you trace the graph of a function, the trace cursor doesn't hit every point on the graph. So tracing is not a reliable way of finding the value of a function at a specified value of the independent variable x. The **CALC** menu, however, contains a command that will evaluate a function at any specified x-value. To access and use this command, perform the following steps:

1. **Graph the functions in a viewing window that contains the specified value of x.**

   Graphing functions and setting the viewing window are explained in Chapter 9. To get a viewing window containing the specified value of x, that value must be between **Xmin** and **Xmax**.

2. **Set the Format menu to ExprOn and CoordOn.**

   Setting the Format menu is explained in Chapter 9.

3. **Press 2nd TRACE to access the Calculate menu.**

4. **Press 1 to select the value option.**

5. **Enter the specified value of x.**

   When using the **value** command to evaluate a function at a specified value of x, that value must be an x-value that appears on the x-axis of the displayed graph — that is, it must be between **Xmin** and **Xmax**. If it isn't, you get an error message.

   Use the keypad to enter the value of x (as illustrated in the first graph in Figure 11-1). If you make a mistake when entering your number, press CLEAR and re-enter the number.

6. **Press ENTER.**

   After you press ENTER, the first highlighted function in the Y= editor appears at the top of the screen, the cursor appears on the graph of that function at the specified value of x, and the coordinates of the cursor appear at the bottom of the screen. This is illustrated in the second graph in Figure 11-1.

7. **Repeatedly press ▲ to see the value of the other graphed functions at your specified value of x.**

   Each time you press ▲, the name of the function being evaluated appears at the top of the screen and the coordinates of the cursor location appears at the bottom of the screen. This is illustrated in the third graph in Figure 11-1.

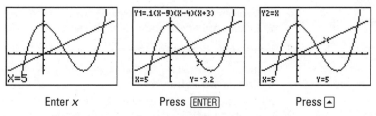

| Enter *x* | Press ENTER | Press ▲ |

Figure 11-1: Steps in evaluating two functions at a specified value of *x*.

After using the **value** command to evaluate your functions at one value of *x*, you can evaluate your functions at another value of *x* by keying in the new value and pressing ENTER. Pressing any function key (such as ENTER or TRACE) *after* evaluating a function deactivates the **value** command.

If you plan to evaluate functions at several specified values of *x*, consider constructing a user-defined table of functional values (as explained in Chapter 10).

Finding the Zeros of a Function

The *zeros* of the function *y* = *f*(*x*) are the solutions to the equation *f*(*x*) = 0. Because *y* = 0 at these solutions, these zeros (solutions) are really just the *x*-coordinates of the *x*-intercepts of the graph of *y* = *f*(*x*). (An *x*-intercept is a point where the graph crosses or touches the *x*-axis.) To find a zero of a function, perform the following steps:

1. **Graph the function in a viewing window that contains the zeros of the function.**

   Graphing a function and finding an appropriate viewing window are explained in Chapter 9. To get a viewing window containing a zero of the function, that zero must be between **Xmin** and **Xmax** and the *x*-intercept at that zero must be visible on the graph.

2. **Set the Format menu to ExprOn and CoordOn.**

   Setting the Format menu is explained in Chapter 9.

3. **Press 2nd TRACE to access the Calculate menu.**

4. **Press 2 to select the zero option.**

5. **If necessary, repeatedly press** ▲ **until the appropriate function appears at the top of the screen.**

6. **Set the Left Bound for the zero you desire to find.**

   To do so, use the ◄ and ► keys to place the cursor on the graph a little to the left of the zero, and then press [ENTER]. A Left Bound indicator appears at the top of the screen (as illustrated by the triangle in the first graph of Figure 11-2).

7. **Set the Right Bound for the zero.**

   To do so, use the ◄ and ► keys to place the cursor on the graph a little to the right of the zero, and then press [ENTER]. A Right Bound indicator appears at the top of the screen, as shown by the right triangle in the second graph of Figure 11-2.

8. **Tell the calculator where you guess the zero is located.**

   This guess is necessary because the calculator uses a numerical routine for finding a zero. The routine is an iterative process that requires a seed (guess) to get it started. The closer the seed is to the zero, the faster the routine finds the zero. To do this, use the ◄ and ► keys to place the cursor on the graph as close to the zero as possible, and then press [ENTER]. The value of the zero appears at the bottom of the screen, as shown in the third graph of Figure 11-2.

The calculator uses scientific notation to denote really large or small numbers. For example, –0.00000001 is displayed on the calculator as –1E–8, and 0.00000005 is displayed as 5E–8.

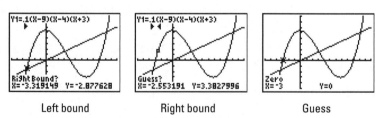

Left bound   Right bound   Guess

Figure 11-2: Steps in finding the zero of a function.

Finding Min & Max

Finding the maximum or minimum point on a graph has many useful applications. For example, the maximum point on the graph of a profit function not only tells you the maximum profit (the *y*-coordinate), it also tells you how many items (the *x*-coordinate) the company must manufacture to achieve this profit. To find the minimum or maximum value of a function, perform the following steps:

1. **Graph the function in a viewing window that contains the minimum and/or maximum values of the function.**

   Graphing a function and finding an appropriate viewing window are explained in Chapter 9.

2. **Set the Format menu to ExprOn and CoordOn.**

   Setting the Format menu is explained in Chapter 9.

3. **Press 2nd TRACE to access the Calculate menu.**

4. **Press 3 to find the minimum, or press 4 to find the maximum.**

5. **If necessary, repeatedly press ▲ until the appropriate function appears at the top of the screen.**

6. **Set the Left Bound of the minimum or maximum point.**

   To do so, use the ◄ and ► keys to place the cursor on the graph a little to the left of the location of the minimum or maximum point, and then press ENTER. A *left bound indicator* (the triangle shown in the first graph of Figure 11-3) appears at the top of the screen.

7. **Set the Right Bound for the zero.**

   To do so, use the ◄ and ► keys to place the cursor on the graph a little to the right of the location of the minimum or maximum point, and then press ENTER. A *right bound indicator* (the rightmost triangle in the second graph of Figure 11-3) appears at the top of the screen.

8. Tell the calculator where you guess the min or max is located.

To do so, use the ◀ and ▶ keys to place the cursor on the graph as close to the location of the minimum or maximum point as possible, and then press ENTER. The coordinates of the minimum or maximum point appears at the bottom of the screen (as in the third graph of Figure 11-3).

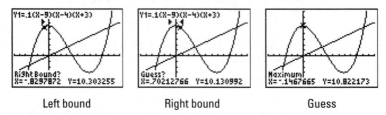

| Left bound | Right bound | Guess |

Figure 11-3: Steps in finding the maximum value of a function.

Finding Points of Intersection

Using the ▶ ◀ ▲ ▼ keys to locate the point of intersection of two graphs gives you an *approximation* of that point, but this method rarely gives you the actual point of intersection. To accurately find the coordinates of the point where two functions intersect, perform the following steps:

1. Graph the functions in a viewing window that contains the point of intersection of the functions.

Graphing a function and finding an appropriate viewing window are explained in Chapter 9.

2. Set the Format menu to ExprOn and CoordOn.

Setting the Format menu is explained in Chapter 9.

3. Press 2nd TRACE to access the Calculate menu.

4. Press 5 to select the intersect option.

5. Select the first function.

If the name of one of the intersecting functions does not appear at the top of the screen, repeatedly press ▲ until it does. This is illustrated in the first graph of Figure 11-4. When the cursor is on one of the intersecting functions, press ENTER to select it.

6. **Select the second function.**

   If the calculator does not automatically display the name of the second intersecting function at the top of the screen, repeatedly press ⊡ until it does. This is illustrated in the second graph of Figure 11-4. When the cursor is on the second intersecting function, press ENTER to select it.

7. **Use the ⊡ and ⊡ to move the cursor as close to the point of intersection as possible.**

   This is illustrated in the third graph in Figure 11-4.

8. **Press ENTER to display the coordinates of the point of intersection.**

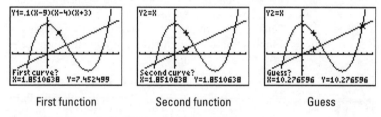

| First function | Second function | Guess |

Figure 11-4: Steps in finding a point of intersection.

Finding the Slope of a Curve

The calculator is not equipped to find the derivative of a function. For example, it cannot tell you that the derivative of x^2 is $2x$. But the calculator is equipped with a numerical routine that evaluates the derivative at a specified value of x. This numerical value of the derivative is the slope of the tangent to the graph of the function at the specified x-value. It is also called the slope of the curve. To find the slope (derivative) of a function at a specified value of x, perform the following steps:

1. **Graph the function in a viewing window that contains the specified value of x.**

   Graphing a function and setting the viewing window are explained in Chapter 9. To get a viewing window containing the specified value of x, that value must be between **Xmin** and **Xmax**.

2. **Set the Format menu to ExprOn and CoordOn.**

   Setting the Format menu is explained in Chapter 9.

3. **Press [2nd][TRACE] to access the Calculate menu.**

4. **Press [6] to select the dy/dx option.**

5. **If necessary, repeatedly press [▲] until the appropriate function appears at the top of the screen.**

   This is illustrated in the first graph in Figure 11-5.

6. **Enter the specified value of x.**

   To do so, use the keypad to enter the value of *x*. As you use the keypad, **X=** appears, replacing the coordinates of the cursor location appearing at the bottom of the screen in the previous step. The number you key in appears after **X=**. This is illustrated in the second graph in Figure 11-5. If you make a mistake when entering your number, press [CLEAR] and re-enter the number.

   If you are interested only in finding the slope of the function in a general area of the function instead of at a specific value of *x*, instead of entering a value of *x*, just use the [◄] and [►] to move the cursor to the desired location on the graph of the function.

7. **Press [ENTER].**

   After pressing [ENTER], the slope (derivative) is displayed at the bottom of the screen. This is illustrated in the third graph in Figure 11-5.

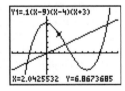 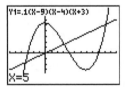 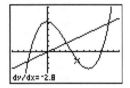

   Select function   Enter *x*   Press [ENTER]

Figure 11-5: Steps in finding the slope at a specified value of *x*.

Evaluating a Definite Integral

If $f(x)$ is positive for $a \le x \le b$, and then the definite integral $\int_a^b f(x)\,dx$ also gives the area between the curve and the x-axis for $a \le x \le b$. To evaluate the definite integral, perform the following steps:

1. **Graph the function $f(x)$ in a viewing window that contains the lower limit a and the upper limit b.**

   Graphing a function and setting the viewing window are explained in Chapter 9. To get a viewing window containing a and b, these values must be between **Xmin** and **Xmax**.

2. **Set the Format menu to ExprOn and CoordOn.**

   Setting the Format menu is explained in Chapter 9.

3. **Press [2nd][TRACE] to access the Calculate menu.**

4. **Press [7] to select the $\int f(x)\,dx$ option.**

5. **If necessary, repeatedly press [▲] until the appropriate function appears at the top of the screen.**

   This process is illustrated in the first graph in Figure 11-6.

6. **Enter the value of the lower limit a.**

   To do so, use the keypad to enter the value of the lower limit a. As you use the keypad, **X=** appears, replacing the coordinates of the cursor location appearing at the bottom of the screen in the previous step. The number you key in appears after **X=**. This is illustrated in the second graph in Figure 11-6. If you make a mistake when entering your number, press [CLEAR] and re-enter the number.

7. **Press [ENTER].**

   After pressing [ENTER], a left bound indicator appears at the top of the screen.

8. **Enter the value of the upper limit b and press [ENTER].**

   After pressing [ENTER], the value of the definite integral appears at the bottom of the screen and the area between the curve and the x-axis, for $a \le x \le b$, will be shaded. This is illustrated in the third graph in Figure 11-6.

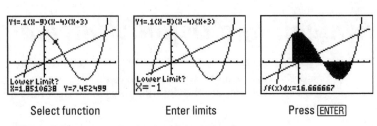

Select function   Enter limits   Press ENTER

Figure 11-6: Steps in evaluating a definite integral.

The shading of the graph produced by using the $\int f(x)\,dx$ option on the Calculate menu does not automatically vanish when you use another Calculate option. To erase the shading, press 2nd PRGM 1 to invoke the **ClrDraw** command on the Draw menu. The graph is then redrawn without the shading.

Chapter 12

Graphing Transformations

. . . .

In This Chapter

▶ Starting and quitting Transformation Graphing

▶ Entering and graphing transformations

▶ Creating a slide show of transformations

▶ Graphing transformations of more than one function

. . . .

*W*ith the Transformation Graphing application that comes preloaded on the TI-84 Plus family of graphing calculators, you can investigate transformations of a graph without leaving the graphing screen. For example, you can investigate the effect of changing the value of one of the variables in an equation such as $y = A\sin(Bx + C) + D$, and without leaving the graphing screen, you can change the value of another variable and instantly see how the graph changes. You can even create a slide show picturing how the graph changes as one variable changes over time. This chapter tells you how to do such things.

Starting Transformation Graphing

To start the Transformation Graphing application, press APPS ALPHA 4, use ▾ to move the cursor to the **Transfrm** application, and press ENTER to select the application. You are confronted with one of the three screens shown in Figure 12-1.

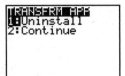

Logo screen   Application   Another application
     is already running   is running

Figure 12-1: What you see when you select the Transformation Graphing
application from the APPS menu.

If no other applications are running, you see the first screen shown
in Figure 12-1. Press any key except 2nd or ALPHA to enter the
Transformation Graphing application. If Transformation Graphing
is already running, you see the second screen in Figure 12-1. Press
2 to re-enter the application. The third screen in Figure 12-1 tells
you that another application is currently running. Press 1 to exit
(overwrite) that application, and then press any key except 2nd or
ALPHA to enter Transformation Graphing.

After you enter Transformation Graphing, you are returned to the
calculator's Home screen, and it looks like the application is not
running. Press Y=, and you see a screen similar to the one in Figure 12-2. The symbols to the left of the functions in this screen
indicate that the Transformation Graphing application is running.
When Transformation Graphing is not running, the graphing style
symbols (\, ◥, ◣, ◢, ⊸, ◊, ⋰) appear to the left of the functions in the
Y= editor. Graphing styles are explained in Chapter 9 and are not
available while Transformation Graphing is running.

```
Plot1 Plot2 Plot3
＊Y₁=6/X^2
＊Y₂=
＊Y₃=
＊Y₄=
＊Y₅=
＊Y₆=
＊Y₇=
```

Figure 12-2: The Y= editor when Transformation Graphing is running.

Quitting Transformation Graphing

Most of the time, you don't even know the Transformation Graphing application is running unless you are actively using the application or unless you press [Y=] to graph a normal function and see the symbols in Figure 12-2 to the left of the functions in the Y= editor. Quitting the application so that you can graph normal functions is about as puzzling as knowing whether or not it is running.

To quit (exit) this application, press [APPS][ALPHA][4], use [▼] to move the cursor to the **Transfrm** application, and press [ENTER] to select the application. When you see the second screen in Figure 12-1, press [1] to quit (uninstall) the application. No, uninstall does not delete the application from your calculator, it just deactivates it.

Entering Functions

Functions are defined in the Y= editor the same way you define normal functions, as explained in Chapter 9. Transformation Graphing allows your functions to have a maximum of four variables and these variables are always A, B, C, and/or D. These letters are entered using the [ALPHA] key. For example, to enter the variable A, press [ALPHA][MATH]. Figure 12-3 shows examples of such functions. For function Y_5 in this figure, Transformation Graphing will not recognize E as a variable; it will treat it as a constant by assigning it whatever value is stored in the calculator in the constant E.

```
Plot1 Plot2 Plot3
►Y₁⊟Asin(BX+C)+D

►Y₂=A(X+B)²+C
►Y₃=AX²+BX+C
►Y₄=AX+B
►Y₅=AX^4+BX^3+CX
²+DX+E
```

Figure 12-3: Examples of definitions of transformations.

Graphing Transformations

The Transformation Graphing application graphs transformations in three different ways called *play types:* Play-Pause (>||), Play (>), and Play-Fast (>>). The symbols next to these play types are the symbols used by Transformation Graphing to indicate the play type on the calculator screen. The second two play types, Play and Play-Fast, are used to display a slide show of your transformations. How to use these play types is explained later in this chapter.

Play-Pause, which is explained in this section, graphs a function and then waits for you to prompt the application to graph a transformation of that function. Without leaving the graphing screen, you can enter a new value for any variable in the definition of the function or you can increment the variable by a predefined step size.

To graph a function and investigate its transformations using the Play-Pause play type, follow these steps:

1. **Press** Y= **and highlight the equal sign of the function you plan to graph.**

   Transformation Graphing can graph only one function at a time. The function whose equal sign is highlighted is the function that will be graphed. In Figure 12-3, Y_1 will be graphed. To graph a different function, use the arrow keys to place the cursor on the equal sign of that function and press ENTER to highlight its equal sign.

2. **Press** WINDOW ▲ **to access the Settings editor and highlight Play-Pause, the first play type.**

   The first line of the Settings editor contains the symbols for the three play types: Play-Pause (>||), Play (>), and Play-Fast (>>). The second two, Play and Play-Fast, are used to display a slide show of your transformations. How to do this is explained later in this chapter.

   If the first play type is not highlighted, use the arrow keys to place the cursor on the >|| symbol and press ENTER to highlight it, as illustrated in Figure 12-4.

Figure 12-4: The Settings editor.

3. **Enter the initial values of your variables A, B, C, and/ or D.**

   In Figure 12-4, the variables A, B, C, and D must be assigned values because I am graphing the first function in Figure 12-3. If I were graphing the second function in Figure 12-3, only the variables A, B, and C would appear in the Settings editor because these are the only variables used in the definition of that function.

   To assign a value to a variable, use the arrow keys to place the cursor after the equal sign of the variable, use the number keys to enter its value, and then press ENTER. You may enter the value as an arithmetic expression. When you press ENTER, the calculator evaluates that expression. In Figure 12-4, I entered the initial value for C as $\pi/2$.

   The first transformation that is graphed is the function defined by these initial values. Because I am graphing the first function in Figure 12-3 using the initial values in Figure 12-4, the first function that I graph will be $y = \sin(x + \pi/2)$.

4. **Highlight the equal sign of the variable that you want to investigate.**

   To highlight the equal sign, use the arrow keys to place the cursor on the equal sign and press ENTER to highlight it. Transformation Graphing allows you to investigate only one variable at a time, so only one equal sign will be highlighted.

   In Figure 12-4, the equal sign of variable A is highlighted, indicating that I want to investigate the amplitude of the first function in Figure 12-3.

5. **Enter a value for Step, the step size.**

   Each time you tell the calculator to graph a transformation, it will increment the chosen variable by this specified step size and graph the resulting function. In my example, Figures 12-3 and 12-4, the calculator will graph $y = \sin(x + \pi/2)$, $y = 2\sin(x + \pi/2)$, $y = 3\sin(x + \pi/2)$, and so on.

6. **Graph the function.**

   You graph the function the same way you graph a normal function. You either define the variables in the Window editor (as explained in Chapter 9) and press $\boxed{\text{GRAPH}}$, or you use one of the Zoom commands explained in Chapter 10. Because I am graphing a trig function in my example, I pressed $\boxed{\text{ZOOM}}\boxed{7}$ to get the **ZTrig** command to graph the function in the first picture in Figure 12-5. As you can see in this picture, the values of the variables defining the function appear in the lower-left corner of the graph.

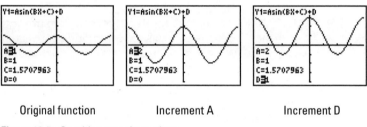

Original function   Increment A   Increment D

Figure 12-5: Graphing transformations.

7. **To graph a transformation of the function, press $\boxed{\blacktriangleright}$ or $\boxed{\blacktriangleleft}$ or enter a new value for one of the variables, and then press $\boxed{\text{ENTER}}$.**

   Each time you press $\boxed{\blacktriangleright}$, the value of **Step** is added to the variable with the highlighted equal sign and the transformation of the graph is drawn. When you press $\boxed{\blacktriangleleft}$, the value of **Step** is subtracted from that variable and the transformation of the graph is drawn. This is illustrated in the second picture in Figure 12-6 where $\boxed{\blacktriangleright}$ was pressed one time.

   While you are graphing transformations, you can investigate a different variable without revisiting the Settings editor. To do this use $\boxed{\blacktriangle}\boxed{\blacktriangledown}$ to place the cursor on the equal sign of that variable and press $\boxed{\text{ENTER}}$. Then each time you press $\boxed{\blacktriangleright}$ or $\boxed{\blacktriangleleft}$, that variable is increased or decreased by the specified step size and the new transformation is drawn.

Other available graphing features

All the commands and features described in Chapters 9, 10, and 11 that are available for graphing normal functions are also available when graphing transformations. For example, you can split the screen and display a graph and a table, you can zoom in on a graph, you can trace a graph, and you can graph a stat plot along with your graph. After using one of these commands, if the transformation variables in the lower-left corner of the screen do not appear, as they do in the figures in this chapter, press GRAPH to make them reappear. When these variables are on the screen, you can use the features available in the Transformation Graphing application.

This is illustrated in the third picture in Figure 12-5 where variable D was increased by the step size.

You can also change the value of a variable without revisiting the Settings editor. To do this, use ▲▼ to place the cursor on the equal sign of that variable, use the number keys to enter a new value, and press ENTER to see the transformation of the function.

Creating a Slide Show

A slide show allows you to view the graphs of a sequence of transformations of a function. Each picture in the slide show displays one transformation, and you can run your slides in slow or fast motion. There is even a feature that allows the previous graphs in the slide show to remain on the screen, as illustrated in the third picture in Figure 12-6.

To create a slide show of transformations of a graph, follow these steps:

1. **Follow Steps 1 through 6 in the previous section, "Graphing Transformations." In Step 2, highlight > for a slow slide show or highlight >> for a fast slide show.**

   The first picture in Figure 12-6 shows that the Settings editor is set for a slow-motion slide show of the transformations of the graph of $y = A\sin(Bx + C) + D$, the first function in Figure 12-3.

  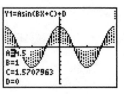

Define variables   Set format   Press [GRAPH]

Figure 12-6: Creating a slide show.

2. **Enter a value for Max, the maximum value of the variable with the highlighted equal sign (that is, the value of that variable at the end of the slide show).**

   There are restrictions on the value you assign to **Max**. If it is too large, when you try to run your slide show, you get the ERR: MEMORY error message. To avoid this error message, the values assigned to **Max**, **Step**, and the variable with the highlighted equal sign should abide by the following inequality: (**Max** – *variable*)/**Step** ≤ 12. In the first picture in Figure 12-6, (**Max** – *variable*)/**Step** = (5 – 1)/0.5 = 8 is well below the maximum bound of 12.

   If you're wondering how I came up with this crazy inequality, here's the explanation. A slide show can consist of a maximum of 13 slides: one slide for the graph of the original function and 12 slides for the graphs of the progressive transformations of that function. If you do the algebra, you can show that the number of transformations in a slide show is (Max – *variable*)/Step where *variable* is the number assigned to the variable with the highlighted equal sign. So this value must be less than or equal to 12, the maximum number transformation slides allowed in a slide show.

3. **Press [2nd][ZOOM] to display the Format menu. In the last line, highlight either TrailOff or TrailOn.**

   If you highlight **TrailOff**, your slide show will look like a motion picture with one transformation appearing on each slide. If you highlight **TrailOn**, the transformations from previous slides appear as dotted graphs while the graph of the current transformation appears as a solid graph, as illustrated in the third picture in Figure 12-6.

If the option you want is not already highlighted, use the arrow keys to place the cursor on that option and press ENTER to highlight it. In the second picture in Figure 12-6, **TrailOn** is highlighted.

4. **Press GRAPH to start the slide show.**

Before the show starts, you see a screen tallying the number of slides in your slide show. After completing the slide show, the calculator keeps rerunning it until you press ON or ENTER, as explained in the next step.

If you do get the ERR: MEMORY error message, reduce the value assigned to **Max** and/or increase the value assigned to **Step** and/or increase the value assigned to the variable with the highlighted equal sign. (See the explanation in Step 2.)

5. **Press and hold ON to terminate the slide show.**

After pressing ON, the Setting editor appears so that you can, if you wish, make changes in this editor.

If you want to pause the slide show, press ENTER. A moving dotted line appears in the upper-right corner, as illustrated in the third picture in Figure 12-6. To resume the show, press ENTER again.

Graphing Transformations of Two or More Functions

Although the Transformation Graphing application is capable of graphing the transformations of only one function at a time, you can get around this problem by defining that function as a sequence of functions, as illustrated in the first picture of Figure 12-7. The last two pictures in this figure show the transformations of this sequence of functions.

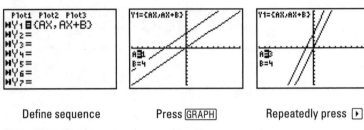

Define sequence   Press GRAPH   Repeatedly press ▶

Figure 12-7: Graphing a sequence of functions.

To define a function as a sequence of functions, the functions in the sequence are separated by commas and the sequence is surrounded by curly brackets, as in the first picture in Figure 12-7. The curly brackets are entered in the calculator by pressing 2nd (and 2nd).

Chapter 13

Graphing Inequalities

. . . .

In This Chapter

▶ Starting and quitting Inequality Graphing

▶ Entering and graphing inequalities

▶ Exploring a graph

▶ Shading intersections and unions

▶ Storing data points

▶ Solving linear programming problems

. . . .

*W*ith the Inequality Graphing application that comes pre-loaded on the TI-84 Plus family of graphing calculators, you can graph functions and inequalities of the form $y \leq f(x)$, $y < f(x)$, $y \geq f(x)$, and $y > f(x)$. You can even graph and shade regions formed by the union or intersection of several inequalities. You can also use this application to solve linear programming problems. If you don't know what linear programming is, see the explanation in the last section in this chapter.

Starting Inequality Graphing

To start the Inequality Graphing application, press APPS ALPHA x^2; if necessary, use ▾ to move the cursor to the **Inequalz** application and press ENTER to select the application. You are confronted with one of the three screens shown in Figure 13-1.

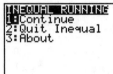

Logo screen Application Another application
     is already running is running

Figure 13-1: What you see when you select the Inequality Graphing application from the APPS menu.

If no other applications are running, you see the first screen in Figure 13-1. Press any key to enter the Inequality Graphing application. If Inequality Graphing is already running, you see the second screen in Figure 13-1. Press $\boxed{1}$ to re-enter the application. The third screen in Figure 13-1 tells you that another application is currently running. Press $\boxed{2}$ to exit that application, and then press any key to enter Inequality Graphing.

After you enter Inequality Graphing, you are placed in the Y= editor so that you can enter functions and inequalities. The functions previously housed in this editor appear on the screen along with the inequality symbols at the bottom of the screen, as illustrated in the first picture in Figure 13-2. If you move the cursor so that it is not on an equal sign, the inequality symbols at the bottom of the screen vanish, as in the second picture in this figure.

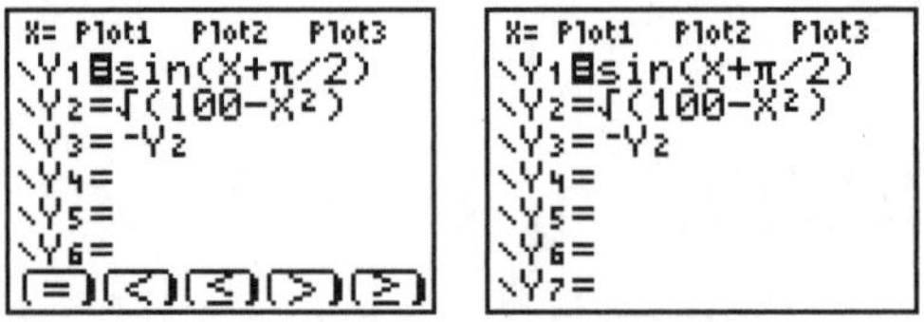

Cursor is Cursor is not
on equal sign on equal sign

Figure 13-2: The Y= editor when Inequality Graphing is running.

Quitting Inequality Graphing

Most of the time, you don't even know the Inequality Graphing application is running unless you are actively using the application or unless you place the cursor on an equal sign in the Y= editor to display the inequality symbols, as in the first picture in Figure 13-2. How to quit the application is about as puzzling as knowing whether or not it is running.

To quit (exit) this application, press APPS ALPHA x^2; if necessary use ▾ to move the cursor to the **Inequalz** application, and press ENTER to select the application. When you see the second screen in Figure 13-1, press ② to quit the application.

Entering Functions and Inequalities

The Inequality Graphing application can graph functions and inequalities of the form $y = f(x)$, $y < f(x)$, $y \le f(x)$, $y > f(x)$, and $y \ge f(x)$. Such functions and inequalities are defined in the Y= editor. The application can also graph equalities and inequalities of the form $x = N$, $x < N$, $x \le N$, $x > N$, and $x \ge N$, provided that N is a number. These equalities and inequalities are defined in the X= editor. Using these editors is explained in the following sections.

Entering inequalities in the Y= editor

To define a function or inequality of the form $y = f(x)$, $y < f(x)$, $y \le f(x)$, $y > f(x)$, and $y \ge f(x)$, follow these steps:

1. Press Y= **to access the Y= editor.**

To erase any unwanted functions or inequalities from the Y= editor, use the arrow keys to place the cursor after the equality or inequality symbol in the definition of the unwanted function or inequality and press CLEAR.

2. **Use the arrow keys to place the cursor on the sign (=, <, ≤, >, or ≥) of the function or inequality you are defining.**

   This is illustrated in the first picture in Figure 13-3, where an inequality is to be defined in **Y₁**.

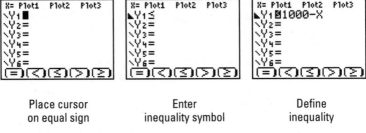

| Place cursor | Enter | Define |
| on equal sign | inequality symbol | inequality |

Figure 13-3: Defining inequalities in the Y= editor.

3. **Press ALPHA and press the key under the appropriate equality or inequality symbol.**

   To get the second picture in Figure 13-3, I pressed ALPHA ZOOM to enter ≤. I pressed ZOOM because that is the key under the ≤ symbol appearing at the bottom of the screen.

   The equality and inequality symbols appear at the bottom of the screen only when the cursor is on the equality or inequality symbol appearing to the right of one of the functions **Y₁** through **Y₉** or **Y₀**.

4. **Press ▶ and enter the definition of the function or inequality.**

   The definition of the function or inequality is entered the same way you enter the definition of a function, as explained in Chapter 9. The third picture in Figure 13-3 shows that the inequality $y \le 1000 - x$ is defined in **Y₁**.

After defining a function or inequality, you can change the inequality sign in this definition by following Steps 2 and 3.

The graphing style of an inequality is determined by the Inequality Graphing application and cannot be changed. The application does however allow you to change the graphing style of a function. Graphing styles and how to change them are explained in Chapter 9.

When you exit the Inequality Graphing application, all inequality signs in the Y= editor are converted to equal signs and the original inequality sign is not reinstated the next time that you run the application.

Entering inequalities in the X= editor

Equalities and inequalities of the form $x = N$, $x < N$, $x \leq N$, $x > N$, and $x \geq N$ *(where N is a number)* are defined in the X= editor the same way inequalities are defined in the Y= editor, as explained in the previous subsection. To access the X= editor, follow these steps:

1. **If you are not currently in the Y= editor, press** Y= **to get there.**

2. **Repeatedly press** ▲ **until the cursor is on X= in the upper-left corner of the Y= editor.**

   This is illustrated in the first picture in Figure 13-4.

3. **Press** ENTER **to access the X= editor.**

| Access X= editor | Define inequality | Press ENTER |

Figure 13-4: Defining inequalities in the X= editor.

The *number* N in the inequality can be entered as an arithmetic expression, as illustrated in the second picture in Figure 13-3. That expression is evaluated by the calculator after you press ENTER, ▲, or ▼, as illustrated in the third picture in this figure.

 To return to the Y= editor from the X= editor, repeatedly press ▲ until the cursor is in the upper-left corner of the screen, and then press ENTER.

When you exit the Inequality Graphing application, all entries made in the X= editor are erased.

Graphing Inequalities

As with functions, if the inequality sign in the definition of the inequality is highlighted, then that inequality will be graphed; if it isn't highlighted, it won't be graphed. The first picture in Figure 13-5 shows that the first two inequalities will be graphed, but the third won't. To change the highlighted status of an inequality sign, place the cursor on that sign and press [ENTER].

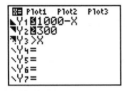  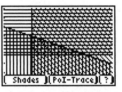

Define inequalities   Set the window   Press [GRAPH]

Figure 13-5: Graphing inequalities.

You graph the inequalities defined in the Y= and X= editors the same way you graph a normal function. You either define the variables in the Window editor (as explained in Chapter 9) and press [GRAPH] or use one of the Zoom commands explained in Chapter 10. When the graph is displayed, you see three options at the bottom of the graph screen, as in the third picture in Figure 13-5. These options are explained in the next section.

The Inequality Graphing application adds the **ShadeRes** variable to the Window editor, as illustrated in the second picture in Figure 13-5. This variable can be set to any integer 3 through 8. A setting of 3 places the lines in the shaded graph close together and 8 places then far apart. The default value is 3, and this setting works just fine for most graphs, as illustrated in the third picture in Figure 13-5.

Exploring a Graph

When the graph is displayed, three options appear at the bottom of the screen, as illustrated in the third picture in Figure 13-5. The

Shades option redraws the graph shading only the union or intersection of the regions, the **Pol-Trace** option traces the points of
intersection appearing in the graph, and the **?** option displays the
rudimentary help screen shown in Figure 13-6. In this section, I
explain how to use the **Shades** and **Pol-Trace** options, and I also
explain what other option are available for exploring and investi-
gating your graph.

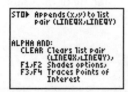

Figure 13-6: The Inequality Graphing help screen.

To hide the three options at the bottom of the graph screen, press
ENTER; to redisplay them, press GRAPH.

Shading unions and intersections

The graph in the third picture in Figure 13-5 is pretty cluttered, as
is the case with most graphs of more than two inequalities. The
Shades option will get rid of the clutter by shading only the union
or the intersection of the regions. To accomplish this, follow these
steps:

1. **Press** ALPHA Y= **or** ALPHA WINDOW **to display the Shades
   menu.**

   Because the **Shades** option at the bottom of the graph
   screen is above the F1 and F2 function keys on the calculator, pressing either ALPHA Y= to select F1 or ALPHA WINDOW
   to select F2 will produce the **Shades** menu, as illustrated in
   the first picture in Figure 13-7.

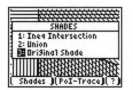   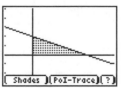

   Press ALPHA Y=   Press 1

Figure 13-7: Graphing the intersection or regions.

2. Press the number of the option you want.

The new graph automatically appears on the screen, as illustrated in the second picture in Figure 13-7. This picture shows the intersection of the regions in the third picture in Figure 13-5.

After graphing the union or intersection of the regions in your graph, you can redisplay the original shading of the graph by selecting the third option in the **Shades** menu.

Finding the points of intersection

The **Pol-Trace** option is used to find the points of intersection appearing on the graph screen. When the calculator finds such a point, you can store the x- and y-coordinates of that point in the calculator. This is quite handy when solving linear programming problems, as explained later in this chapter. To find and store the points of intersection in an inequality graph, follow these steps:

1. Press [ALPHA][ZOOM] **or** [ALPHA][TRACE] **to select the Pol-Trace option.**

Because the **Pol-Trace** option at the bottom of the graph screen is above the F3 and F4 function keys on the calculator, this option can be selected by pressing either [ALPHA][ZOOM] to select F1 or [ALPHA][TRACE] to select F2.

After selecting this option, the cursor moves to one point of intersection and the coordinates of that point are displayed at the bottom of the screen, as illustrated in the first picture of Figure 13-8. In the upper-left corner of the screen, you see the names of the intersecting inequalities.

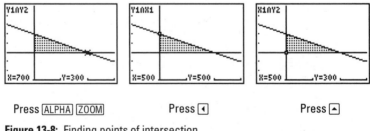

Press [ALPHA] [ZOOM]   Press [◄]   Press [▲]

Figure 13-8: Finding points of intersection.

2. **Press** STO▶ **to store the coordinates of the point of intersection.**

   If you don't need to store these coordinates, you can skip this step. If you do press STO▶, you get a message saying, "Point appended to ((INEQX, (INEQY)." This tells you that the *x*-coordinate is stored in the list named INEQX and the *y*-coordinate is stored in list INEQY. Accessing, using, and managing these lists is explained later in this chapter in the section, "Storing Data Points." Press ENTER to get rid of the message and return to the graph.

   If the point is already stored in the calculator, you get the "Duplicate Point" message. Press ENTER to get rid of the message. The Inequality Graphing application will not store the point a second time.

3. **Use the arrow keys to move to the next point of intersection and, if you desire, press** STO▶ **to store its coordinates.**

   Pressing ◀ or ▶ moves the cursor to the next point of intersection on the graph of the left inequality in the upper-left corner of the screen. This is illustrated in the first and second pictures in Figure 13-8. In the first picture in this figure, the left inequality in the upper-left corner of the screen is Y1. After I pressed ▶, the cursor jumped to the other point of intersection on this line, as illustrated in the second picture. Because this line has only two points of intersection, if I were to press ▶ again, the cursor would go back to the point of intersection in the first picture in this figure.

   Pressing ▲ or ▼ changes the left inequality in the upper-left corner of the screen. This may or may not move the cursor. If the cursor doesn't move, press ◀ or ▶ to move the cursor to the next point of intersection. For example, to get from the second to the third picture in Figure 13-8, I pressed ▲ to change the left inequality to X1. But this gave me the intersection same point of intersection. So I pressed ◀ to get the other point of intersection on line X1, as illustrated in the third picture in this figure.

   If **Pol-Trace** is not able to find all points of intersection appearing on the graph screen, the "Pol-Trace is not perfect" sidebar in this chapter gives you a solution to this problem.

4. **Press** CLEAR **when you are finished using Pol-Trace.**

Pol-Trace is not perfect

The Pol-Trace feature found in the Inequality Graphing application has no trouble finding the points of intersection of linear inequalities. However, if your inequalities are not linear, **Pol-Trace** may not be able to find all points of intersection. But this isn't a problem, because you can always use the **Intersect** tool in the **Calc** menu to find the points of intersection that **Pol-Trace** couldn't find. And the points found by the **Intersect** tool can be stored in the calculator the same way that points found by **Pol-Trace** are stored. Using the **Intersect** tool to find points of intersection is explained in Chapter 11. The "Storing Data Points" section tells you how to store points of intersection found using the **Intersect** tool.

Other ways to explore a graph

All the commands and features described in Chapters 9, 10, and 11 that are available for graphing and exploring normal functions are also available when graphing and exploring inequalities. For example, you can split the screen and display a graph and a table, you can zoom in on a graph, you can trace a graph, you can find the coordinates of maximum and minimum points, and you can do much, much more. Many of these commands are housed in the **Zoom** and **Calc** menus. Using these commands and features is explained in Chapters 9, 10, and 11.

Storing Data Points

When you start Inequality Graphing for the first time, the application creates two lists, INEQX and INEQY, to house the *x*- and *y*-coordinates of data points that you store in the calculator. When you exit Inequality Graphing, these data lists are not deleted from the calculator. So when you start the application again at a later time, any data previously stored in these lists will still be there, provided that you didn't delete the lists from the memory of the calculator.

The last section in this chapter, "Solving Linear Programming Problems," gives a real-world example of why you would want to store data points in lists. In this section, I tell you how to store data points in these lists, clear the contents of these lists, and view the data in the lists. Chapter 16 gives you a more detailed explanation of dealing with data lists. Among other things, Chapter 16 tells you how to manually enter or edit data in a list, how to delete data from a list, and how to sort data. Chapter 16 also tells you how to delete a data list from the calculator's memory. But if you do delete the INEQX and INEQY data lists, the next time you start Inequality Graphing, the application will re-create these lists. So why bother deleting them?

Clearing the INEQX and INEQY lists

When the Inequality Graphing application stores a data point, it appends that point to the other points already stored in the INEQX and INEQY lists. When you exit Inequality Graphing, the application does not clear the contents of these lists. So if you are graphing a new set of inequalities and want to store data points associated with the graph, it's a good idea to clear the old data points from these lists.

To clear the contents of the INEQX and INEQY lists, press GRAPH ALPHA CLEAR. The graph screen appears and the INEQX and INEQY lists remain in the calculator as empty data lists.

If an inequality graph is displayed on the screen, simply press ALPHA CLEAR to clear the INEQX and INEQY data lists. If any other screen is displayed, such as the Y= editor, you must press GRAPH ALPHA CLEAR to clear these lists.

Storing points in INEQX and INEQY

The Inequality Graphing application can store any data point whose coordinates appear at the bottom of the graph screen, as illustrated in the pictures in Figure 13-8. Such points are found using **Trace**, **Pol-Trace**, or any of the first five tools in the **Calc** menu. (**Trace** is explained in Chapter 10, **Pol-Trace** is explained earlier in this chapter, and the tools in the **Calc** menu are explained in Chapter 11.)

A data point can be stored in the calculator only when the cursor is on that point and the coordinates of the cursor location appear at the bottom of the graph screen, as shown in Figure 13-8. When this is the case, press STO▸ to store the coordinates of the data point. You usually get a message saying, "Point appended to ((INEQX, (INEQY)" or "Duplicate point." The first message tells you that the x-coordinate of your data point is stored in the list named INEQX and the *y*-coordinate is stored in list INEQY. Press ENTER to get rid of the message and return to the graph. If the point is already stored in the calculator, you get the "Duplicate Point" message. Press ENTER to get rid of the message. The Inequality Graphing application will not store the point a second time.

If you get the "List Editor full" message when you store a data point, this tells you that your data has been stored but there are too many lists in the Stat List editor to display the INEQX and INEQY lists. This is easily remedied by deleting two lists form the Stat List editor and then recalling the INEQX and INEQY lists. How to do this is explained in Chapter 16. If you delete two lists from the Stat List editor and don't recall the INEQX and INEQY lists, the Inequality Graphing application automatically places them in the Stat List editor the next time you save a data point.

If you get the "((INEQX, (INEQY) already full" message when you store a data point, this tells you that these lists already contain 999 entries, the maximum number of entries allowed in any list. Before storing any more data in these lists, you will have to delete some entries from the lists. How to do this is explained in Chapter 16.

Viewing stored data

Press STAT 1 to view the data stored in lists INEQX and INEQY, as illustrated in Figure 13-9. If the Stat List editor already contains 19 or 20 lists, then there is not enough room for the editor to display these two lists. This situation is remedied by deleting a few lists from the Stat List editor and then recalling the INEQX and INEQY lists. How to do this is explained in Chapter 16.

INEQX	INEQY	REVNU ?
700	300	------
500	300	
500	500	

INEQX(4) =

Figure 13-9: Viewing lists INEQX and INEQY.

Solving Linear Programming Problems

Linear programming is a method for finding the maximum or minimum value of a multivariable function that is constrained by a system of inequalities. The following example should help you understand this rather technical definition of linear programming.

> A chocolate company sells real and imitation chocolate chips to a local cookie factory. On any given day, the cookie factory needs at least 500 pounds of real chocolate chips and at least 300 pounds of imitation chocolate chips. The real chocolate chips sell for $1.25 a pound and the imitation chocolate chips sell for $0.75 a pound. If the truck that takes the chocolate chips to the cookie factory can carry at most 1,000 pounds of chocolate chips, how many pounds of each kind of chocolate chips should the chocolate company ship to the cookie factory in order to maximize its revenue?

In this example, the chocolate factory's revenue is the function revenue = $1.25x + 0.75y$ where x is the number of pounds of real chocolate chips and y is the number of pounds of imitation chocolate chips that the chocolate company ships to the cookie factory. The constraints stated in this example are: $500 \leq x$, $300 \leq y$, and $x + y \leq 1000$. In other words, this example asks you to find the maximum value of revenue = $1.25x + 0.75y$ subject to the system of constraints $x \geq 500$, $y \geq 300$, and $y \leq 1000 - x$.

How do you solve a linear programming problem? The following theorem gives the answer.

Linear Programming Theorem: If an optimum (maximum or minimum) value of a function constrained by a system of inequalities exists, then that optimum value occurs at one or more of the vertices of the region defined by the constraining system of inequalities.

This theorem tells us to evaluate the function at the points of intersection of the constraining system of inequalities. The smallest value found is the minimum value of the function and the largest is its maximum value. To get the Inequality Graphing application to help you solve a linear programming problem, follow these steps:

1. **Graph the system of constraints.**

   How to do this is explained earlier in this chapter. For the example at the beginning of this section, the graph of the system of constraints ($x \geq 500$, $y \geq 300$, and $y \leq 1000 - x$) appears in the third picture in Figure 13-5.

2. **Graph the intersection of the regions in the graph.**

   How to do this is explained earlier in this chapter. For the example at the beginning of this section, the graph of the intersection appears in the second picture in Figure 13-7.

3. **Find and store the points of intersection in the graph.**

   How to do this is explained earlier in this chapter. For the example at the beginning of this section, the process of finding the points of intersection is illustrated in Figure 13-8.

4. **Display the stored points of intersection.**

   How to do this is explained earlier in this chapter. For the example at the beginning of this section, the stored points of intersection appear in Figure 13-9.

5. **Create a list to the right of list INEQY and give it a name.**

   The name you give the list should describe the function in the linear programming problem. In the next step this function will be evaluated at the stored points of intersection.

   If an empty, unnamed list does not appear to the right of list INEQY, place the cursor in the heading of the third column and press [2nd][DEL] to insert a blank column, enter a name, and then press [ENTER]. If an empty, unnamed list does appear in the third column, place the cursor in the heading of that column, enter a name, and then press [ENTER]. Should you need it, a more detailed explanation of creating and naming lists can be found in Chapter 16.

   For the example at the beginning of this section, the created list is named REVNU for revenue, as illustrated in Figure 13-9.

6. **Use a formula to define the entries in the new list.**

   The formula you enter is the formula that defines the function you want to optimize. In the example at the beginning of this section, that formula is $1.25x + 0.75y$, the definition of the revenue function. Because x is housed in list INEQX and y in INEQY, this formula is entered into the calculator as $1.25*(INEQX + 0.75*(INEQY$.

To use a formula to define a list, place the cursor on the name of the list in the column heading. Because formulas must be surrounded by quotes, press [ALPHA][+] to enter the first quotation mark. Then enter the formula. To enter the name of a list, such as (INEQX, press [2nd][STAT] to display a list of the names of the lists in the Stat List editor. Repeatedly press [▾] to highlight the number to the left of the list and press [ENTER] to insert the name of the list in your formula. After entering the formula, press [ALPHA][+] to enter the closing quotation mark.

7. Press [ENTER] to evaluate the function at the points of inter-section of the constraining system of inequalities.

According to the Linear Programming Theorem, if the function has a maximum and/or minimum value, those values appear in the list you just created. As illustrated in Figure 13-10, the chocolate factory in the example at the beginning of this section can maximize its revenue by shipping 700 pounds of real chocolate chips and 300 pounds of imitation chocolate chips.

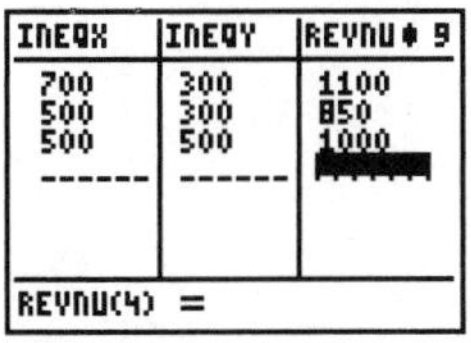

Figure 13-10: Solution to a linear programming problem.

Part IV

Probability and Statistics

"Okay — let's play the statistical probabilities of this situation. There are 4 of us and 1 of him. Phillip will probably start screaming, Nora will probably faint, you'll probably yell at me for leaving the truck open, and there's a good probability I'll run like a weenie if he comes toward us."

In this part . . .

This part gives you a look at calculating permutations and combinations, as well as generating random numbers and simulating tossing coins, rolling dice, picking marbles, and drawing cards.

I also show you how to graph and analyze one- and two-variable statistical data sets. And if you want to do regression modeling (curve-fitting) — hey, who doesn't? — I show you how to do that, too.

Chapter 14

Probability

- -

In This Chapter

▶ Evaluating permutations and combinations

▶ Generating random numbers

- -

Do you need to calculate the number of ways you can arrange six people at a table or the number of ways you can select four people from a group of six people? Or do you just need an unbiased way of selecting people at random? If so, this is the chapter for you.

Permutations and Combinations

A *permutation,* denoted by **nPr**, answers the question: "From a set of **n** different items, how many ways can you select *and* order (arrange) **r** of these items?" A *combination,* denoted by **nCr**, answers the question: "From a set of **n** different items, how many ways can you select (independent or order) **r** of these items?" To evaluate a permutation or combination, follow these steps:

1. **On the Home screen, enter n, the total number of items in the set.**

    If you're not already on the Home screen, press 2nd MODE to exit (quit) the current screen and enter the Home screen.

2. **Press MATH ▶ ▶ ▶ to access the Math Probability menu.**

3. **Press 2 to evaluate a permutation or press 3 to evaluate a combination.**

4. **Enter r, the number of items selected from the set, and press ENTER to display the result.**

Figure 14-1 illustrates this procedure. Notice that the last two lines in the figure tell you that it's impossible to select 7 items from a set of only 5 items.

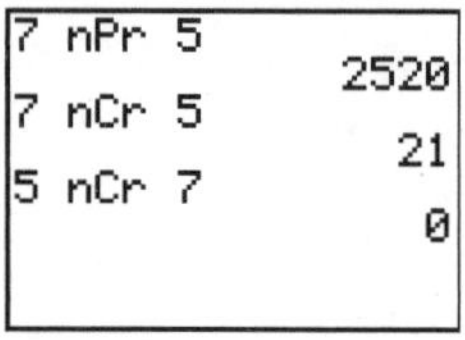

```
7 nPr 5
            2520
7 nCr 5
              21
5 nCr 7
               0
```

Figure 14-1: Evaluating permutations and combinations.

Generating Random Numbers

When generating random numbers, you usually want to generate numbers that are integers contained in a specified range, or decimal numbers that are strictly between 0 and 1.

Generating random integers

To generate random integers that fall between the integers **a** and **b**:

1. **Press MATH▶ ▶ ▶ 5 to select the randInt command from the Math Probability menu.**

2. **Enter the value of the lower limit a, press ⬚, and enter the upper limit b.**

3. **Press ENTER to generate the first random integer. Repeatedly press ENTER to generate more random integers.**

This is illustrated in the first picture in Figure 14-2.

Pressing any key except ENTER stops the calculator from generating random integers.

Generating random decimals

To generate random decimal numbers that are strictly between 0 and 1, press [MATH][▶][▶][▶][1] to select the **rand** command from the Math Probability menu. Then repeatedly press [ENTER] to generate the random numbers. The second picture in Figure 14-2 illustrates this process.

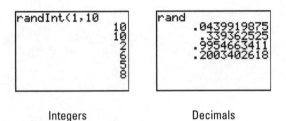

Integers   Decimals

Figure 14-2: Generating random numbers.

Chapter 15

Simulating Probabilities

● ●

In This Chapter

▶ Tossing coins

▶ Rolling dice

▶ Picking marbles from a pot

▶ Spinning a spinner

▶ Drawing cards from a deck

● ●

*W*ith the Probability Simulation application that comes pre-loaded on the TI-84 Plus family of calculators, you can simulate tossing coins, rolling dice, picking marbles from a pot, spinning a spinner, and drawing cards from a deck. It even allows you to rig the simulation with weighted coins and unfair dice.

As the application performs simulations, it collects the data associated with these simulations and displays it in a graph or table. It can even save the data for you so that you can perform a statistical analysis of the data at a later time. In this chapter, I tell you how to get the Probability Simulation application to do all these neat things.

Starting and Quitting Probability Simulation

To start the Probability Simulation application, press [APPS][ALPHA][8], use [▼] to move the cursor to the **Prob Sim** application, and press [ENTER] to select the application and display the logo screen, as illustrated in the first screen in Figure 15-1. Press any key to start the Probability Simulation application and display the Main menu screen, as illustrated in the second picture in this figure.

Logo screen   Main menu

Figure 15-1: Screens you see when you start Probability Simulation.

You quit the Probability Simulation application by using the **QUIT** command at the bottom of the Main menu, as illustrated in the second picture in Figure 15-1. If you are not in the Main menu, repeatedly press [Y=] until this menu appears. Then press [GRAPH] to exit the application. When asked if you really want to quit, press [Y=] to select the **YES** option.

Using the Probability Simulation Application

Before you toss coins, roll dice, pick marbles, spin spinners, or draw cards, you need to know how to access the commands at the bottom of the screen, how to seed the random number generator, and what the **ESC** command does. These things are explained in this section; tossing coins, rolling dice, picking marbles, spinning spinners, drawing cards, and generating random numbers are explained later in this chapter.

Executing the commands at the bottom of the screen

At the bottom of each screen, you see a line of five boxes containing from two to five commands, as illustrated in the second picture in Figure 15-1 where the boxes contain four commands (**OK**, **OPTN**, **ABOUT**, and **QUIT**) with no command in the second box. Under these boxes are five calculator keys: [Y=], [WINDOW], [ZOOM], [TRACE], and [GRAPH]. You execute the command by pressing the calculator key that is under the box. For example, in the second picture in Figure 15-1, the **OPTN** command is executed by pressing [ZOOM].

Seeding the random number generator

The calculator doesn't really generate random numbers; it uses a formula to generate a sequence of numbers that appear to be random. Each number in this sequence is dependent on the number that precedes it. Thus the whole sequence is determined by the first number in the sequence. This number is called the seed; assigning a value to the seed is called seeding the random number generator. If you seed two different TI-84's with the same number, the random number generator will produce the same sequence of numbers on each calculator. Now that isn't very random, is it?

The outcome of each simulation performed by the Probability Simulation application, whether it be tossing a coin or spinning a spinner, is determined by a random number generated by Probability Simulation's random number generator. Usually, you don't need to seed the random number generator to ensure that you get a "random" outcome. You can just accept whatever number the calculator uses as a seed because it uses the last random number it generated as the seed.

However, if you want to ensure that a simulation is replicated on two or more TI-84's, set the seed to the same number on each calculator. Or if you want to ensure that a simulation is not replicated, set the seed to a random number of your choice.

To seed the random number generator, follow these steps:

1. **Go to Probability Simulation's Main menu.**

   The Main menu, pictured in the second screen in Figure 15-1, is the first screen you see when you start the Probability Simulation application. If you are not in the Main menu, repeatedly press [Y=] until this menu appears.

2. **Press [ZOOM] to execute the OPTN command.**

   A blinking cursor appears, waiting for you to enter a number.

3. **Use the keypad to enter any positive integer.**

4. **Press [GRAPH] to select the OK option.**

   The random number generator is seeded by the number you entered, and you are returned to the Main menu.

Going back to the previous screen using the ESC command

The **ESC** command sends you back to the previous screen. If it is available, it is always the first command in the command line at the bottom of the screen. So it is always executed by pressing [Y=].

Understanding the Settings Editor

The Probability Simulation application contains four simulators (Tossing Coins, Rolling Dice, Picking Marbles from an urn, and Spinning a Spinner) that work pretty much the same way. This section contains information common to these four simulators. If you'd like to skip this section for now and start using one of these simulators, by all means do so. The directions for the Settings editor in each simulator are explained later in this chapter; they refer you back to this section when needed.

Trial Set

Most Settings editors in the Probability Simulation application contain the **Trial Set** option. With this option, you tell the application how many trials you want it run whenever you tell it to toss coins, roll dice, pick marbles, or spin a spinner. For example, if you are tossing two coins and **Trial Set** is 5, the first time you tell the application to toss the coins, it tosses the two coins five times, thus executing five trials. The next time you tell it to toss the coins, it tosses the coins five more times for a total of ten trials, and so on. Similarly, if you are rolling dice and **Trial Set** is 5, then each time you tell the application to roll dice, it will roll the dice five times.

If **Trial Set** is 1, then, after you tell the application to perform the first trial, you are given the option of tossing the coins one time, ten times, or 50 times. (You can see an example of this in the second picture of Figure 15-5, later in this chapter.) If **Trial Set** is greater than 1, then each time you tell the application to execute a trial, it executes the number of trials specified by the **Trial Set** setting.

Graph and table settings

Most of the Settings editors in the Probability Simulation application contain options that you can use to tell the application how you want it to display the graph and the table of the data it collects. These options are

✔ **Graph:** With this option, the application graphs your data as a histogram and gives you the choice between having the *y*-axis of the histogram display the *frequency* of an outcome or the *probability* of an outcome. For example, if you toss one coin eleven times and it lands heads up six times, then in a frequency histogram the bar depicting the "heads" outcome is six units tall; in a probability histogram, it is 6/11 units tall. When setting the options in the Settings editor, select **Freq** if you want the graph displayed as a frequency histogram; select **Prob** for a probability histogram.

✔ **StoTbl:** This option tells the application how many rows you want to see when your data is displayed in a table. You are given a choice between seeing no rows, all the rows, or only 50 rows. If you select 50 rows, only the bottom 50 rows of the table (your most recent data) can be viewed as you scroll through the data in a table. But let's face it, the TI-84 is a powerful puppy; it can handle displaying *all* the rows in the table. So there is no harm in setting the **StoTbl** option to **All**. It won't slow things down one bit.

✔ **ClearTbl:** This option is pretty obvious; it affords you the opportunity to tell the application if you want to clear the table or not. Your only choices are **Yes** and **No**. However, if you make changes to other options in the Settings editor, **ClrTbl** is automatically set to **Yes**.

✔ **Update:** This option enables you to tell the application to update the graph and table after 1, 20, or 50 trials, or at the end of the probability experiment. Because the TI-84 is a fast calculator, set this to 1.

Weighted outcomes

The Advanced Settings editor is where you tell the application if you want it to toss fair or weighted coins, roll fair or weighted dice, or spin a spinner divided into equal or unequal sections. The first picture in Figure 15-2 depicts the weights for a fair marble and the second picture shows the weights for a spinner divided into four equal sections.

To bias a coin, die, or spinner, change the weight of the outcome. For example, to bias a die so that it is twice a likely to display 6 as it is to display any other number, set the weights of sides 1 through 5 to 1 and the weight of side 6 to 2.

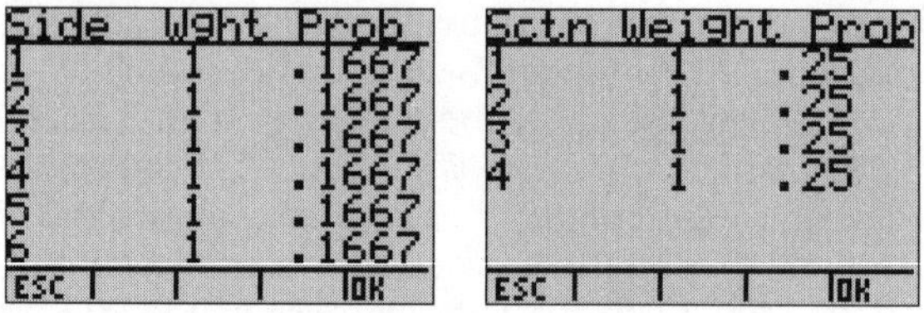

Side	Wght	Prob		Sctn	Weight	Prob
1	1	.1667		1	1	.25
2	1	.1667		2	1	.25
3	1	.1667		3	1	.25
4	1	.1667		4	1	.25
5	1	.1667				
6	1	.1667				
ESC		OK		ESC		OK

Evenly weighted marble   Evenly divided spinner

Figure 15-2: Fair (unbiased) dice and spinner.

To change the weights of the outcomes listed in the Advanced Settings editor, use the arrow keys to place the cursor on the existing weight in the second column of the Advanced Settings editor, use the keypad to enter the new weight, and then press [ENTER]. The number you enter for the weight must be a positive integer. As you enter the weights, the application updates the probability of the outcome in the third column.

Tossing Coins

The Probability Simulation application can simulate tossing from one to three coins at a time. It can even toss weighted coins. When tossing only one coin at a time, the application keeps track of the number of heads and tails that occur as the coin is repeatedly tossed. When tossing more than one coin at a time, the application keeps track of only the number of heads that occur.

The data from the repeatedly tossing coins can be displayed in a histogram or in a table. The application even gives you the option of saving your data so you can, if you choose, statistically analyze it at a later time. Chapter 17 tells you how to perform such an analysis and the "Saving your data" sidebar in this chapter tells you how to — you guessed it — save your data. This section tells you how to use the Toss Coins simulator.

Simulating the tossing of coins

To toss coins, follow these steps:

1. **Start the Probability Simulation application and press** [1] **to select the Toss Coins option in the Main menu.**

   You see the Toss Coins Home screen, as illustrated in the first picture in Figure 15-3.

To use the Toss Coins simulator after using another simulator, repeatedly press [Y=] until you see the Main menu (second picture in Figure 15-1), and then press [1] to select the Toss Coins simulator.

| Home screen | Settings editor | Advanced Settings editor |

Figure 15-3: The Toss Coins simulator's Home screen and editors.

2. **Press [ZOOM] to display the Settings editor. Change the settings in Settings editor as appropriate.**

   The second picture in Figure 15-3 shows the Settings editor. Should you need it, the "Understanding the Settings Editor" section, earlier in this chapter, explains the function of all options except the **Coins** option. The **Coins** option lets you tell the application to toss 1, 2, or 3 coins each time it tosses coins.

   To enter a number in **Trial Set**, use the arrow keys to place the cursor on the existing number, use the keypad to enter a new positive integer, and then press [ENTER]. To select other options, use the arrow keys to place the cursor on the option, and then press [ENTER] to select the option.

3. **Press [WINDOW] to display the Advanced Settings editor. Enter the weights for your coins.**

   The screen you see is similar to the third picture in Figure 15-3. If you are tossing more than one coin, the application requires that all of the coins be weighted in the same way. For example, if you want one coin to be twice as likely to land heads up and you are tossing three coins, then all three coins must be twice as likely to land heads up. Should you need it, the "Understanding the Settings Editor" section, earlier in this chapter, explains how to weight your coins.

4. **Press [GRAPH] to say OK to the weights in the Advanced Settings editor. Press [GRAPH] again to say OK to the settings in the Settings editor.**

   You see the Toss Coins Home screen, as illustrated in the first picture in Figure 15-3.

5. **Press** WINDOW **to toss coins.**

You see a screen similar to the first or second picture in Figure 15-4. If one coin was tossed only one time, then only one bar appears in the histogram.

6. **Continue tossing coins.**

If in Step 2, you set **Trial Set** to a number greater than one, then after tossing the first set of coins, you see a screen similar to the first picture in Figure 15-4. Press WINDOW to toss more coins.

If **Trial Set** is 1, then after tossing the first set of coins, you see a screen similar to the second picture in Figure 15-4. Press WINDOW to toss one more set of coins, ZOOM to toss ten more sets of coins, or TRACE to toss 50 more sets of coins.

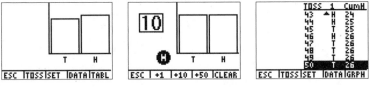

Figure 15-4: The Toss Coins simulator's graph and table.

Reading the graph and table

The cumulative data from tossing coins is stored in both a histogram and a table. The histogram, by default, is displayed on the screen without any values on the *y*-axis. The "Histograms and tables" sidebar in this chapter tells you how to display and read the histogram and the table. Here are some specifics about the Toss Coins histogram and table:

✔ **Toss Coins histogram:** If you are tossing only one coin, the histogram displays the cumulative outcomes of tails and heads from repeated tossing of the coin, as illustrated in the first and second pictures in Figure 15-4. If you are tossing more than one coin, the histogram displays only cumulative outcomes of heads. For example, if you are tossing two coins, the histogram displays the outcomes of no heads, one head, or two heads.

✔ **Toss Coins table:** The number of the toss appears in the first column of the table. If only one coin is tossed, the second column contains the outcome (H for heads or T for tails) for that coin and the last column contains the cumulative number of heads, as illustrated in the third picture of Figure 15-4. If more than one coin is tossed, the middle columns contain the outcome (H or T) for each coin and the last column contains the total number of heads for that particular toss of the coins.

Rolling Dice

The Probability Simulation application can simulate rolling from one to three dice at a time. It can even roll weighted dice. When rolling only one die at a time, the application keeps track of the number of times each number on the die lands up as the die is repeatedly rolled. When rolling more than one die at a time, the application keeps track of the sum of the numbers on the dice.

The data from the repeatedly rolling the dice can be displayed in a histogram or in a table. The application even gives you the option of saving your data so you can, if you choose, statistically analyze it at a later time. Chapter 17 tells you how to perform such an analysis, and the "Saving your data" sidebar in this chapter tells you how to — you guessed it — save your data. This section tells you how to use the Roll Dice simulator.

Histograms and tables

The Toss Coins, Roll Dice, Pick Marbles, and Spin Spinner simulators in the Probability Simulation application display cumulative data in both a histogram and a table. The histogram, by default, is displayed on the screen without any values on the *y*-axis.

To view the *y*-values of the histogram, press ▶. The first bar in the histogram is shaded and the *y*-value is displayed. Continue to press ▶ to display the *y*-values of the other bars. Pressing ▶ after the last bar takes you back to the first bar in the histogram. Pressing ◀ can also be used to display the *y*-values of the bars in the histogram.

To display the table of the data, you must be in the simulator's Home screen. You know you are in the Home screen when **TABL** is the last command at the bottom of the screen, as illustrated in the first picture of Figure 15-4. If you are not in the Home screen, as illustrated in the second picture of Figure 15-4, press Y= to display the Home screen.

To display the table from the simulators Home screen, press GRAPH to execute the **TABL** command. To display the histogram after displaying the table, press GRAPH again to execute the **GRPH** command.

Simulating the rolling of dice

To roll dice, follow these steps:

1. **Start the Probability Simulation application and press ②
   to select the Roll Dice option in the Main menu.**

   You see the Roll Dice Home screen, as illustrated in the first
   picture in Figure 15-5.

   To use the Roll Dice simulator after using another simulator,
   repeatedly press Y= until you see the Main menu (second
   picture in Figure 15-1), and then press ② to select the Roll
   Coin simulator.

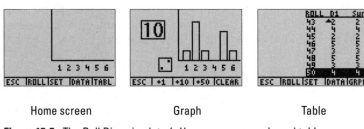

| Home screen | Graph | Table |

Figure 15-5: The Roll Dice simulator's Home screen, graph, and table.

2. **Press ZOOM to display the Settings editor. Change the settings in Settings editor as appropriate.**

   You see a screen similar to the Toss Coins simulator's
   Settings editor, as illustrated in the second picture in Figure 15-3.

   Should you need it, the "Understanding the Settings Editor"
   section, earlier in this chapter, explains the function of all
   options except the **Dice** and **Sides** options. The **Dice** option
   lets you tell the application to roll 1, 2, or 3 dice each time
   it rolls dice. The **Sides** option lets you roll normal six-sided
   dice or exotic dice having 8, 10, 12, or 20 sides. If you are
   rolling more than one die, all your dice must have the same
   number of sides.

   To enter a number in **Trial Set**, use the arrow keys to place
   the cursor on the existing number, use the keypad to enter
   a new positive integer, and then press ENTER. To select
   other options, use the arrow keys to place the cursor on
   the option and press ENTER to select the option.

   Don't forget the **Update** option. The down arrow in the
   lower-right corner of the screen indicates that you should
   repeatedly press ⊡ to reach this option.

3. **Press** WINDOW **to display the Advanced Settings editor. Enter the weights for your dice.**

   The screen you see lists the sides of a die in the first column, its weight in the second column, and the probability of that side landing face up in the third column. If you are rolling more than one die, the application requires that all of the dice be weighted in the same way. Should you need it, the earlier section, "Understanding the Settings Editor," explains how to weight your dice.

4. **Press** GRAPH **to say OK to the weights in the Advanced Settings editor. Press** GRAPH **again to say OK to the settings in the Settings editor.**

   You see the Roll Dice Home screen, as illustrated in the first picture in Figure 15-5. If you are rolling more than one die, you see a jumble of numbers on the screen. This is explained in the next section, "Reading the graph and table."

5. **Press** WINDOW **to roll dice.**

   You see a screen similar to the second picture in Figure 15-5. If in Step 2 you set **Trial Set** to 1, then only one bar appears in the histogram. If you set **Trial Set** to a number greater than one, then the command line at the bottom of the screen is the same command line as in the first picture in this figure.

6. **Continue rolling dice.**

   If in Step 2 you set **Trial Set** to a number greater than one, press WINDOW to roll more dice.

   If **Trial Set** is 1, then after rolling the first set of dice, you see a screen similar to the second picture in Figure 15-5. Press WINDOW to roll one more set of dice, ZOOM to roll ten more sets of dice, or TRACE to roll 50 more sets of dice.

Reading the graph and table

The cumulative data from rolling dice is stored in both a histogram and a table. The histogram, by default, is displayed on the screen without any values on the *y*-axis. The "Histograms and tables" sidebar in this chapter tells you how to display and read the histogram and the table. Here are some specifics about the Roll Dice histogram and table:

✔ **Roll Dice histogram:** If you are rolling only one die, the histogram displays the cumulative outcomes of the side of the die that landed face-up. This is illustrated in the second picture in Figure 15-5 for a six-sided die. If you are rolling more than one die, the histogram displays cumulative outcomes of the sum of the face-up sides of the dice. For example, if you are rolling three dice, the possible outcomes (sums of face-up sides) are the integers 3 through 15. These numbers appear below the histogram with the two-digit numbers displayed in a column. The right arrow indicates that there are too many bars in the histogram to display on the screen. Repeatedly press ▶ to see these bars.

✔ **Roll Dice table:** The number of the roll appears in the first column of the table. The middle columns contain the outcome (number that landed face-up) for each die, and the last column contains sum of the outcomes for the dice in that roll. If you are rolling only one die, the middle and last column will, of course, be the same, as illustrated in the third picture in Figure 15-5.

Picking Marbles from an Urn

The Probability Simulation application can simulate picking one marble at a time from an urn that contains from two to five different types (colors) of marbles. You even get to specify how many marbles of each type are in the urn and you get to tell the application whether or not a marble picked from the urn is placed back in the urn before the next selection is made. The application keeps track of the type of marble picked from the urn.

The data from the repeatedly picking marbles can be displayed in a histogram or in a table. The application even gives you the option of saving you data so that you can, if you choose, statistically analyze it at a later time. Chapter 17 tells you how to perform such an analysis, and the "Saving your data" sidebar in this chapter tells you how to — you guessed it — save your data. This section tells you how to use the Pick Marbles simulator.

Simulating picking marbles

To pick marbles from an urn, follow these steps:

1. **Start the Probability Simulation application and press ③ to select the Pick Marbles option in the Main menu.**

   You see the Pick Marbles Home screen, as illustrated in the first picture in Figure 15-6.

To use the Pick Marbles simulator after using another simulator, repeatedly press [Y=] until you see the Main menu (second picture in Figure 15-1) and then press [3] to select the Pick Marbles simulator.

 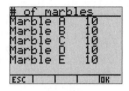 

Home screen   Advance Settings   Table
                           screen

Figure 15-6: The Pick Marbles simulator's Home screen, Advanced Settings screen, and table.

2. **Press [ZOOM] to display the Settings editor. Change the settings in Settings editor, as appropriate.**

   You see a screen similar to the Toss Coins simulator's Settings editor, as illustrated in the second picture in Figure 15-3.

   Should you need it, the earlier section, "Understanding the Settings Editor," explains the function of all options except the **Types** and **Replace** options. The **Types** option lets you tell the application how many different types (colors) of marbles in the urn. The urn can contain from two to five different kinds of marbles. The **Replace** option lets you tell the simulator if a marble is put back in the urn (**Yes**) or not (**No**) before another marble is picked from the urn.

   To enter a number in **Trial Set**, use the arrow keys to place the cursor on the existing number, use the keypad to enter a new positive integer, and then press [ENTER]. To select other options, use the arrow keys to place the cursor on the option, and then press [ENTER] to select the option.

   Don't forget the **Update** option. The down arrow in the lower-right corner of the screen indicates that you should repeatedly press [▾] to reach this option.

3. **Press [WINDOW] to display the Advanced Settings editor. Enter the number of each type of marble in the urn.**

   The Advanced Settings editor is illustrated in the second picture in Figure 15-6. To change the number of marbles of a certain type, use the arrow keys to place the cursor on the number appearing next to that type, use the keypad to enter a new positive integer, and then press [ENTER].

4. **Press** GRAPH **to say OK to the weights in the Advanced Settings editor. Press** GRAPH **again to say OK to the settings in the Settings editor.**

   You see the Pick Marbles Home screen. If you set the **Replace** option to **Yes**, the letter R appears in the upper-left corner of the screen, as illustrated in the first picture in Figure 15-6.

5. **Press** WINDOW **to pick marbles.**

   The histogram appears on the screen. If in Step 2 you set **Trial Set** to 1, then only one bar appears in the histogram.

6. **Continue picking marbles.**

   If in Step 2 you set **Trial Set** to a number greater than one, press WINDOW to pick more marbles.

   If **Trial Set** is 1, then after picking the first marble, the command line at the bottom of the screen is the same as the command line in the second picture in Figure 15-5. Press WINDOW to pick one more marble, ZOOM to pick ten more marbles, or TRACE to pick 50 more marbles.

   If in Step 2 you set **Replace** to **No**, then the urn could eventually run out of marbles. When this happens, the simulator displays the "no more marbles" message and will, of course, not allow you to pick any more marbles from the urn. To pick more marbles after seeing this message, start a new simulation of picking marbles by following Steps 2 through 6. In Step 2 if you don't see the **SET** command, press Y= to get back to the Pick Marbles simulator's Home screen.

Reading the graph and table

The cumulative data from picking marbles is stored in both a histogram and a table. The histogram, by default, is displayed on the screen without any values on the *y*-axis. The "Histograms and tables" sidebar in this chapter tells you how to display and read the histogram and the table. Here are some specifics about the Pick Marbles simulator's histogram and table:

- **Pick Marbles histogram:** Each bar in the histogram records the data for each type of marble in the urn.

- **Pick Marbles table:** This is illustrated in the third picture of Figure 15-6. The first column displays the number of the pick and the second column shows what type of marble was picked.

Saving your data

The data that appears in any Probability Simulation table can be saved to lists so that you can, after exiting the application, statistically analyze this data. Chapter 16 tells you how to place the saved data in the Stat editor and Chapter 17 tells you how to analyze the data.

To save the data, go to the simulator's Home screen. (You know you are in the Home screen when **DATA** is the fourth command at the bottom of the screen. If you are not in the Home screen, press Y= to display the Home screen.) Then press TRACE to display the Save Data screen. The names of the files (lists) you see are approximately the same as the column headings in the simulator's table. You cannot rename these lists. Press GRAPH to tell the application that it is OK to save the data to the lists specified on the Save Data screen.

The list names for the data in each simulator are different. So, for example, if you save data after tossing coins and then save data after rolling dice, the data from each simulation will remain in the calculator. But the list names in a given simulator are the same. So, for example, if you save data after tossing coins and then save data again after tossing more coins, the data from the second simulation will — without warning — overwrite the data from the first simulation. If you don't want this to happen, consider renaming the lists saved in the first simulation before saving the data from the second simulation. To rename the lists, you must first exit the Probability Simulation application. Then create a user-named data list using a new list name and recall the old list to that user-named list. The user-named list is automatically saved under its list name. Chapter 16 tells you how to create user-named lists and how to recall lists.

Spinning a Spinner

The Probability Simulation application can simulate spinning a spinner that is divided into two to eight sections of equal or unequal areas. It will not simulate the spinner landing on the boundary of two sections. An outcome of this simulator is the section on which the spinner landed.

The data from the repeatedly spinning the spinner can be displayed in a histogram or in a table. The application even gives you the option of saving your data so you can, if you choose, statistically analyze it at a later time. Chapter 17 tells you how to perform such an analysis and the "Saving your data" sidebar in this chapter tells you how to — you guessed it — save your data. This section tells you how to use the Spin Spinners simulator.

Simulating spinning spinners

To spin a spinner, follow these steps:

1. **Start the Probability Simulation application and press** 4 **to select the Spin Spinners option in the Main menu.**

   You see the Spin Spinner simulator's Home screen, as illustrated in the first picture in Figure 15-7.

   To use the Spin Spinner simulator after using another simulator, repeatedly press Y= until you see the Main menu (second picture in Figure 15-1), and then press 4 to select the Spin Spinners simulator.

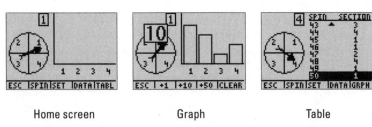

Home screen   Graph   Table

Figure 15-7: The Spin Spinner simulator's Home screen, graph, and table.

2. **Press** ZOOM **to display the Settings editor. Change the settings in Settings editor as appropriate.**

   You see a screen similar to the Toss Coins simulator's Settings editor, as illustrated in the second picture in Figure 15-3.

   Should you need it, the earlier section, "Understanding the Settings Editor," explains the function of all options except the **Sections** option. This option lets you tell the application how many sections you want the spinner to have. It can have from two to eight sections.

   To enter a number in **Trial Set** or **Sections**, use the arrow keys to place the cursor on the existing number, use the keypad to enter a new positive integer, and then press ENTER. To select other options, use the arrow keys to place the cursor on the option and press ENTER to select the option.

3. **Press** WINDOW **to display the Advanced Settings editor. Enter the weight of each section of the spinner.**

   The number of the section is displayed in the first column of the Advanced Settings editor, its weight appears in the second column, and the probability of the spinner landing on that section appears in the third column. The weight corresponds to the area of the spinner occupied by that section. For example, if you want a spinner to have three sections with one section occupying half the area of the spinner and the other two sections each occupying a fourth of the spinner, set the weight of one section to two and the weight of the other two sections to one.

To change a number in the weight column, use the arrow keys to place the cursor on the existing number, use the keypad to enter a new positive integer, and then press ENTER.

4. **Press GRAPH to say OK to the weights in the Advanced Settings editor. Press GRAPH again to say OK to the settings in the Settings editor.**

   You see the Spin Spinner Home screen.

5. **Press WINDOW to spin the spinner.**

   You see a screen similar to the second picture in Figure 15-7. The number on which the spinner last landed appears at the top of the screen.

6. **Continue spinning the spinner.**

   If in Step 2 you set **Trial Set** to a number greater than one, press WINDOW to spin the spinner the number of times specified in **Trial Set**.

   If **Trial Set** is 1, then after the first spin of the spinner the command line at the bottom of the screen is the same as the command line in the second picture in Figure 15-7. Press WINDOW to spin the spinner one time, ZOOM to spin the spinner ten more time, or TRACE to spin it 50 more times.

Reading the graph and table

The cumulative data from spinning the spinner is stored in both a histogram and a table. The histogram, by default, is displayed on the screen without any values on the *y*-axis. The "Histograms and tables" sidebar in this chapter tells you how to display and read the histogram and the table. Here are some specifics about the Spin Spinner simulator's histogram and table:

- ✔ **Spin Spinner histogram:** Each bar in the histogram records the data for each section of the spinner.

- ✔ **Spin Spinners table:** This is illustrated in the third picture of Figure 15-7. The first column displays the number of the spin and the second column shows where the spinner landed.

Drawing Cards from a Deck

The Probability Simulation application can simulate drawing a card from one to three decks of cards. It even allows you to specify whether or not the card is placed back in the deck before another card is drawn. And those decks of cards can consist of 52 or 32 cards. A deck of 32 cards is a 52-card deck without any twos, threes, fours, fives, or sixes.

The application keeps track of the card picked each time the simulation is run and the data is displayed in a table. The application even gives you the option of saving your data so you can, if you choose, statistically analyze it at a later time. Chapter 17 tells you how to perform such an analysis, and the "Saving your data" sidebar in this chapter tells you how to — you guessed it — save your data. This section tells you how to use the Draw Cards simulator.

Simulating drawing cards

To draw cards from one or more decks of cards, follow these steps:

1. **Start the Probability Simulation application and press 5 to select the Draw Cards option in the Main menu.**

   You see the **Draw Cards** Home screen, as illustrated in the first picture in Figure 15-8.

    To use the **Draw Cards** simulator after using another simulator, repeatedly press Y= until you see the Main menu (second picture in Figure 15-1), and then press 5 to select the **Draw Cards** simulator.

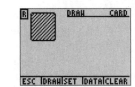 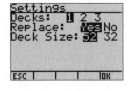 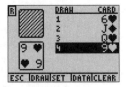

Home screen   Settings editor   Table

Figure 15-8: The **Draw Cards** simulator's Home screen, Settings editor, and table.

2. **Press ZOOM to display the Settings editor. Change the settings in Settings editor, as appropriate.**

You see the screen in the second picture in Figure 15-8. **Decks** tells the application how many decks of cards you want to use, **Replace** tells the application if you want the card placed back in the deck or decks of cards before another card is drawn, and **Deck Size** tells the application how many cards are in the deck or decks of cards you are using. To select these options, use the arrow keys to place the cursor on the option and press ENTER to select the option.

3. **Press GRAPH to say OK to the settings in the Settings editor.**

   You see the Draw Cards Home screen. If you set the **Replace** option to **Yes**, the letter R appears in the upper-left corner of the screen, as illustrated in the first picture in Figure 15-8.

4. **Press WINDOW to draw cards.**

   Each time you press WINDOW, the card drawn is displayed in the table on the screen, as illustrated in the third picture in Figure 15-8.

If in Step 2 you set **Replace** to **No**, then the deck could eventually run out of cards. When this happens the simulator displays the "no more cards" message and will, of course, not allow you draw any more cards. When this happens you have three options: Go do something else, press GRAPH to clear the table and start over with the same type of simulation, or press ZOOM to set up a different type of simulation.

Saving the Draw Cards simulator's data

The "Saving your data" sidebar in this chapter tells you how to save the data stored in any table appearing in the Probability Simulation application. When you save the data from the Draw Cards simulator, it is saved in three lists: Draw, Value, and Suit. The Draw list records the number of the draw. The Value list records the numerical value of the card. The numerical value of an Ace is 1, a Jack is 11, a Queen is 12, and a King is 13. The Suit list records a Heart as 1, a Club as 2, a Spade as 3, and a Diamond as 4.

Chapter 16

Dealing with Statistical Data

● ●

In This Chapter

▶ Entering data into the calculator

▶ Deleting and editing data in a data list

▶ Saving and recalling a data list

▶ Sorting data lists

● ●

*T*he calculator has many features that provide information about the data that has been entered in the calculator. It can graph data as a scatter plot, histogram, or box plot. The calculator can calculate the median and quartiles. It can even find a regression model (curve fitting) for your data. It can do this and much, much more. This chapter tells you how to enter your data in the calculator; Chapter 17 shows you how to use the calculator to analyze that data.

Entering Data

What you use to enter statistical data into the calculator is the Stat List editor — a relatively large spreadsheet that can accommodate up to 20 columns (data lists). And each data list (column) can handle a maximum of 999 entries. Pictures of the Stat List editor appear in Figure 16-1.

To use stat lists to enter your data into the calculator, follow these steps:

1. **Press** ⌷STAT⌷⌷5⌷⌷ENTER⌷ **to execute the SetUpEditor command.**

   The SetUpEditor command clears all data lists (columns) from the Stat List editor and replaces them with the six default lists L_1 through L_6. Any lists that are cleared from the editor by this command are still in the memory of the calculator; they just don't appear in the Stat List editor.

2. **Press** STAT 1 **to enter the Stat List editor.**

If no one has ever used the Stat List editor in your calculator, then the Stat List editor will look like the first picture in Figure 16-1. If the Stat List editor has been used before, then some of the default lists L_1 through L_6 may contain data, as in the second picture in Figure 16-1.

L1	L2	L3	1
▄▄▄▄▄	------	------	

L1(1) =

L1	L2	L3	1
1890	-1.8	------	
1891	0		
1892	0		
1893	-.92		
1894	-4.63		
1895	-1.94		
1896	0		

L1(1)=1890

Empty lists   Lists with data

Figure 16-1: The Stat List editor.

3. **If necessary, clear lists L_1 through L_6 or create a user-named list.**

The calculator requires that each data set (list) have a name. You can use the default names L_1 through L_6, or you can create your own name for a data list. If you want to create your own name, the section, "Creating User-Named Data Lists," tells you how.

If you want to use one of the default names L_1 through L_6 for your data list, but that list already contains data, then you must first clear the contents of the list before you enter new data into it. (The next section, "Deleting and Editing Data," tells you how to clear a data list.)

4. **Enter your data. Press** ENTER **after each entry.**

Use the ▶ ◀ ▲ ▼ keys to place the cursor in the column where you want to make an entry. Use the keypad to enter your number and press ENTER when you're finished. A column (list) can accommodate up to 999 entries.

To quickly enter data that follows a sequential pattern (such as 1, 2, 3, ..., 100 or 1, 4, 9, ..., 1600, or 10, 20, ..., 200), see the section, "Using Formulas to Enter Data."

Deleting and Editing Data

Sooner or later you'll have to remove or modify the data that you've placed in a data list. The following list shows you how to do so:

✔ **Deleting a data list from the memory of the calculator:**

To permanently remove a data list from the memory of the calculator, press 2nd + 2 to enter the Memory Management menu. Then press 4 to see the data lists that are stored in memory. Use ▼ to move the indicator to the list you want to delete, and then press DEL to delete that list. When you're finished deleting lists from memory, press 2nd MODE to exit (quit) the Memory Management menu and return to the Home screen.

Although the calculator does allow you to delete a default list (L_1 through L_6) from memory, in reality, it deletes only the contents of the list and not its name.

✔ **Clearing the contents of a data list:**

When you clear a data list, the list's contents (and not its name) will be erased, leaving an empty data list in the calculator's memory. To clear the contents of a data list in the Stat List editor, use the ▶ ◀ ▲ ▼ keys to place the cursor on the name of a list appearing in a column heading, and then press CLEAR ENTER.

✔ **Deleting a column (list) in the Stat list editor:**

To delete a column (list) from the Stat List editor, use the ▶ ◀ ▲ ▼ keys to place the cursor on the name of the list appearing in the column headings, and then press DEL. The list will be removed from the Stat List editor but not from the memory of the calculator.

✔ **Deleting an entry in a data list:**

To delete an entry from a data list, use the ▶ ◀ ▲ ▼ keys to place the cursor on that entry, and then press DEL to delete the entry from the list.

✔ **Editing an entry in a data list:**

To edit an entry in a data list, use the ▶ ◀ ▲ ▼ keys to place the cursor on that entry, press ENTER, and then edit the entry or key in a new entry. If you key in the new entry, the old entry is automatically erased. Press ENTER when you're finished editing or replacing the old entry.

Creating User-Named Data Lists

To name a data list in the Stat List editor, follow these steps:

1. **If necessary, press** STAT 1 **to enter the Stat List editor.**

2. **Use the** ▶ ◀ ▲ ▼ **keys to place the cursor on the column heading where you want your user-named list to appear.**

   Your user-named list is created in a new column that appears to the left of the column highlighted by the cursor (as shown in the first picture in Figure 16-2).

3. **Press** 2nd DEL **to insert the new column.**

   The second picture in Figure 16-2 shows this procedure.

4. **Enter the name of your data list and press** ENTER.

   The name you give your data list can consist of one to five characters that must be letters, numbers, or the Greek letter θ. The first character in the name must be a letter or θ.

   The ▢ after **Name** = indicates that the calculator is in Alpha mode. In this mode, when you press a key, you enter the green letter above the key. To enter a number, exit the mode by pressing ALPHA again, and then enter the number. To enter a letter after entering a number, you must press ALPHA to put the calculator back in Alpha mode (as in the third picture in Figure 16-2). Press ENTER when you're finished entering the name.

L1	**L2**	L3	2
1890	⁻1.8	------	
1891	0		
1892	0		
1893	⁻.92		
1894	⁻4.63		
1895	⁻1.94		
1896	0		
L2 ={⁻1.8,0,0, ⁻...			

L1	▬▬▬	L2	2
1890		⁻1.8	
1891		0	
1892		0	
1893		⁻.92	
1894		⁻4.63	
1895		⁻1.94	
1896		0	
Name=▢			

L1	▬▬▬	L2	2
1890		⁻1.8	
1891		0	
1892		0	
1893		⁻.92	
1894		⁻4.63	
1895		⁻1.94	
1896		0	
Name=YEAR			

Indicate column   Press 2nd DEL   Enter name

Figure 16-2: Steps for creating a user-named data list.

If the name you give your data list is the name of a data list stored in memory, then after entering that name and pressing ENTER, the data in the list stored in memory will be automatically entered in the Stat List editor.

After you have named your data list, you can press ▼ and start entering your data. Or, if appropriate, you can use a formula to generate the data. (See the next section, "Using Formulas to Enter Data.") And if the data you want to put in the newly named list is in another column of the Stat List editor — or in a list stored in memory under another name — you can paste that data into your newly named list. (See the section, "Saving and Recalling Data Lists," later in this chapter.)

Using Formulas to Enter Data

Figure 16-3 illustrates how you would place the sequence 10, 20, ..., 200 in list L_1. The formula used in this example is simply x. The initial and terminal values of x are naturally 10 and 200, respectively. And, as you may guess, x is incremented by 10.

To use a formula to define your data:

1. **If necessary, press** STAT 1 **to enter the Stat List editor.**

2. **Use the** ▶◀▲▼ **keys to place the cursor on the column heading where you want your data to appear and press** ENTER **.**

3. **Press** 2nd STAT ▶ 5 **to access the seq command.**

4. **Enter your formula as a function of a single variable, press** , **, and then enter the name of the variable and press** , **.**

   The first picture in Figure 16-3 shows this process; here the formula is x and the variable is x.

5. **Enter the initial value of your variable, press** , **, enter the terminal value of your variable, press** , **, enter the increment for the variable, and then press**) **.**

   The second picture in Figure 16-3 shows this process.

6. **Press** ENTER **to enter your data in the calculator.**

   This procedure is shown in the third picture in Figure 16-3.

L1	L2	L3	1	L1	L2	L3	1	L1	L2	L3	1
------	------	------		------	------	------		10	------	------	
								20			
								30			
								40			
								50			
								60			
								70			
L1 =seq(X,X,				L1 =...,10,200,10)				L1(1)=10			

Figure 16-3: Steps for using a formula to define a data set.

Saving and Recalling Data Lists

Saving your data lists is the first step in the direction of calling them up again when you want to use or change them. The following list shows you how to do so:

✔ **Saving data lists:**

After you enter data into the Stat List editor, that data is automatically stored in the memory of the calculator under the list name that appears as the column heading for that list. You don't have to take any further steps to ensure that the calculator saves your data. However, if you clear the contents of a data list (as described in the section, "Deleting and Editing Data"), the calculator retains the name of the data list in memory but deletes the contents of that list.

If you've entered your data in one of the default lists L_1 through L_6 and would like to save it as a named list, first create a user-named data list; you should get a result that resembles the first picture in Figure 16-4. Then press ENTER 2nd and press the number key for your data list (as in the second picture in Figure 16-4). Finally, press ENTER to insert the data in the default data list into the newly named data list. The third picture in Figure 16-4 shows this process.

✔ **Recalling data lists:**

You can use the SetUpEditor command to set up the Stat List editor with the data lists you specify. To do this, press STAT 5 to invoke the SetUpEditor command. Enter the names of the data lists, separated by commas. Then press ENTER STAT 1 to see the data lists (as shown in Figure 16-5).

If you're already in the Stat List editor, you can recall a saved data list by creating a data list that has the same name as the saved data list. (For pointers on how to do so, see the section, "Creating User-Named Data Lists.")

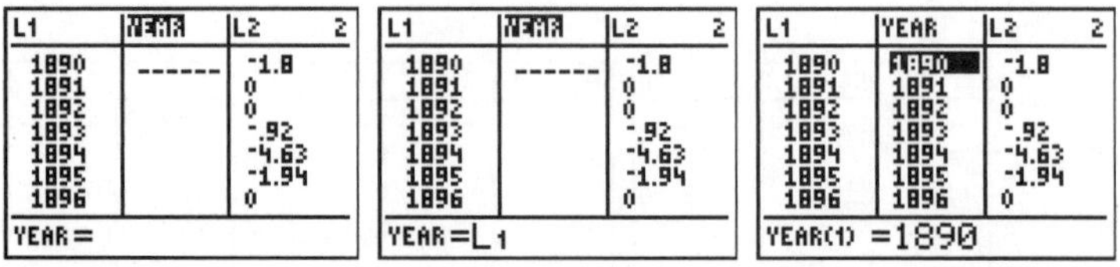

Create named list   Enter default list   Press ENTER

Figure 16-4: Steps for copying data from one list to another.

nums	Lone	DEP 1
1	21	32
2	36	45
3	44	50
4	38	49
5	52	60
6	45	56
7	29	34

SetUpEditor NUMS
,LONE,DEP

nums(1) =1

Specify lists   View lists

Figure 16-5: Recalling saved data lists.

You can save a data list on your PC and recall it at a later date. (Chapter 18 tells you how.) You can also transfer a data list from one calculator to another, as described in Chapter 19.

Sorting Data Lists

To sort data lists, follow these steps:

1. **Press** STAT.

2. **Press** 2 **to sort the list in ascending order, or press** 3 **to sort it in descending order.**

3. **Enter the list name.**

   To sort a default named list such as L_1, press 2nd 1 to enter its name. If you're sorting a user-named list, first press 2nd STAT ▶ ▲ ENTER to insert the letter **L** and then enter the name of the list. Inserting the letter **L** tells the calculator that what follows this letter is a data list, as shown in the first line in the first picture in Figure 16-6.

   If you want to sort rows according to the contents of the data list you entered in Step 3, then (after completing Step 3) enter the names of the other lists, separated by commas. For example, the third line in the first picture in Figure 16-6 is the command needed to rearrange the rows in Figure 16-5 so that the data in the second column is in ascending order.

4. **Press**) ENTER **to sort the list, then press** STAT 1 **to view the sorted list.**

   The second picture in Figure 16-6 shows the rows in Figure 16-5 rearranged so that the second column is in ascending order.

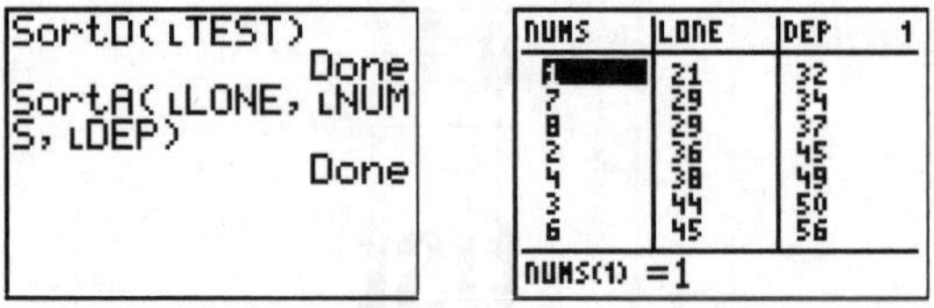

Sort command   Sorted data

Figure 16-6: Sorting data.

Chapter 17

Analyzing Statistical Data

. . . .

In This Chapter

▶ Plotting statistical data

▶ Creating histograms and box plots to describe one-variable data

▶ Creating scatter and line plots to describe two-variable data

▶ Tracing statistical data plots

▶ Finding the mean, median, standard deviation, and other neat stuff

▶ Finding a regression model for your data (curve fitting)

. . . .

*I*n descriptive statistical analysis, you usually want to plot your data and find the mean, median, standard deviation, and so on. You may also want to find a regression model for your data (a process also called *curve fitting*). This chapter tells you how to get the calculator to do these things for you.

Plotting One-Variable Data

The most common plots used to graph one-variable data are histograms and box plots. In a *histogram,* the data is grouped into classes of equal size; a bar in the histogram represents one class. The height of the bar represents the quantity of data contained in that class, as in the first picture in Figure 17-1.

A *box plot* (as in the second picture in Figure 17-1) consists of a box-with-whiskers. The box represents the data existing between the first and third quartiles. The box is divided into two parts, with the division line defined by the median of the data. The whiskers represent the locations of the minimum and maximum data points.

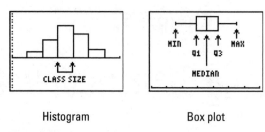

Histogram   Box plot

Figure 17-1: One-variable statistical plots.

Constructing a histogram

To construct a histogram of your data, follow these steps:

1. **Store your data in the calculator.**

   Entering data in the calculator is described in Chapter 16. Your data does not have to appear in the Stat List editor to plot it, but it does have to be in the memory of the calculator.

2. **Turn off any Stat Plots or functions in the Y= editor that you don't want to be graphed along with your histogram.**

   To do so, press Y= to access the Y= editor. The calculator graphs any highlighted Plots in the first line of this editor. To remove the highlight from a Plot so that it won't be graphed, use the ▶◀▲▼ keys to place the cursor on the on the Plot and then press ENTER to toggle the Plot between highlighted and not highlighted.

   The calculator graphs only those functions in the Y= editor defined by a highlighted equal sign. To remove the highlight from an equal sign, use the ▶◀▲▼ keys to place the cursor on the equal sign in the definition of the function, and then press ENTER to toggle the equal sign between highlighted and not highlighted.

3. **Press 2nd Y= to access the Stat Plots menu and enter the number (1, 2, or 3) of the plot you want to define.**

   The first picture in Figure 17-2 shows this process, where **Plot1** is used to plot the data.

Select plot number   Define plot   Press ZOOM 9

Figure 17-2: Steps for creating a histogram.

4. **Highlight On or Off.**

   If **On** is highlighted, the calculator plots your data. If you
   want your data to be plotted at a later time, highlight **Off**.
   To highlight an option, use the ▶◀▲▼ keys to place the
   cursor on the option, and then press ENTER.

5. **Press ▼, use ▶ to place the cursor on the type of plot you
   want to create, and then press ENTER to highlight it.**

   Select ⬚ to construct a histogram.

6. **Press ▼, enter the name of your data list (Xlist), and
   press ENTER.**

   If your data is stored in one of the default lists L_1 through
   L_6, press 2nd, key in the number of the list, and then press
   ENTER. For example, press 2nd 1 if your data is stored in L_1.

   If your data is stored in a user-named list, key in the name
   of the list and press ENTER when you're finished. Notice (as
   in Figure 17-2) that the calculator is already in Alpha mode,
   waiting for the first letter in the name of your list.

7. **Enter the frequency of your data.**

   If you entered your data without paying attention to duplicate data values, then the frequency is 1. On the other
   hand, if you did pay attention to duplicate data values, you
   most likely stored the frequency in another data list. If so,
   enter the name of that list the same way you entered the
   Xlist in Step 6.

8. **Press ZOOM 9 to plot your data using the ZoomStat
   command.**

ZoomStat finds an appropriate viewing window for plotting your data, as in the third picture in Figure 17-2. The next step shows you how to redefine the class size in a histogram.

9. **Press** WINDOW**, set Xscl equal to the class size you desire, and then press** GRAPH**.**

The class size (**Xscl**) must be ≥ (**Xmax – Xmin**)/47. If it isn't, you get the ERR: STAT error message.

10. **If necessary, adjust the settings in the Window editor.**

The data plotted in Figure 17-2 consists of test scores. For such data, you naturally want the class size (**Xscl**) to be 10. But when the histogram is graphed again using this class size (as in the first picture in Figure 17-3), the viewing window doesn't accommodate the histogram. To correct this, adjust the settings in the Window editor (as described in Chapter 9). The second picture in Figure 17-3 shows the result of adjusting these settings.

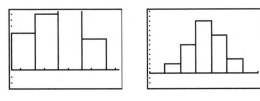

Adjust **Xscl**   Adjust window

Figure 17-3: Steps for defining the class size in a histogram.

Constructing a box plot

To construct a box plot for your data, follow Steps 1 through 8 for constructing a histogram. In Step 5, select the Box Plot symbol ⊞⊢. If you adjust the viewing window as explained in Chapter 9, you can display a histogram and a box plot in the same viewing window (as shown in the first picture in Figure 17-4).

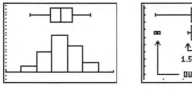 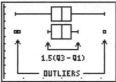

Histogram   Modified box plot

Figure 17-4: A box plot with a histogram and with a modified box plot.

 If your data has *outliers* (data values that are much larger or smaller than the other data values), consider constructing a modified box plot instead of a box plot. Figure 17-4 illustrates both a standard box plot and a modified box plot of the same data (in the second picture). In a modified box plot, the whiskers represent data in the range defined by 1.5(Q3 − Q1), and the outliers are plotted as points beyond the whiskers. The steps for constructing box plots and modified box plots are the same, except in Step 5 you select the modified box plot symbol ⊿.

Plotting Two-Variable Data

The most common plots used to graph two-variable data sets are the scatter plot and the *xy*-line plot. The *scatter plot* plots the points (*x*, *y*) where *x* is a value from one data list **(Xlist)** and *y* is the corresponding value from the other data list **(Ylist)**. The *xy-line plot* is simply a scatter plot with consecutive points joined by a straight line.

To construct a scatter plot or an *xy*-line plot, follow these steps:

1. **Follow Steps 1 through 6 in the previous subsection ("Constructing a histogram") with the following difference:**

   In Step 5, highlight ⌖ to construct a scatter plot or highlight ⊞ to construct an *xy*-line plot.

2. **Enter the name of your Ylist and press** ENTER.

3. Choose the type of mark used to plot points.

You have three choices: a small square, a small plus sign, or a dot. To select one, use ▶ to place the cursor on the mark and press ENTER.

4. Press ZOOM 9 to plot your data using the ZoomStat command.

ZoomStat finds an appropriate viewing window for plotting your data. This is illustrated in Figure 17-5.

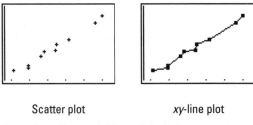

Scatter plot   *xy*-line plot

Figure 17-5: Two-variable statistical plots.

Tracing Statistical Data Plots

Before tracing a statistical data plot, press 2nd ZOOM and, if necessary, highlight the **CoordOn** in the second line of the Format menu and highlight **ExprOn** in the last line. This allows you to see the name of the data set being traced and the location of the cursor. To highlight an entry, use the ▶◀▲▼ keys to place the cursor on the entry and press ENTER.

To trace a statistical data plot, press TRACE. In the upper-left corner of the screen, you see the Stat Plot number (P1, P2, or P3) and the name(s) of the data list(s) being traced. If you have more than one stat plot on the screen, repeatedly press ▲ until the plot you want to trace appears in the upper-left corner of the screen.

Use the ▶◀ keys to trace the plot. What you see depends on the type of plot:

✔ **Tracing a histogram:** As you trace a histogram, the cursor moves from the top center of one bar to the top center of the next bar. At the bottom of the screen, you see the values of **min**, **max**, and **n**. This tells you that there are **n** data points x such that **min** $\leq x <$ **max**. This is illustrated in the first picture in Figure 17-6.

✔ **Tracing a box plot:** As you trace a box plot from left to right, the values that appear at the bottom of the screen are **minX** (the minimum data value), **Q1** (the value of the first quartile), **Med** (the value of the median), **Q3** (the value of the third quartile, and **maxX** (the maximum data value). This is illustrated in the second picture in Figure 17-6.

✔ **Tracing a modified box plot:** As you trace a modified box plot from left to right, the values that appear at the bottom of the screen are **minX** (the minimum data value), and then you see the values of the other outliers, if any, to the left of the interval defined by 1.5(Q3 – Q1). The next value you see at the bottom of the screen is the value of the left bound of the interval defined by 1.5(Q3 – Q1). Then, as with a box plot, you see the values of the first quartile, the median, and the third quartile. After that you see the value of the right bound of the interval defined by 1.5(Q3 – Q1), the outliers to the right of this, if any, and finally you see **maxX** (the maximum data value).

✔ **Tracing a scatter plot or an *xy*-line plot:** As you trace a scatter plot or an *xy*-line plot, the coordinates of the cursor location appear at the bottom of the screen. As shown in Figure 17-6, the *x*-coordinate is a data value for the first data list named at the top of the screen; the *y*-coordinate is the corresponding data value from the second data list named at the top of the screen.

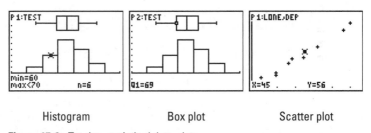

| Histogram | Box plot | Scatter plot |

Figure 17-6: Tracing statistical data plots.

Analyzing Statistical Data

The calculator can perform one- and two-variable statistical data analysis. For one-variable data analysis, the statistical data variable is denoted by **x**. For two-variable data analysis, the data variable for the first data list is denoted by **x** and the data variable for the second data list is denoted by **y**. Table 17-1 lists the variables calculated using one-variable data analysis (**1-Var**), as well as those calculated using two-variable analysis (**2-Var**).

Table 17-1	One- and Two-Variable Data Analysis	
1-Var	*2-Var*	*Meaning*
$\bar{x}$	$\bar{x}, \bar{y}$	Mean of data values
Σx	$\Sigma x, \Sigma y$	Sum of data values
Σx^2	$\Sigma x^2, \Sigma y^2$	Sum of squares of data values
Sx	Sx, Sy	Sample standard deviation
σx	$\sigma x, \sigma y$	Population standard deviation
n	n	Total number of data points
minx	minX, minY	Minimum data value
maxX	maxX, maxY	Maximum data value
Q1		First quartile
Med		Median
Q3		Third quartile
	Σxy	Sum of x*y

One-variable data analysis

To analyze one-variable data, follow these steps:

1. **Store your data in the calculator.**

   Entering data in the calculator is described in the previous chapter. Your data does not have to appear in the Stat List editor to analyze it, but it does have to be in the memory of the calculator.

2. **Press** STAT ▶ 1 **to select the 1-Var Stats command from the Stat Calculate menu.**

3. **Enter the name of your data list (Xlist).**

   If your data is stored in one of the default lists L_1 through L_6, press 2nd, key in the number of the list, and then press ENTER. For example, press 2nd 1 if your data is stored in L_1.

If your data is stored in a user-named list, first press
[2nd][STAT][▶][▲][ENTER] to insert the letter **L**, and then enter
the name of the list. Inserting the letter **L** tells the calculator that what follows this letter is a data list. To enter the
name of the list, use the [ALPHA] key to insert letters (as
shown in the first picture of Figure 17-7).

4. **If necessary, enter the name of the frequency list.**

   If the frequency of your data is 1, you can skip this step and
   go to the next step. If, however, you stored the frequency
   in another data list, press [,] and enter the name of that frequency list (just as you entered the **Xlist** in Step 3). The
   second picture in Figure 17-7 shows this process.

5. **Press [ENTER] to view the analysis of your data.**

   This is illustrated in the third picture in Figure 17-7. Use the
   [▼][▲] keys to view the other values that don't appear on the
   screen.

Enter list   Enter frequency   Press [ENTER]

Figure 17-7: Steps for one-variable data analysis.

Two-variable data analysis

To analyze two-variable data, follow these steps:

1. **Follow Steps 1 through 3 in the previous subsection ("One-
   variable data analysis") with the following difference:**

   In Step 2, press [STAT][▶][2] to select the **2-Var Stats** command.

2. **Press [,] and enter the name of the Ylist.**

3. **Follow Steps 4 and 5 in the previous subsection ("One-
   variable data analysis").**

Regression Models

Regression modeling is the process of finding a function that approximates the relationship between the two variables in two data lists. (An example appears in Figure 17-8, where a straight line approximates the relationship between the lists.) Table 17-2 shows the types of regression models the calculator can compute.

Table 17-2	Types of Regression Models	
TI-Command	*Model Type*	*Equation*
Med-Med	Median-median	$y = ax + b$
LinReg(ax+b)	Linear	$y = ax + b$
QuadReg	Quadratic	$y = ax^2 + bx + c$
CubicReg	Cubic	$y = ax^3 + bx^2 + cx + d$
QuartReg	Quartic	$y = ax^4 + bx^3 + cx^2 + dx + e$
LinReg(a+bx)	Linear	$y = a + bx$
LNReg	Logarithmic	$y = a + b*\ln(x)$
ExpReg	Exponential	$y = ab^x$
PwrReg	Power	$y = ax^b$
Logistic	Logistic	$y = c/(1 + a*e^{-bx})$
SinReg	Sinusoidal	$y = a*\sin(bx + c) + d$

To compute a regression model for your two-variable data, follow these steps:

1. **If necessary, turn on Diagnostics.**

   When the Diagnostics command is turned on, the calculator displays the correlation coefficient (**r**) and the coefficient of determination (**r²** or **R²**) for appropriate regression models (as shown in the second picture in Figure 17-8). By default, this command is turned off. After you turn this command on, it stays on until you turn it off. Here's how to turn on Diagnostics:

   a. **Press** 2nd 0 x^{-1} **to access the Catalog menu and to advance the Catalog to the entries beginning with the letter D.**

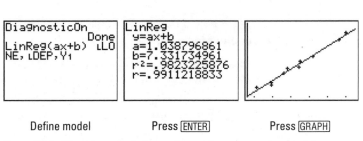

Define model   Press ENTER   Press GRAPH

Figure 17-8: Steps for calculating and graphing a regression model.

> b. **Repeatedly press ⊡ to advance the Catalog indicator to the DiagnosticOn command.**
>
> c. **Press ENTER to paste this command on the Home screen, and press ENTER again to execute this command.**
>
> The first picture in Figure 17-8 shows this procedure.

2. **If necessary, put the calculator in Function (Func) mode.**

   If the regression model is a function that you want to graph, you must first put the calculator in Function mode. (Setting the mode is explained in Chapter 1.)

3. **If you haven't already done so, graph your two-variable data in a scatter plot or an *xy*-line plot.**

   An earlier section of this chapter ("Plotting Two-Variable Data") explains how to do so.

4. **Select a regression model from the Stat Calculate menu.**

   To do so, press STAT ▶ to access the Stat Calculate menu. Repeatedly press ⊡ until the number or letter of the desired regression model is highlighted, and press ENTER to select that model.

5. **Enter the name for the Xlist data, press ⌷, and then enter the name of the Ylist data.**

   The appropriate format for entering list names is explained in Step 3 in the earlier section, "One-variable data analysis."

6. **If necessary, enter the name of the frequency list.**

   To determine whether to enter a frequency list, see Step 4 in the subsection earlier section, "One-variable data analysis."

7. **Press ⌷ and enter the name of the function (Y_1, ... , Y_9, or Y_0) in which the regression model is to be stored.**

   To enter a function name, press VARS ▶ 1, and then enter the number of the function (as in the first picture in Figure 17-8).

8. **Press** ENTER **to calculate and view the equation of the regression model.**

   This is illustrated in the second picture in Figure 17-8. The equation of the regression model is automatically stored in the Y= editor under the name you entered in Step 7.

9. **Press** GRAPH **to see the graph of your data and regression model.**

   This process is illustrated in the third picture in Figure 17-8.

Part V
Communicating with PCs and Other Calculators

The 5th Wave   By Rich Tennant

"You can sure do alot with a TI–84 Plus, but I never thought dressing one up in G.I. Joe clothes and calling it your little desk commander would be one of them."

In this part . . .

This part gets you ready to transfer files between your calculator and a PC, or between your calculator and another calculator. I also tell you how to download and install the free TI Connect software you can use to (among other things) transfer files to and from your PC.

Chapter 18

Communicating with a PC Using TI Connect™

. . . .

In This Chapter

▶ Downloading the TI Connect software

▶ Installing and running the TI Connect software

▶ Connecting your calculator to your computer

▶ Transferring files between your calculator and your computer

▶ Upgrading the calculator's operating system

. . . .

*Y*ou need two things to enable your calculator to communicate with your computer: TI Connect (software) and a TI-Graph Link cable. TI Connect is free; the TI-Graph Link cable came bundled with your calculator. If you are no longer in possession of the link cable, you can purchase one at the Texas Instruments online store at www.education.ti.com.

Downloading TI Connect

The TI Connect software is on the TI Resource CD that most likely came with your calculator. However, the version on this CD may not be current. The following steps tell you how to download the current version of TI Connect from the Texas Instruments Web site, as it existed at the time this book was published:

1. **Go to the Texas Instruments Web site (**www.education. ti.com**).**

2. **In the Know What You're Looking For? drop-down list, select TI Connect.**

3. **Click the Downloads link in the column to the left of the page.**

4. **Click either the Download TI Connect for Windows link or the Download TI Connect for Macintosh link (depending on the type of computer you use, Windows or Macintosh).**

5. **If you haven't already logged onto the TI Web site, the Sign In page appears. If you're already a member, enter your e-mail address and password; if you're not a member, sign up — it's free.**

6. **Click the appropriate language.**

7. **Follow the directions given during the downloading process. Make a note of the directory in which you save the download file.**

Installing and Running TI Connect

After you've downloaded TI Connect, you install it by double-clicking the downloaded TI Connect file you saved in your computer. Then follow the directions given by the installation program you just launched.

When you start the TI Connect program, you see the many subprograms it contains. To see what these subprograms are used for, click the **HELP** button in the lower-right corner of the screen. In this chapter, I explain how to use TI Device Explorer to transfer files between your calculator and your PC.

Each of the subprograms housed in TI Connect have excellent Help menus that tell you exactly how to use the program.

Connecting Calculator and PC

You use the TI-Graph Link cable that came with your calculator to connect your calculator to your computer. If you don't already have a TI-Graph Link cable, you can purchase one at the Texas Instruments online store at www.education.ti.com.

The TI-84 Link cable that came with your calculator is a USB-to-USB cable. Because the ends of this cable are of different sizes, it's easy to figure out how to connect your calculator to your computer; the small end fits in the right slot on the top of your calculator and the other end plugs into one of your computer's USB ports.

The TI-83 I/O-to-USB can be used to connect your calculator to your computer. The plug end of this cable fits into the top left slot on your calculator.

Transferring Files

After you've connected the calculator to your computer, the TI Device Explorer program housed in TI Connect can transfer files between the two devices. This allows you to archive calculator files on your computer.

To transfer files between your calculator and PC, start the TI Connect software and click the TI Device Explorer program. A directory appears, listing the files on your computer. Expanding this directory works the same on your calculator as on your computer. When transferring files, you're usually interested in transferring the files housed in the in the following directories: Graph Database, List, Matrix, Picture, and Program. If any of these directories don't appear on-screen, that means no files are housed in that directory.

To copy or move files from your calculator to your PC, highlight the files you want to transfer, click **Action**, and select either **Copy to PC** or **Move to PC**. When the **Browse for Folder** window appears, select the location to which your files will be transferred and click **OK**.

To copy files to the calculator from a PC running Windows, you don't need to be in the TI Device Explorer program. Just open Windows Explorer, highlight the files you want to copy, right-click the highlighted files, select **Send To**, and click **Connected TI Device**. When asked if you want the files sent to **RAM** or **Archive**, select **Archive**. Files stored in the Archive memory of the calculator cannot be executed or edited, so I am assuming that your transfer files are not in need of editing. If I am wrong, select **RAM**. Directions for transferring files from a Macintosh to the calculator can be found in the TI Device Explorer Help menu.

The Help menu in TI Device Explorer is packed with useful information. In it, you will find directions for editing and deleting calculator files and directions for backing up all files on your calculator.

Upgrading the OS

Texas Instruments periodically upgrades the operating systems of the TI-84 Plus family of calculators. To get the calculator to upgrade the operating system, start the TI Connect software and click the TI Device Explorer program. Click the Help menu at the top of the screen and select **TI Device Explorer Help**. Click **Upgrading the device operating system** and follow the on-screen directions.

Chapter 19

Communicating Between Calculators

. . . .

In This Chapter

▶ Linking calculators so files can be transferred between them

▶ Determining what files can be transferred

▶ Selecting files to be transferred

▶ Transferring files between calculators

. . . .

*Y*ou can transfer data lists, programs, matrices, and other such files from one calculator to another if you link the calculators with the unit-to-unit link cable that came with your calculator. This chapter describes how to make such transfers.

Linking Calculators

Calculators are linked using the unit-to-unit link cable that came with the calculator. If you're no longer in possession of the cable, you can purchase one at the Texas Instruments online store at www.education.ti.com.

The unit-to-unit link cable for the TI-83 can be used to link a TI-83 to a TI-84. It can also be used to link two TI-84's.

The unit-to-unit link cable connects to the TI-84 calculator at the port at the top of the calculator. On the TI-83, it connects to the port at the bottom of the calculator. If you want your TI-84 to link with a TI-83, you need an I/O-to-I/O cable — that's the cable having a plug on both ends.

If you get an error message when transferring files from one calculator to another, the most likely cause is that the unit-to-unit link cable isn't fully inserted into the port of one calculator.

Transferring Files

You can transfer files between your TI-84 and another TI-84, TI-83 Plus, or TI-83 Plus Silver Edition. After connecting two calculators, you can transfer files from one calculator (the sending calculator) to another (the receiving calculator). To select and send files, follow these steps:

1. **Press [2nd][X,T,Θ,n] on the sending calculator to access the Link Send menu.**

   The **Link Send** menu appears in the first picture in Figure 19-1.

2. **Use [▾][▴] to select the type of file you want to send, and then press [ENTER].**

   The first picture in Figure 19-1 shows the types of files you can send. The down arrow visible after number 7 in this list of menu items indicates that there are more menu items than can be displayed on-screen. Repeatedly press [▾] to view these other menu items.

   If you want to send all files on the calculator to another calculator, select **All+** and proceed to Step 4.

3. **Use [▾][▴] to move the cursor to a file you want to send and press [ENTER] to select that file. Repeat this process until you have selected all the files in this list that you want to send to another calculator.**

   The calculator places a small square next to the files you select, as in the second picture of Figure 19-1. In this picture, lists L_1, L_2, and L_3 are selected in the **List Select** menu.

```
SEND RECEIVE
1▓All+…
2:All-…
3:Pr9m…
4:List…
5:Lists to TI82…
6:GDB…
7↓Pic…
```

```
SELECT TRANSMIT
■ L₁        LIST
■ L₂        LIST
■ L₃        LIST
▸ L₄        LIST
  L₅        LIST
  L₆        LIST
  FREQ      LIST
```

Link Send menu   List Select menu

Figure 19-1: Selecting files for transmission between calculators.

4. **On the receiving calculator, press** [2nd][X,T,Θ,n][▶][ENTER].

You see a screen that says **waiting**, and in its upper-right corner, a moving broken line indicates that the receiving calculator is waiting to receive files.

Always put the receiving calculator in Receiving mode before you transfer files from the sending calculator.

5. **On the sending calculator, press** [▶][ENTER] **to send the files to the receiving calculator.**

As files are transferred, you may receive the **DuplicateName** menu, as illustrated in the first picture of Figure 19-2. This indicates that the receiving calculator already contains a file with the same name. Because the default names for stat lists are stored in the calculator, you always get this message when transferring a list, even if the list on the receiving calculator is empty.

When you get the **DuplicateName** menu, select the appropriate course of action:

- If you select **Overwrite**, any data in the existing file is overwritten by the data in the file being transferred.

- If you select **Rename**, a new file is created and stored under the name you specify, as in the second picture in Figure 19-2.

The 🔲 after **Name** = indicates that the calculator is in Alpha mode: When you press a key, what you enter is the green letter above the key. To enter a number, press [ALPHA] to take the calculator out of Alpha mode and then enter the number. To enter a letter after entering a number, you must press [ALPHA] to put the calculator back in Alpha mode. Press [ENTER] when you're finished entering the name.

When renaming a file that is being transferred to the receiving calculator, the calculator has a strange and confusing way of warning you that a file having the same name already exists on the receiving calculator. When you press [ENTER] after entering the name, the calculator erases the name and makes you start over with entering a name. No warning message tells you that a file having the same name already exists on the calculator. If this happens to you, simply enter a different name.

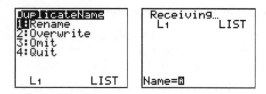

DuplicateName menu   Renaming a file

Figure 19-2: Dealing with duplicate file names.

Figure 19-3 illustrates a completed transfer of files between two calculators. The first picture in the figure shows the files that were sent; the second picture shows the files that were received. During the transfer of the files, L_2 was renamed **DATA.**

Sending calculator   Receiving calculator

Figure 19-3: Transferring files between two calculators.

If you want to terminate the transfer of files while it is in progress, press [ON] on either calculator. Then press [ENTER] when you're confronted with the Error in Xmit error message. If you put one calculator in Receiving mode and then decide not to transfer any files to that calculator, press [ON] to take it out of Receiving mode.

Transferring Files to Several Calculators

After transferring files between two calculators (as described in the previous section), you can then use the sending and/or receiving calculator to transfer the same files to a third calculator, usually without having to reselect the files. (If the initial transfer consisted of files selected from the **A-** submenu of the **Link Send** menu, then you will have to reselect the files.)

To transfer files to a third calculator, follow these steps:

1. **After making the initial transfer of files between the sending and receiving calculators, wait until Step 4 before pressing any keys on the calculator that will be used to transfer the files to a third calculator.**

   After the initial transfer of files is complete, the screens on the sending and receiving calculators look similar to those in Figure 19-4, only with different files. If you press any key on the calculator, other than those specified in Step 3, the files you're planning on sending to a third calculator will no longer be selected and you will have to reselect them.

2. **Link the third calculator to either the sending or receiving calculator.**

3. **On the third calculator, press** 2nd X,T,Θ,n ▶ ENTER.

4. **On the other calculator, press** 2nd X,T,Θ,n **and select the same menu item that was used in the initial transfer of files. Press** ▶ ENTER **to complete the transfer of the files to the third calculator.**

   The files from the previous transfer are still selected, provided that in the interim you made no new selection from the **Link Send** menu (as shown in Figure 19-4). The selected files in this figure are the files that were sent to the receiving calculator in the initial transfer of files (refer to Figure 19-3).

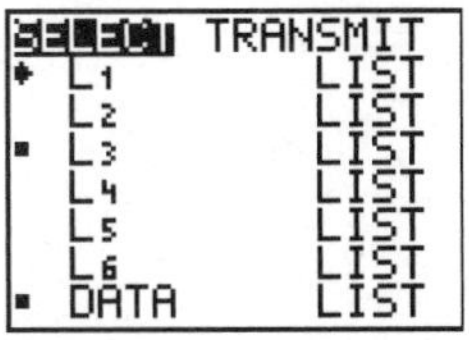

Figure 19-4: Transferring files to a third calculator.

Part VI

The Part of Tens

I'm mathematically dyslexic. But it's not that unusual - 100 out of every 15 people are.

In this part . . .

This part wraps up some handy items in packages of (approximately) ten. I tell you how to download and install application programs that enhance the capabilities of your calculator, and briefly describe ten of my favorites. I also list the most common errors that crop up while using the calculator, and explain the most common error messages the calculator may give you.

And if that's not enough, I tell you about all those chapters that I would have loved to put in this book but couldn't because of lack of space. But don't worry; I put them on the Dummies Web site just for you!

Chapter 20

Eight Topics That Didn't Make the Book

In This Chapter

▶ Topics that you can find on Wiley's Web site

▶ Topics that you can find in *TI-83 Plus Graphing Calculator For Dummies*

*T*he TI-84 Plus calculator offers more things to discuss than would fit in a book this size, so I had to leave some stuff out. In fact, all the other things I wanted to tell you about would have filled another book almost a big as this one. Luckily, I have been able to house some of these topics on the book's companion Web site. (The address for this site is provided in the Introduction.) The other topics I wanted to tell you about can be found in the *TI-83 Plus Graphing Calculator For Dummies* book. This chapter tells you what you can find on the Web site and what you can find in *TI-83 Plus Graphing Calculator For Dummies*.

Topics on Wiley's Web Site

The address for the Web site housing the topics in the following list can be found in the Introduction of this book. Here's what I've put on this Web site:

✔ **Doing Geometry Using Cabri Jr.:**

Part II of this book tells you about doing geometry using the GeoMaster application that comes preloaded on the TI-84 Plus family of calculators. The online Bonus Chapters 1, 2, 3, and 4 (collectively known as "Doing Geometry Using Cabri Jr."), tells you how to go about doing geometry using the Cabri Jr. application that also comes preloaded on your calculator.

If you are using a TI-83 Plus calculator that does not have the GeoMaster or Cabri Jr. application, you can download these applications form TI's Web site. Chapter 21 tells you how to do this.

🖊 **Programming the Calculator:**

This section on the Web site explains how to write programs on your calculator. It also tells you how to first write the program on a computer and then transfer it to your calculator.

Topics in the TI-83 For Dummies Book

The *TI-83 Plus Graphing Calculator For Dummies* book, written, of course, by yours truly, contains many topics of interest to a user of the TI-84. The keystrokes in these topics are the same for both calculators (TI-83 or TI-84). So you will have no problem when consulting the *TI-83 Plus Graphing Calculator For Dummies* book on the following topics:

🖊 **Dealing with Finances:**

Part III of the *TI-83 Plus Graphing Calculator For Dummies* book contains three chapters that explain how to use the financial features on the calculator to answer many important questions, which run the gamut from "Should I lease or borrow?" to "How much should I invest if I want to retire as a millionaire?" I also discuss how to calculate the best interest rate, find internal rates of return, use the (Time-Value-of-Money) TVM Solver, and cope with round-off errors.

🖊 **Dealing with Complex Numbers:**

Chapter 4 in the *TI-83 Plus Graphing Calculator For Dummies* book tells you how to enter and understand the format for complex numbers.

🖊 **Drawing on a Graph:**

Chapter 12 in the *TI-83 Plus Graphing Calculator For Dummies* book tells you how to draw line segments on a graph and how to write text on the graph. It also tells you how to draw circles and function on the graph and how to save your drawings.

✔ **Graphing Sequences:**

Chapters 13 and 14 in the *TI-83 Plus Graphing Calculator For Dummies* book explain how to graph and analyze sequences. A sequence is also called an iterative function, recursive function, or recurrence relation. Whatever you want to call it, the *TI-83 Plus Graphing Calculator For Dummies* book tells you how to deal with it.

✔ **Graphing Parametric Equations:**

Chapter 15 of the *TI-83 Plus Graphing Calculator For Dummies* book explains how to graph and analyze parametric equations. It also explains how to trace a graph, create tables, and save your graph for future use.

✔ **Graphing Polar Equations:**

Chapter 16 of the *TI-83 Plus Graphing Calculator For Dummies* book explains how to graph and analyze polar equations. As with the chapter on graphing parametric equations, this chapter also explains how to trace a graph, create tables, and save your graph for future use. You are also shown how to convert between rectangular and polar coordinates.

Chapter 21

Ten Great Applications

In This Chapter

▶ Reviewing ten applications for the calculator

▶ Finding and downloading applications

▶ Installing applications on your calculator

*T*he Texas Instruments Web site contains over 40 applications that you can download and install on your calculator. Most of these application programs are free; those that aren't free are very inexpensive.

Texas Instruments may have already installed some of these programs on your calculator, even those that aren't free. To see what application programs are already on your calculator, press APPS.

In the following section, I briefly describe some application programs you can download from the Texas Instruments Web site. At the end of this chapter, I tell you how to find, download, and install those programs.

Ten Great Applications

Here are ten great applications you can download from the Texas Instruments Web site:

- **Advanced Finance:** This program turns your calculator into a financial calculator.

- **Cabri Jr.:** This is an interactive, dynamic geometry program that allows you to export geometric figures between the calculator and the Cabri Geometry II Plus software for Windows.

✔ **Catalog Help:** This handy program gives you the syntax for entering the argument required by a calculator function.

✔ **CellSheet:** This program turns your calculator into a spreadsheet. If you also download the free TI CellSheet Converter software, then you can transfer your spreadsheet files between your calculator and Microsoft Excel or Appleworks.

✔ **GeoMaster:** This is a geometry program that draws circles, triangles, and polygons. It also measures angles, calculates areas, and performs geometric transformations. How to use this application is explained in Part III of this book.

✔ **Inequality Graphing:** As the name implies, this program graphs inequalities. Using this application is covered in Chapter 13.

✔ **NoteFolio:** This program turns your calculator into a word processor. Because using the calculator keys is more difficult than typing on a keyboard, I suggest purchasing a TI Keyboard so you can key in words the way you do on a computer. And don't forget to download the NoteFolio Creator software so you can transfer files between the calculator and Microsoft Word.

✔ **Organizer:** This program is a personal organizer that you can use to schedule events, create to-do lists, and save phone numbers and e-mail addresses.

✔ **Probability Simulation:** This program simulates rolling dice, tossing coins, spinning a spinner, or drawing a card from a deck of cards. Chapter 15 tells you how to use this application.

✔ **StudyCards:** This program creates electronic flash cards. Be sure also to download the free TI StudyCard Creator software that allows you to create the flash cards on your PC.

Downloading an Application

The following steps tell you how to download application programs from the Texas Instruments Web site, as it existed at the time this book was published. To download and install applications, follow these steps:

1. **Go to the Texas Instruments Web site at** `www.education.ti.com`.

2. **In the Know What You're Looking For? drop-down list, select Apps & OS versions.**

3. **Click the link that matches type of calculator you have.**

4. **Click the link for the application you want to download.**

5. **Click Download Instructions and read the instructions on how to download applications.**

   The download instructions are the same for each application, so you need read the instructions only once.

6. **Click the Guidebook to download it.**

   Save the application Guidebook (manual) on your computer or print it.

7. **Click Download under the picture of the calculator and follow the directions you're given. Make a note of the directory in which you save the file you download.**

   After you accept the License Agreement, you're asked to log in. If you aren't a member of the site, sign up — it's free.

Installing an Application

To install applications on your calculator, you need the TI Connect software and a TI-Graph Link cable. Downloading and installing the software and connecting your calculator to your PC using the TI-Graph Link cable are explained in Chapter 18. Directions for copying the application file to your calculator are also found in Chapter 18.

Chapter 22

Eight Common Errors

● ●

In This Chapter

▶ Incorrectly negating numbers

▶ Improperly indicating the order of operations

▶ Forgetting you're in Radian mode

▶ Graphing Stat Plots when functions are active and vice versa

● ●

*E*ven the best calculating machine is only as good as its input. This chapter identifies eight common errors made when using the calculator.

Using ⊟ Instead of ⊡ to Indicate That a Number Is Negative

If you press ⊟ instead of ⊡ at the beginning of an entry, the calculator assumes you want to subtract what comes after the minus sign from the previous answer. If you use ⊟ instead of ⊡ in the interior of an expression to denote a negative number, the calculator responds with the ERR: SYNTAX error message.

Indicating the Order of Operations Incorrectly by Using Parentheses

When evaluating expressions, the order of operations is crucial. To the calculator, for example, -3^2 equals -9. This may come as quite a surprise to someone expecting the more standard evaluation, where $(-3)^2$ equals 9. The calculator first performs the operation in parentheses, then it squares the number, and after that, it performs the unary operation of negating a number. Unless you're careful, this won't provide the answer you're looking for. To guard against this error, you may want to review the detailed list of the order in which the calculator performs operations (given in Chapter 2). Also, when graphing rational functions, users who are new to the calculator often make the basic mistake of omitting the parentheses that must be used to set the numerator apart from the denominator.

Improperly Entering the Argument for Menu Functions

If an argument is improperly entered, a menu function won't work. A prime example is the **fMin** function housed in the Math MATH menu. Do you remember what to place after this function so that you can use it? If you don't, you get the ERR: ARGUMENT error message.

Texas Instruments offers a really invaluable (and free!) application called Catalog Help that you can install on your calculator. It reminds you of the appropriate argument that each function requires. I highly recommend installing it on your calculator. Chapter 21 tells you how to do this.

Entering an Angle in Degrees While in Radian Mode

Actually, you *can* do so legitimately, but you have to let the calculator know that you're overriding the Angle mode by placing a degree symbol after your entry. Chapter 3 tells you how to do so.

Graphing Trigonometric Functions While in Degree Mode

This, too, is a mistake unless you do it just right: In the Window editor, you have to set the limits for the x-axis as $-360 \le x \le 360$. Pressing ZOOM 7 or ZOOM 0 to have the calculator graph the function using the **ZTrig** or **ZoomFit** command produces similar results.

But this works when you're graphing pure trig functions such as sin
x. If you're graphing something like sin $x + x$, life is a lot easier if you
graph it in Radian mode.

Graphing Functions When Stat Plots Are Active

If you get the ERR: INVALID DIM error message when you graph a
function, this is most likely caused by a Stat Plot that the calculator is trying to graph along with your function. Chapter 9 tells you
how to inactivate that Stat Plot.

Graphing Stat Plots When Functions or Other Stat Plots Are Active

If you get the ERR: INVALID DIM error message when you graph a
Stat Plot, this is most likely caused by a function or another Stat
Plot that the calculator is trying to graph along with your function.
Chapter 17 tells you how to inactivate those functions or Stat Plots.

Setting the Window Inappropriately for Graphing

If you get the ERR: WINDOW RANGE error message when graphing
functions, this is most likely caused by setting **Xmin** ≥ **Xmax** or by
setting **Ymin** ≥ **Ymax** in the Window editor. Setting the Window
editor is explained in Chapter 9.

Chapter 23

Eleven Common Error Messages

In This Chapter

▶ Listing the eleven most common error messages

▶ Getting familiar with the eleven most common error messages

▶ Avoiding the eleven most common errors (but you knew that)

*T*his chapter gives a list of eleven (ten with an extra one thrown in for good measure) common error messages the calculator may give you.

ARGUMENT

You usually get this message when you are using a function housed in one of the menus on the calculator. This message indicates that you have not properly defined the argument needed to use the function.

Texas Instruments has a really invaluable application called Catalog Help that you can install on your calculator and use to remind you of the appropriate argument required by these functions. The Catalog Help program is free, so I highly recommend that you install it on your calculator. Chapter 21 explains how to do this.

BAD GUESS

This message indicates that the guess you've given to the calculator isn't within the range of numbers that you specified. This is one of those times when the calculator asks you to guess the solution. One example is when you're finding the maximum value or the zero of a function within a specified range (see Chapter 11). Another is when you're finding the solution to an equation where that solution in contained in a specified range (see Chapter 4).

One other time that you can get this message is when the function is undefined at (or near) the value of your guess.

DATA TYPE

This type of error occurs if, for example, you enter a negative number when the calculator requires a positive number.

DIM MISMATCH

You usually get this message when you attempt to add, subtract, or multiply matrices that don't have compatible dimensions.

DOMAIN

You usually get this message when you're using a function housed on a menu of the calculator. If that function is, for example, expecting you to enter a number in a specified range, you get this error message if that number isn't in the specified range.

INVALID

This is the catchall error message. Basically, it means that you did something wrong when defining something (for example, you used function Y_3 in the definition of function Y_2, but forgot to define function Y_3).

INVALID DIM

You get this invalid-dimension message if (for example) you attempt to raise a nonsquare matrix to a power or enter a decimal for an argument of a function when the calculator is expecting an integer.

NO SIGN CHNG

When you're using the Equation Solver (detailed in Chapter 4) you get this message when the equation has no real solutions in your specified range. When using the Finance application (discussed in Part II of *TI-83 Plus Graphing Calculator For Dummies*) you get this message when you don't use the correct sign for cash flow.

SINGULAR MAT

You get this message when you try to find the inverse of a matrix whose determinant is zero.

SYNTAX

This is another catchall error message. It usually means you have a typo somewhere.

WINDOW RANGE

This, of course, means that the Window is improperly set. This problem is usually (but not always) caused by improperly setting **Xmin** ≥ **Xmax** or **Ymin** ≥ **Ymax** in the Window editor. For a look at the proper way to set the Window for functions, check out the explanations in Chapter 9.

Appendix A

Creating and Editing Matrices

* *

In This Chapter

▶ Defining a matrix

▶ Editing a matrix

▶ Displaying the contents of a matrix

▶ Augmenting two matrices

▶ Copying one matrix to another matrix

▶ Deleting a matrix from the memory of the calculator

* *

A *matrix* is a rectangular array of numbers arranged in rows and columns. With matrices, a system of equations can be easily manipulated or solved. The dimensions, r × c, of a matrix are defined by the number of rows and columns in the matrix. The calculator allows you to define up to ten matrices. Each matrix can have dimensions of up to 99 × 99 and can contain only real-number entries.

Defining a Matrix

To define a matrix, follow these steps:

1. **Press [2nd][x⁻¹][▶][▶] to enter the Matrix editor menu.**

   The first picture in Figure A-1 shows the names of matrices used by the calculator. The dimensions appearing to the right of the first two matrices in this picture indicate that these two matrices have already been defined and are stored in the memory of the calculator.

2. **Key in the number (1 through 9, or 0) of the matrix you want to define or redefine.**

   If you select an already-defined matrix, the following steps redefine that matrix by overwriting any existing entries. The redefined matrix replaces the original matrix in the memory of the calculator.

   If all ten matrices in the Matrix editor are defined and you don't want to sacrifice any of them in order to define a new matrix, consider saving some of the already-defined matrices on your PC. Chapter 18 tells you how to do so.

3. **Enter the dimensions of the matrix. Press [ENTER] after each entry.**

   The dimensions, r × c, of a matrix indicate the number of rows and columns in the matrix. The number of rows is entered first.

4. **Enter the elements in the matrix. Press [ENTER] after each entry.**

   The calculator enters elements one row at a time. When you press [ENTER] after entering the last element in the first row, the calculator moves to the beginning of the second row and waits for you to make another entry.

   Before accepting an entry, the calculator displays the row and column of the entry at the bottom of the screen. It also displays the value assigned to that entry. To change that value, just key in the new value and press [ENTER]. The new value can also be entered as an arithmetic expression such as $9^2 + 7$. To leave that value as it is, just press [ENTER], as in the second picture in Figure A-1.

5. **When you're finished defining your matrix, press [2nd][MODE] to exit the Matrix editor and return to the Home screen.**

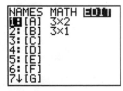
Select matrix

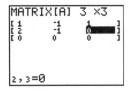
Define matrix

Figure A-1: Steps for defining a matrix.

Editing a Matrix

To edit an already-defined matrix, follow these steps:

1. **Follow Steps 1 and 2 in the previous section.**

2. **Use the ▶◀▲▼ to place the cursor on the entry to be edited.**

3. **Key in the new number and press [ENTER].**

4. **When you're finished editing your matrix, press [2nd][MODE] to exit (quit) the Matrix editor and return to the Home screen.**

Displaying Matrices

To display a matrix on the Home screen, first press [2nd][MODE] to access the Home screen. Then press [2nd][x⁻¹] and enter the number of the matrix to be displayed. Finally, press [ENTER] to display the matrix, as in the first two pictures in Figure A-2. If the Home screen isn't large enough to contain the whole matrix, use the ▶◀▲▼ keys to view the missing elements.

To view the contents of a matrix in the Matrix editor instead of on the Home screen, follow the first two steps in the "Defining a Matrix" section at the beginning of this chapter.

Augmenting Two Matrices

Augmenting two matrices allows you to append one matrix to another matrix. Both matrices must be defined and have the same number of rows. To augment two matrices, follow these steps:

1. **If necessary, press [2nd][MODE] to access the Home screen.**

2. **Press [2nd][x⁻¹]▶[7] to select the augment command from the Matrix Math menu.**

3. **Enter the name of the first matrix and then press [,].**

   The first matrix is the matrix that appears on the left in the augmented matrix. To enter its name, press [2nd][x⁻¹]

and key in the number of the matrix name. This is illustrated in the third picture in Figure A-2.

4. **Enter the name of the second matrix and then press** ⌐⌐.

5. **Store the augmented matrix under a specified matrix name.**

To do so press ⌐STO►⌐, enter the name of the matrix in which you plan to store the augmented matrix, and then press ⌐ENTER⌐.

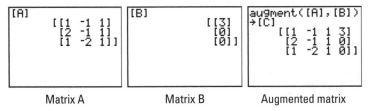

| Matrix A | Matrix B | Augmented matrix |

Figure A-2: Augmenting two matrices.

Copying One Matrix to Another

There are several situations in which you may want to copy the contents of one matrix to another. One of these is when you want to define a new matrix by adding rows and columns to an existing matrix. To do so, copy the existing matrix to a new matrix and then redefine the new matrix to have the number of rows and columns you desire. Defining and redefining matrices is described in the first section of this chapter.

To copy one matrix to another matrix, follow these steps:

1. **If necessary, press** ⌐2nd⌐⌐MODE⌐ **to access the Home screen.**

2. **Press** ⌐2nd⌐⌐x⁻¹⌐ **and key in the number of the matrix you plan to copy.**

3. **Press** ⌐STO►⌐.

4. **Press** ⌐2nd⌐⌐x⁻¹⌐ **and key in the number of the matrix that will house the copy.**

If you copy the contents of a matrix to another matrix, the contents of that other matrix will be erased and replaced with the contents of the matrix you're copying. If all ten matrices in the Matrix editor are defined and you don't want to sacrifice any of them in order to make a copy of a matrix, consider saving some of the already defined matrices on your PC. Chapter 18 tells you how to do so.

5. Press ENTER **to save a copy of the matrix under the new name.**

The third picture in Figure A-2 illustrates using STO▸ to save the contents of one matrix in another matrix.

Deleting a Matrix from Memory

To delete a matrix from the memory of the calculator, follow these steps:

1. Press 2nd + 2 5 **to access the list of matrices that are in the memory of the calculator.**

2. Repeatedly press ▾ **to place the indicator next to the matrix you want to delete and press** DEL.

3. When you're finished deleting matrices, press 2nd MODE **to exit (quit) the Memory Manager and return to the Home screen.**

Appendix B

Using Matrices

In This Chapter

▶ Using matrices in arithmetic expressions

▶ Finding a scalar multiple of a matrix

▶ Negating a matrix

▶ Using the identity matrix in an arithmetic expression

▶ Using matrices to solve a system of equations

▶ Converting a matrix to reduced row-echelon form

Matrix Arithmetic

When evaluating arithmetic expressions that involve matrices, you usually want to perform the following basic operations: scalar multiplication, negation (additive inverse), addition, subtraction, multiplication, and inversion (multiplicative inverse). You may also want to raise a matrix to an integral power or find its transpose. And you may want to use the identity matrix in an arithmetic expression.

Here's how you enter matrix operations in an arithmetic expression:

1. **Define the matrices in the Matrix editor.**

   This operation is explained in the first section of Appendix A.

2. **Press 2nd MODE to access the Home screen.**

   All matrix operations are performed on the Home screen.

3. **If you want to clear the Home screen, repeatedly press CLEAR.**

**4. Enter the operations you want to perform and press
[ENTER] when you're finished.**

As with algebraic expressions, the Home screen is where
you evaluate arithmetic expressions that involve matrices.
To paste the name of a matrix into an expression, press
[2nd][x⁻¹] and key in the number of the matrix name. Here's
how you enter the various operations into the arithmetic
expression:

- **Entering the scalar multiple of a matrix:**

  To enter the scalar multiple of a matrix in an arithmetic expression, enter the value of the scalar and
  then enter the name of the matrix as shown in the
  first picture in Figure B-1.

- **Negating a matrix:**

  To negate a matrix, press [(-)] and then enter the
  name of the matrix as shown in the second picture
  in Figure B-1.

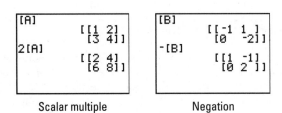

Scalar multiple   Negation

Figure B-1: The scalar multiple and the negation of a
matrix.

- **Entering the identity matrix:**

  You don't have to define an identity matrix in the
  Matrix editor in order to use it in an algebraic expression. To enter an identity matrix in an expression,
  press [2nd][x⁻¹][▶][5] to select the **identity** command
  from the Matrix Math menu. Then enter the size of
  the identity matrix. For example, enter **2** for the 2×2
  identity matrix, as in the first picture in Figure B-2.

- **Adding or subtracting matrices:**

  When adding or subtracting matrices, the matrices
  must have the same dimensions. If they don't, you
  will get the ERR: DIM MISMATCH error message.

Entering the addition and subtraction of matrices is straightforward; just combine the matrices by pressing ⊞ or ⊟, as appropriate. The second picture in Figure B-2 illustrates this process.

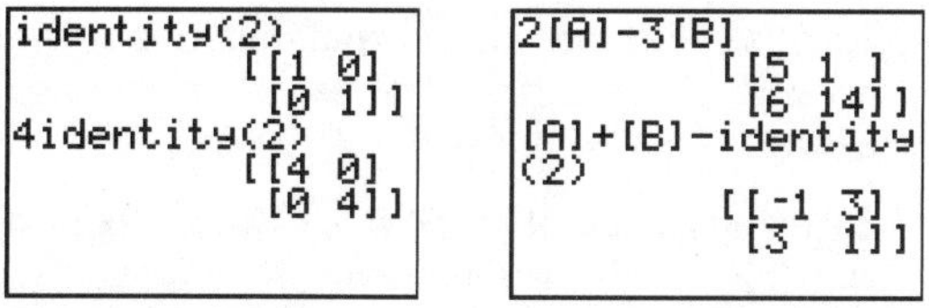

```
identity(2)
         [[1 0]
          [0 1]]
4identity(2)
         [[4 0]
          [0 4]]
```
```
2[A]-3[B]
         [[5 1 ]
          [6 14]]
[A]+[B]-identity
(2)
         [[-1 3]
          [3  1]]
```

Identity matrix   Adding and subtracting

Figure B-2: The identity matrix and addition/subtraction of matrices.

- **Multiplying two matrices:**

  When finding the product A*B of two matrices, the number of columns in the first matrix A must equal the number or rows in the second matrix B. If this condition isn't satisfied, you will get the ERR: DIM MISMATCH error message.

  The multiplication of matrices is straightforward; just indicate the product by using juxtaposition by pressing ⌧, as in the first picture in Figure B-3.

- **Finding the inverse of a matrix:**

  When finding the inverse of a matrix, the matrix must be *square* (number of rows = number of columns) and *nonsingular* (nonzero determinant). If it is not square, you will get the ERR: INVALID DIM error message. If is singular (determinant = 0), you will get the ERR: SINGULAR MAT error message. Evaluating the determinant of a matrix is explained in the next section.

  Entering the inverse of a matrix is straightforward; just enter the name of the matrix and then press [x⁻¹], as in the second picture of Figure B-3.

- **Raising a matrix to a positive integral power.**

  When finding the power of a matrix, the matrix must be square. If it isn't, you will get the ERR: INVALID DIM error message.

Only non-negative integers can be used for the power of a matrix. If the exponent isn't a nonnegative integer, you will get the ERR: DATA TYPE error message. If you raise a square matrix to the zero power, you will get the identity matrix.

To raise a square matrix to a negative power, raise the inverse of the matrix to the corresponding positive power.

Entering the positive power of a matrix is straightforward; just enter the name of the matrix, press ⌐∧⌐, and enter the power, as in the third picture of Figure B-3.

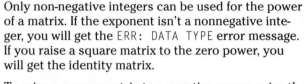

| Product of a matrix | Inverse of a matrix | Power of a matrix |

Figure B-3: The product and powers of matrices.

- **Transposing of a matrix.**

  To transpose a matrix in an arithmetic expression, enter the name of the matrix and then press ⌐2nd⌐⌐x⁻¹⌐⌐▶⌐⌐2⌐ to select the Transpose command from the Matrix Math menu as illustrated in the first picture in Figure B-4.

Finding the Determinant

When finding the determinant of a matrix, the matrix must be square (number of rows = number of columns). If it isn't, you get the ERR: INVALID DIM error message.

To evaluate the determinant of a matrix, follow these steps:

1. **If necessary, press ⌐2nd⌐⌐MODE⌐ to access the Home screen.**

2. **Press ⌐2nd⌐⌐x⁻¹⌐⌐▶⌐⌐1⌐ to select the det command from the Matrix Math menu.**

3. **Enter the name of the matrix and then press ⌐)⌐.**

   To enter the name of the matrix, press ⌐2nd⌐⌐x⁻¹⌐ and key in the number of the matrix name.

4. Press ENTER **to evaluate the determinant.**

This procedure is illustrated in the second picture in Figure B-4.

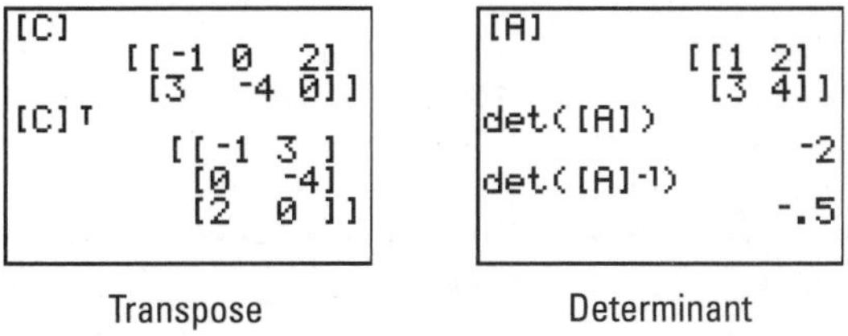

```
[C]
        [[-1  0   2]
         [3  -4   0]]
[C]ᵀ
        [[-1  3 ]
         [0  -4]
         [2   0 ]]
```

```
[A]
                [[1 2]
                 [3 4]]
det([A])
                      -2
det([A]⁻¹)
                     -.5
```

Transpose   Determinant

Figure B-4: The transpose and determinant of a matrix.

Solving a System of Equations

$$a_{11}x + a_{12}y + a_{13}z = b_1$$

$$a_{21}x + a_{22}y + a_{23}z = b_2$$

$$a_{31}x + a_{32}y + a_{33}z = b_3$$

Three matrices are associated with a system of linear equations: the coefficient matrix, the solution matrix, and the augmented matrix. For example, **A**, **B**, and **C**, are (respectively) the coefficient matrix, solution matrix, and augmented matrix for the system of equations just given.

$$A = \begin{bmatrix} a_{11} & a_{12} & a_{13} \\ a_{21} & a_{22} & a_{23} \\ a_{31} & a_{32} & a_{33} \end{bmatrix} \; B = \begin{bmatrix} b_{11} \\ b_{21} \\ b_{31} \end{bmatrix} \; C = \begin{bmatrix} a_{11} & a_{12} & a_{13} & b_1 \\ a_{21} & a_{22} & a_{23} & b_2 \\ a_{31} & a_{32} & a_{33} & b_3 \end{bmatrix}$$

Systems of linear equations can be solved by first putting the augmented matrix for the system in reduced row-echelon form. The mathematical definition of reduced row-echelon form isn't important here. It is simply an equivalent form of the original system of equations, which, when converted back to a system of equations, gives you the solutions (if any) to the original system of equations.

For example, when the reduced row-echelon matrix in the first picture in Figure B-5 is converted to a system of equations, it gives the solutions $x = -3$, $y = 3$, and $z = 9$. The matrix in the second picture in Figure B-5 converts to the system $x - z = 0$ and $y - z = -2$. This arrangement indicates that the system has an infinite number of solutions — namely, all solutions in which $x = z$ and $y = z - 2$, where

z is any real number. The third picture in Figure B-5 illustrates a system that has no solution — the last line of the matrix says that $0 = 1$, which is clearly impossible!

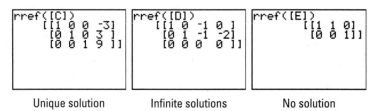

| Unique solution | Infinite solutions | No solution |

Figure B-5: Converting a matrix to reduced row-echelon form.

To solve a system of equations, follow these steps:

1. **Define the augmented matrix in the Matrix editor.**

   The augmented matrix for the system of equations is explained at the beginning of this section. (Appendix A explains how to define a matrix in the Matrix editor.)

   You can define the coefficient and solution matrices for the system of equations and then augment these matrices to form the augmented matrix. (For more about augmenting matrices, see Appendix A.)

2. **Press [2nd][MODE] to access the Home screen.**

3. **Press [2nd][x^{-1}][▶][ALPHA][APPS] to select the rref command. (On the TI-83, press [MATRX][▶][ALPHA][MATRX].)**

   You can also select the **rref** command by pressing [2nd][x^{-1}][▶], repeatedly pressing [▼] until the cursor is next to the **rref** command, and then pressing [ENTER].

4. **Enter the name of the matrix and then press [ )].**

   To enter the name of the matrix, press [2nd][x^{-1}] and key in the number of the matrix name.

5. **Press [ENTER] to put the augmented matrix in reduced row-echelon form.**

6. **To find the solutions (if any) to the original system of equations, convert the reduced row-echelon matrix to a system of equations.**

   The beginning of this section describes converting a reduced row-echelon matrix to a system of equations.

Index

• Symbols and Numerics •

: (colon) linking expressions, 28
, (comma) in numbers, avoiding, 22
( ) (parentheses)
  for exponential functions, 23
  fractional notation and, 22
  in Math menu functions, 30
  order of operations and, 23, 24,
    233–234
  for square-root function, 23
π key, 22
π, radians as fractional multiple of, 35
2nd key. *See* secondary functions

• A •

a + b*i* mode, 18
aborting processes
  in GeoMaster, 53, 54
  overview, 11, 13
ABOUT command, 172
abs function, 33
absolute value, finding, 33
accuracy issues for graphs, 110–112
addition
  entering expressions, 21–22
  of like measurements (GeoMaster),
    88–89
  of matrices, 248–249
  order of operations, 23–24
  vector sum (GeoMaster), 90
Advanced Finance application, 229
Advanced Settings editor (Probability
    Simulation application)
  overview, 175–176
  Pick Marbles simulator, 183
  Roll Dice simulator, 181
  Spin Spinner simulator, 186–187
  Toss Coins simulator, 177
Alpha key, 11–12
Alpha mode, 11–12, 52
angle bisectors, constructing
    (GeoMaster), 68–69

Angle menu
  degree/DMS conversion, 36–37
  degree/radian conversion, 35–36
  entering angles in DMS measure, 37
  overriding mode of angles, 37
  overview, 34–35
angles
  Degree versus Radian mode and, 234
  degree/DMS conversion, 36–37
  degree/radian conversion, 35–36
  entering in DMS measure, 37
  measuring in GeoMaster, 86–87
  overriding mode of, 37, 234
animate style for graphs, 109
answer, starting expressions
    with last, 25
applications. *See also specific*
    applications
  downloading, 10, 230–231
  installing, 231
  list of available, 229–230
Archive memory, transferring PC
    files to, 215
arcs (GeoMaster), 62–63
area (GeoMaster)
  of circle, triangle, or simple polygon,
    82–84
  of intersection of two polygons, 85–86
  of polygon with intersecting sides,
    84–85
arithmetic expressions
  combining, 28
  editing evaluated expressions, 14
  entering, 21–22
  evaluating, 21–22
  in inequalities, 153
  inserting in functions, 30–31
  inserting numbers from stored
    variables, 27
  matrices in, 247–250
  mini-programs, 28
  order of operations, 23–24, 233–234
  recalling last command, function, or
    expression, 14, 25–26
  starting with last answer, 25
  storing variables, 26–27

arrow keys, 2, 10, 12
assigning values to variables, 26–27, 41–42
augment command, 243
augmenting two matrices, 243–244
AxesOff command, 106
AxesOn command, 106

• B •

backup battery, 10
batteries, 9–10
"Batteries are low" message, 10
biasing. *See* weighting probability simulations
bisectors, 68–69
bound variable, 42
bounds for equation solutions, 42
box plots, 199–200, 202–203, 205
busy indicator, 13

• C •

cables
  TI-Graph Link, 213, 214–215, 231
  unit-to-unit link, 217–218
Cabri Jr. application, 5, 47–49, 225–226, 229
Calculate (CALC) menu
  definite integral command, 137–138
  dy/dx command, 136
  Inequality Graphing application and, 158
  intersect command, 134–135
  maximum command, 133–134
  minimum command, 133–134
  value command, 130–131
  zero command, 131–132
calculator-to-calculator communication. *See* communicating between calculators
calculator-to-PC communication. *See* communicating with a PC
card-drawing simulator. *See* Draw Cards simulator
Catalog Help application, 230
Catalog, using, 18–19
CellSheet application, 230

circles (GeoMaster)
  constructing, 60–61
  finding area, 82–84
  finding equation of, 91
  moving, 62
  resizing, 62, 73
Clear All command, 55
Clear key, 11, 53, 54
clearing. *See also* deleting
  all data lists, 191
  constructions in GeoMaster, 61
  data list contents, 193
  in GeoMaster, 53, 54
  GeoMaster screen, 55
  Home screen, 11, 13, 21
  INEQX and INEQY lists, 159
  mistakes when entering, 11
  tables, 126, 175
ClearTbl option, 175
Clock menu, 16, 18
clock, setting, 18
coefficient of determination, 208
coin-tossing simulator. *See* Toss Coins simulator
colon (:) linking expressions, 28
combinations, 167–168
combining expressions, 28
comma (,) in numbers, avoiding, 22
commands. *See also specific commands*
  editing already-evaluated commands, 14
  entering from Catalog, 18–19
  recalling last command, 14, 25–26
communicating between calculators
  linking calculators, 217–218
  transferring files to another calculator, 218–220
  transferring files to several calculators, 220–221
communicating with a PC
  connecting calculator and PC, 214–215
  downloading TI Connect software, 213–214
  installing TI Connect software, 214
  purchasing a link cable, 213
  starting TI Connect software, 214
  transferring files, 215
  upgrading the calculator OS, 216
complex numbers, 18, 226
Connected mode, 17

constructing geometric objects.
   See GeoMaster application
contrast adjustment for screen, 10
conventions in this book, 2
converting
   between decimals and fractions, 31
   between degrees and DMS, 36–37
   between degrees and radians, 35–36
coordinates of a point (GeoMaster)
   finding, 91
   placing points by, 58
CoordOff command, 105–106
CoordOn command, 105–106
copying one matrix to another, 244–245
correlation coefficient, 208
CPX submenu (Math menu), 30
cube function, 31
cube-root function, 31–32
cursor
   in Alpha mode, 12
   with 2nd key active, 11

• *D* •

data lists. *See* Stat List editor;
      statistical data
Dec function, 31
decimals
   converting between fractions and, 31
   generating random, 169
definite integral, 32, 33, 137–138
degree function, 35
Degree mode
   degree/DMS conversion, 36–37
   degree/radian conversion, 36
   graphing trig functions in, 234–235
   overriding, 37
   overview, 17
   trig functions and, 18
degrees
   degree/DMS conversion, 36–37
   degree/radian conversion, 35–36
deleting. *See also* clearing
   constructions in GeoMaster, 61
   entire entry, 13
   files in GeoMaster, 52–53
   Graph Databases, 116
   matrices from memory, 245
   objects in GeoMaster, 78
   part of an entry, 13
   statistical data, 193

derivative of a function, approximating,
      32–33
determinant of a matrix, finding,
      250–251
dice-rolling simulator. *See* Roll Dice
      simulator
differentiation, numerical, 32–33
dilating geometric objects (GeoMaster),
      97–98
displaying
   function and graph together, 114–115
   functions in tables, 122–126
   graph and table together, 126–127
   Home screen, 21
   matrices, 243
   panning in Function mode, 122
   tables in probability simulators, 179
   Zoom commands, 117–121
distance, finding (GeoMaster), 81–82
division expressions, entering, 21–22
DMS (degrees, minutes, seconds)
      measure, 36–37
Dot mode, 17
downloading
   applications, 10, 230–231
   Cabri Jr. application information,
      5, 225–226
   low batteries and, 10
   TI Connect software, 213–214
Draw Cards simulator, 188–189
DRAW menu (GeoMaster), 53, 57. *See
      also specific tools*
Draw Store menu, 115, 116
drawing line segments on a graph, 226
DuplicateName menu, 219–220
dy/dx command, 136

• *E* •

e key, 22
Edwards, C. C.
   *TI-83 Plus Graphing Calculator For
      Dummies*, 5, 226–227
   *TI-84 Plus Graphing Calculator For
      Dummies*, 1–5
Engineering (Eng) mode, 16
Enter key, 11, 12
entering
   angles in DMS measure, 37
   arithmetic expressions, 21–22
   editing entries, 13–14

entering *(continued)*
  equations in Equation Solver, 40–41
  expressions, 21–22
  fractions, 22
  functions, 18–19, 103–104, 141
  inequalities, 151–154
  inserting characters, 14
  letters and words, 11–12
  negative numbers, 22
  pasting function names, 104
  recalling last command, function, or
      expression, 14, 25–26
  setting the clock, 18
  statistical data, 191–192, 194–195
  typing over characters, 14
Equation Solver
  accessing, 40
  assigning values to variables, 41–42
  basic steps, 39–40
  defining solution bounds, 42
  entering or editing the equation, 40–41
  error messages, 43
  finding multiple solutions, 44
  guessing a solution, 42–43
  left–rt value, 43
  setting the mode, 40
  solving the equation, 43
erasing. *See* deleting
error messages
  common, 237–239
  ERR: ARGUMENT, 234, 237
  ERR: BAD GUESS, 43, 238
  ERR: DATA TYPE, 238, 250
  ERR: DIM MISMATCH, 238, 248, 249
  ERR: DOMAIN, 238
  ERR: INVALID, 238
  ERR: INVALID DIM, 235, 239, 249, 250
  ERR: MEMORY, 146
  ERR: NO SIGN CHNG, 43, 239
  ERR: SINGULAR MAT, 239, 249
  ERR: SYNTAX, 22, 233, 239
  ERR: WINDOW RANGE, 235, 239
  ERROR in tables, 125
  for fnInt function, 33
  for nDeriv function, 33
  negation versus subtraction key and,
      22, 233
  for slide shows, 146
errors, common, 233–235
ESC command, 174
exiting. *See* quitting
exponential functions, keys for, 23

expressions. *See* arithmetic expressions
ExprOff command, 106
ExprOn command, 106

• *F* •

FILE menu (GeoMaster)
  Clear All command, 55
  New File command, 51
  Open File command, 51
  overview, 53
files. *See also* transferring files
  creating (GeoMaster), 51–52
  deleting (GeoMaster), 52–53
  opening (GeoMaster), 52
financial features, 226
Float mode, 17
fMax function, 32
fMin function, 32, 234
fnInt function, 32, 33
Format menu, 105–106
formulas, entering data using, 195
fPart function, 34
Frac function, 31
fractional part of number, finding, 34
fractions
  converting between decimals and, 31
  entering, 22
  radians as fractional multiple of π, 35
Full screen mode, 18
Function (Func) mode
  entering functions, 103–104
  overview, 17
  panning in, 122
  X,T,Θ,n key in, 12
functions. *See also* graphing functions;
      specific functions
  defining as a sequence of functions,
      147–148
  displaying in tables, 122–126
  entering from Catalog, 18–19
  entering in Function mode, 103–104
  entering in Inequality Graphing
      application, 151–154
  entering in Transformation Graphing
      application, 141
  in Equation Solver, 41
  hyperbolic, Catalog for, 23
  improper arguments for, 234
  inserting Math menu functions, 30–31
  keys for, 22–23

in Math menu, 23
order of operations, 23–24
recalling last function, 25–26
referencing other functions in, 104
tracing a graph, 121–122
using Math menu functions, 30
value, finding, 129–131
viewing graph on same screen,
     114–115
zeros, finding, 131–132

• G •

gcd (greatest common divisor),
     finding, 34
gcd function, 34
GeoMaster application
  accessing menus, 53
  angle bisectors, constructing, 68–69
  Cabir Jr. versus, 47–49
  circles, constructing, 60–61
  Clear key, 54
  creating files, 51–52
  deleting constructions, 61
  deleting files, 52–53
  deleting objects, 78
  detaching points from objects, 71
  determining if lines are parallel or
     perpendicular, 74–75
  determining if three points are
     collinear, 76–77
  freestanding points, constructing,
     57–58
  Graph key, 54
  hiding objects, 77–78
  irregular polygons, constructing, 63–65
  labeling objects, 73
  labeling points, 58
  lines, segments, rays, and vectors,
     constructing, 59–60
  measurements, 82–91
  midpoints, constructing, 71–72
  moving objects, 72–74
  overview, 230
  parallel lines, constructing, 66–68
  perpendicular bisectors,
     constructing, 68
  perpendicular lines, constructing,
     66–68
  points of intersection, constructing,
     70–71

points on objects, constructing, 71
quitting, 50–51
recalling files, 52
redisplaying hidden objects, 78
re-entering after dirty exit, 51
re-entering after using menus, 50
regular polygons, constructing, 65–66
reshaping objects, 63, 73
resizing circles, 62, 73
saving your work, 51–52
starting, 49–50
transforming geometric objects, 93–99
triangles and arcs, constructing, 62–63
using menus, 50, 53–55
vector sum, constructing, 90
viewing window adjustment, 79
Graph Databases, 115–116
Graph key in GeoMaster, 54
Graph option, 175
graphing functions. *See also* Inequality
     Graphing application;
     Transformation Graphing
     application
  accuracy issues, 110–112
  animate style, 109
  definite integral, finding, 137–138
  deleting Graph Databases, 116
  entering functions to graph, 103–104
  error messages, 235
  for graphing transformations, 144
  highlighting functions to graph, 110
  line styles, 108
  minimum and maximum point,
     finding, 133–134
  multiple functions, 108–110
  parametric equations, 227
  Path style, 109
  piecewise-defined functions, 112–113
  points of intersection of two graphs,
     finding, 134–135
  polar equations, 227
  recalling Graph Databases, 116
  saving Graph Databases, 115–116
  sequences, 227
  shading styles, 109
  single functions, 105–108
  slope of a curve, finding, 135–136
  Stat Plots active and, 235
  tracing a graph, 121–122
  trig functions, 113–114, 234–235

graphing functions *(continued)*
  viewing function on same screen,
    114–115
  viewing table on same screen, 126–127
  Zoom commands for viewing, 117–120
graphing inequalities. *See* Inequality
    Graphing application
graphing styles, 108–109, 152
graphing transformations. *See*
    Transformation Graphing
    application
greatest common divisor (gcd),
    finding, 34
greatest-integer function, 34
GridOff command, 106
GridOn command, 106
G-T mode, 18, 126–127

• *H* •

hiding objects (GeoMaster), 77–78
histograms
  Probability Simulation application,
    178, 179, 181–182, 184, 187
  statistical data, 199, 200–202, 204
Home screen
  clearing, 11, 13, 21
  defined, 13
  displaying, 21
  expressions evaluated on, 21
  for probability simulators, 179
  returning to, 11, 13
  with Transformation Graphing
    application running, 140
Horiz mode, 18, 114–115
hyperbolic functions, 19

• *I* •

identity matrices, 248
Inequality Graphing application
  arithmetic expressions in
    inequalities, 153
  clearing INEQX and INEQY lists, 159
  entering inequalities in the X= editor,
    153–154
  entering inequalities in the Y= editor,
    151–153
  exiting other applications, 150, 235
  finding points of intersection, 156–158

graphing inequalities, 154
graphing styles, 152
highlighting inequalities to graph, 154
overview, 149, 230
Pol-Trace option, 155, 156–158
quitting, 151
Shades option, 155–156
solving linear programming problems,
    161–163
starting, 149–150
storing data points, 158–160
viewing stored data, 160
Zoom and Calc commands with, 158
INEQX and INEQY lists, 158, 159–160
Insert mode, 14
installing
  applications, 231
  TI Connect software, 214
int function, 34
integers
  finding the integer part of a
    number, 34
  generating random, 168
integration, numerical, 32, 33
Internet resources
  Cabri Jr. application information, 5,
    225–226
  downloading applications, 230–231
  programming the calculator, 5, 226
  Texas Instruments online store,
    213, 217
  TI Connect software, 213–214
  *TI-84 Plus Graphing Calculator For
    Dummies* site, 5
  upgrading the calculator OS, 216
  Wiley Web site, 5, 225–226
intersect command, 134–135
intersection. *See also* points of
    intersection
  finding area of intersection of two
    polygons (GeoMaster), 85–86
  finding area of polygon with
    intersecting sides (GeoMaster),
    84–85
  shading (Inequality Graphing
    application), 155–156
inverse functions, key for, 23
inverse of a matrix, 249
inverse trig functions, keys for, 22–23
iPart function, 34
iterative equations. *See* sequences

• **K** •

keys
  accessing secondary functions, 11
  Alpha, 11–12
  arrow keys, 2, 10, 12
  Clear, 11
  conventions in this book, 2
  e, 22
  Enter, 11, 12
  for functions, 22–23
  important keystrokes, 11
  On, 10
  π, 22
  pressing one at a time, 11
  2nd, 11
  using the keyboard, 10–11
  writing words, 11–12
  X,T,Θ,n, 12

• **L** •

labeling (GeoMaster), 58, 73
LabelOff command, 106
LabelOn command, 106
lcm function, 34
least common multiple (lcm),
      finding, 34
left–rt value (Equation Solver), 43
length, finding (GeoMaster), 81–82
letters, entering, 11–12
line style for graphs, 108
linear equations, solving a system of,
      251–252
linear programming problems, solving,
      161–163
lines (GeoMaster). *See also*
      measurements (GeoMaster)
  constructing between points, 59–60
  determining if parallel or
      perpendicular, 74–75
  determining if three points are
      collinear, 76–77
  finding equation of, 91
  perpendicular and parallel line
      construction, 66–68
  of reflection, 94
link cables
  TI-Graph Link, 213, 214–215, 231
  unit-to-unit link, 217–218

Link Send menu, 218, 220, 221
locating points (GeoMaster), 58

• **M** •

marble-picking simulator. *See* Pick
      Marbles simulator
Math menu
  accessing, 29
  changing submenus, 29
  CPX submenu, 30
  Equation Solver, 40
  functions in, 23
  inserting functions, 30–31
  MATH submenu, 29, 31–33
  NUM submenu, 29, 33–34
  PRB submenu, 30
  using functions, 30
Math Probability menu, 168, 169
MATH submenu (Math menu), 29, 31–33
matrices
  adding, 248–249
  in arithmetic expressions, 247–250
  augmenting two matrices, 243–244
  copying one to another, 244–245
  defined, 241
  defining, 241–242
  deleting from memory, 245
  displaying, 243
  editing, 243
  finding the determinant, 250–251
  further information, 227
  identity, 248
  inverse of, 249
  multiplying, 249
  negating, 248
  raising to a positive integral power,
      249–250
  scalar multiple, 248
  solving a system of equations, 251–252
  subtracting, 248–249
  transposing, 250
Matrix editor, 241–243
Matrix Math menu, 243
max function, 34
maximum. *See* minimum and maximum
maximum command, 133–134
MEAS menu (GeoMaster), 53, 81.
      See also specific tools

measurements (GeoMaster)
  adding and subtracting, 88–89
  of angles, 86–87
  area, 82–86
  coordinates of a point, 91
  equation of a line or circle, 91
  length and distance, 81–82
  slope, 89–90
  vector sum, 90
memory
  deleting data lists from, 193
  deleting GeoMaster files from, 52–53
  deleting Graph Databases from, 116
  deleting matrices from, 245
  transferring PC files to, 215
menus. *See also specific menus*
  in GeoMaster, 50, 53–55
  improper arguments for functions, 234
  overview, 14–15
midpoints, constructing (GeoMaster),
    71–72
min function, 34
minimum and maximum
  points on graph, finding, 133–134
  solving linear programming problems,
    161–163
  values, finding in list of numbers, 34
  values, finding location of, 32
minimum command, 133–134
mini-programs, writing, 28
MISC menu (GeoMaster), 53, 57. *See
    also specific tools*
Mode menu, 16–18
modes. *See also specific modes*
  for Equation Solver, 40
  overriding mode of angles, 37, 234
  setting, 16–18
  X,T,Θ,*n*, 12
moving objects (GeoMaster), 62, 63,
    72–74
multiplication
  entering expressions, 21–22
  of matrices, 249
  order of operations, 23–24

• *N* •

naming
  data lists, 194
  files in GeoMaster, 52

files transferred between calculators,
    219–220
  Graph Databases, 116
  labels in GeoMaster, 73
nDeriv function, 32–33
negating matrices, 248
negation key, subtraction key versus,
    22, 233
New File command, 51
Normal mode, 16
NoteFolio application, 230
NUM submenu (Math menu), 29, 33–34

• *O* •

OK command, 172
On key, 10
one-variable statistical data
  analyzing, 205–207
  plotting, 199–203
  tracing plots, 204–205
Open File command, 51
OPTN command, 172, 173
order of operations, 23–24, 233–234
Organizer application, 230
OS (operating system), upgrading, 216
outliers, 203
overriding, 234
overriding mode of angles, 234
overtyping characters, 14
Overwrite command, 219

• *P* •

parallel lines (GeoMaster)
  constructing, 66–68
  determining, 74–75
parametric equations, graphing, 227
Parametric (Par) mode, 12, 17
parentheses [( )]
  for exponential functions, 23
  fractional notation and, 22
  in Math menu functions, 30
  order of operations and, 23, 24,
    233–234
  for square-root function, 23
pasting function names, 104
Path style for graphs, 109
PC. *See* communicating with a PC
permutations, 167–168

perpendicular bisectors, constructing
(GeoMaster), 68
perpendicular lines (GeoMaster)
bisectors, 68
constructing, 66–68
determining, 74–75
π key, 22
π, radians as fractional multiple of, 35
Pick Marbles simulator
displaying tables, 179
graph and table settings, 174–175
Home screen, 179, 182–183
overview, 182
reading the graph and table, 184
saving data, 185
Settings editors, 183
simulating picking marbles, 182–184
Trial Set option, 174
weighted outcomes, 175–176
piecewise-defined functions, graphing,
112–113
points (GeoMaster)
detaching from objects, 71
determining if collinear, 76–77
finding coordinates, 91
freestanding, constructing, 57–58
of intersection, constructing, 70–71
labeling, 58
midpoints, constructing, 71–72
on objects, constructing, 71
placing precisely, 58
of rotation, 95–96
points of intersection
finding in Inequality Graphing
application, 156–158
linear programming problems, 162, 163
between objects, constructing, 70–71
between two graphs, finding, 134–135
Pol-Trace option, 155, 156–158
polar equations, graphing, 227
polar form, for complex number
display, 18
Polar mode, 12
PolarGC command, 105
polygons (GeoMaster)
constructing irregular, 63–65
constructing regular, 65–66
finding intersection of sides, 84–85
with intersecting sides, finding area,
84–85
intersection of two, finding area, 85–86

simple, finding area, 82–84
simple, defined, 83
PRB submenu (Math menu), 30
probability. *See also* Probability
Simulation application
combinations, 167–168
permutations, 167–168
random number generation, 168–169
Probability Simulation application. *See
also specific simulators*
ClearTbl option, 175
displaying tables in simulators, 179
Draw Cards simulator, 188–189
executing commands at bottom of
screen, 172
graph and table settings, 174–175
Graph option, 175
histograms, 179
Home screen for simulators, 179
overview, 171, 230
Pick Marbles simulator, 182–184
quitting, 172
returning to previous screen, 174
Roll Dice simulator, 179–182
saving your data, 185, 189
seeding the random number
generator, 173
Settings editors, 174–176
simulators, 174
Spin Spinner simulator, 185–187
starting, 171–172
StoTble option, 175
Toss Coins simulator, 176–179
Trial Set option, 174
Update option, 175
weighted outcomes, 175–176
programming the calculator, 5, 226

QUIT command, 172
quitting
aborting processes, 13
GeoMaster, 50–51
Inequality Graphing application, 151
Probability Simulation application, 172
slide shows for transformations, 147
stopping file transfer in progress, 220
Transformation Graphing application,
141

• R •

r function, 36
Radian mode
  converting degrees to radians, 35
  entering angle in degrees in, 234
  for graphing trig functions, 18, 113, 114
  overriding, 37, 234
  overview, 17
radians, 35–36
RAM, transferring PC files to, 215
rand command, 169
randInt command, 168
random number generation, 168–169,
    173
rays, constructing (GeoMaster), 59–60
re^θi mode, 18
Real mode, 18
recalling
  files in GeoMaster, 52
  Graph Databases, 116
  last command, function, or
    expression, 14, 25–26
  saved data lists, 196–197
rectangular form, for complex number
    display, 18
RectGC command, 105
redefining the bound variable, 42
redisplaying hidden objects
    (GeoMaster), 78
reflecting geometric objects
    (GeoMaster), 94–95
regression modeling, 208–210
Remember icon, 5
removing. See deleting
Rename command, 219
renaming. See naming
reshaping objects (GeoMaster), 63, 73
resizing circles (GeoMaster), 62, 73
reusing. See also recalling
  last answer to start expressions, 25
  last command, function, or
    expression, 14, 25–26
Roll Dice simulator
  displaying tables, 179
  graph and table settings, 174–175
  Home screen, 179, 180
  overview, 179
  reading the graph and table, 181–182
  saving data, 185
  Settings editors, 180–181
  simulating rolling dice, 180–181

Trial Set option, 174
  weighted outcomes, 175–176
roots
  cube-root function, 31–32
  order of operations, 23–24
  square-root function, 23
  xth root function, 30, 32
rotating geometric objects
    (GeoMaster), 95–97
round function, 33

• S •

saving
  data lists, 196
  files in GeoMaster, 51–52
  Graph Databases, 115–116
  Probability Simulation table data,
    185, 189
scalar multiple of a matrix, 248
scatter plots, 203–204, 205
Scientific (Sci) mode, 16
screen. See also viewing window
  busy indicator, 13
  clearing, 11, 13
  contrast adjustment, 10
  graph accuracy and size of, 110
scrolling menus, 15
secondary functions, 2, 11. See also
    specific functions
segments, constructing (GeoMaster),
    59–60
seq command, 195
Sequence (Seq) mode, 12, 17
sequences, 17, 227
Sequential mode, 17
Set Clock mode, 18
Settings editors
  Draw Cards simulator, 188–189
  Pick Marbles simulator, 183
  Probability Simulation application,
    overview, 174–176
  Roll Dice simulator, 180–181
  Spin Spinner simulator, 186–187
  Toss Coins simulator, 177
  Transformation Graphing application,
    142–144, 145–146
ShadeRes variable, 154
Shades option, 155–156
shading graphs, 109, 154, 155–156
simple polygons, finding area, 82–84
Simultaneous (Simul) mode, 17

slide shows for transformations, 145–147
slope of a curve, finding, 135–136
slope of a function, approximating, 32–33
slope of a line, finding (GeoMaster), 89–90
solving equations
  in Equation Solver, 39–44
  guessing a solution, 42–43
  of a line or circle (GeoMaster), 91
  system of equations, 251–252
sorting data lists, 197–198
Spin Spinner simulator
  displaying tables, 179
  graph and table settings, 174–175
  Home screen, 179, 186
  overview, 185
  reading the graph and table, 187
  saving data, 185
  Settings editors, 186–187
  simulating spinning spinners, 186–187
  Trial Set option, 174
  weighted outcomes, 175–176
square function, key for, 23
square-root function, key for, 23
starting
  GeoMaster application, 49–50
  Inequality Graphing application, 149–150
  Probability Simulation application, 171–172
  slide shows for transformations, 147
  TI Connect software, 214
  Transformation Graphing application, 137–138
Stat List editor
  clearing all data lists, 191
  clearing contents of data list, 193
  creating user-named data lists, 194–195
  deleting a column, 193
  deleting an entry in a data list, 193
  editing data list entries, 193
  entering data, 192
  formulas for entering data, 195
  recalling saved data lists, 196–197
  saving data lists, 196
  sorting data lists, 197–198
Stat Plots, graphing functions and, 105
Stat Plots menu, 200

statistical data
  analyzing one-variable data, 205–207
  analyzing two-variable data, 205–206, 207
  box plots, constructing, 202–203
  clearing all data lists, 191
  clearing contents of data list, 193
  creating user-named data lists, 194–195
  deleting a column in Stat List editor, 193
  deleting an entry in a data list, 193
  deleting data lists from memory, 193
  editing data list entries, 193
  entering data, 191–192
  formulas for entering data, 195
  histograms, constructing, 200–202
  outliers, 203
  plotting one-variable data, 199–203
  plotting two-variable data, 203–204
  recalling saved data lists, 196–197
  regression modeling, 208–210
  saving data lists, 196
  scatter plots, constructing, 203–204
  sorting data lists, 197–198
  tracing plots, 204–205
  xy-line plots, constructing, 203–204
stopping. *See* quitting
storing numbers in variables, 26–27, 41–42
StoTble option, 175
StudyCards application, 230
subtraction
  of like measurements (GeoMaster), 88–89
  of matrices, 248–249
  negation versus subtraction key and, 22, 233
  order of operations, 23–24
subtraction key, negation key versus, 22, 233
systems of linear equations, solving, 251–252

● *T* ●

Table Setup editor, 123–124
tables
  automatically generated, 124–125
  clearing, 126, 175
  displaying functions in, 122–126

tables *(continued)*
  displaying in Probability Simulation
    application, 179
  ERROR in, 125
  Pick Marbles simulator, 184
  Roll Dice simulator, 182
  settings in Probability Simulation
    application, 175
  Spin Spinner simulator, 187
  Toss Coins simulator, 178–179
  user-generated, 125
  viewing graph on same screen,
    126–127
Technical Stuff icon, 5
tessellating the plane (GeoMaster),
  98–99
Texas Instruments
  downloading applications from,
    230–231
  downloading TI Connect software
    from, 213–214
  online store, 213, 217
  OS upgrade from, 216
TI Connect software
  connecting calculator and PC, 214–215
  downloading, 213–214
  installing applications and, 231
  installing the software, 214
  starting, 214
  transferring files, 215
  upgrading the calculator OS, 216
*TI-83 Plus Graphing Calculator For
  Dummies* (Edwards, C. C.), 5,
  226–227
*TI-84 Plus Graphing Calculator For
  Dummies* (Edwards, C. C.)
  assumptions about the reader, 3
  conventions, 2
  icons in margins, 4–5
  organization, 3–4
  overview, 1
  using, 2, 5
  Web site, 5
TI-Graph Link cable, 213, 214–215, 231
tiling the plane (GeoMaster), 98–99
time, setting, 18
Toss Coins simulator
  displaying tables, 179
  graph and table settings, 174–175
  Home screen, 176–177, 179
  overview, 176

reading the graph and table, 178–179
  saving data, 185
  Settings editors, 177
  simulating tossing of coins, 176–178
  Trial Set option, 174
  weighted outcomes, 175–176
tracing
  graphs, 121–122
  statistical data plots, 204–205
transcendental numbers, keys for, 22
transferring files
  to another calculator, 218–220
  between PC and calculator, 215
  to several calculators, 220–221
  stopping transfer in progress, 220
Transformation Graphing application
  entering functions, 141
  graphing transformations of a single
    function, 142–145
  graphing transformations of multiple
    functions, 147–148
  other graphing features with, 145
  overview, 139
  Play and Play-Fast play types, 142,
    145–147
  Play-Pause play type, 142–145
  quitting, 141
  Settings editor, 142–144, 145–146
  slide show creation, 145–147
  starting, 137–138
transforming geometric objects
    (GeoMaster)
  dilating, 97–98
  reflecting, 94–95
  rotating, 95–97
  tiling the plane, 98–99
  translating, 93–94
translating geometric objects
    (GeoMaster), 93–94
transposing matrices, 250
TRFM menu (GeoMaster), 53. *See also
  specific tools*
Trial Set option
  overview, 174
  Pick Marbles simulator, 183, 184
  Roll Dice simulator, 180, 181
  Spin Spinner simulator, 186, 187
  Toss Coins simulator, 177, 178
triangles (GeoMaster)
  changing shape, 63
  constructing, 62–63

finding area, 82–84
moving, 63
trigonometric functions
Degree mode and, 234–235
graphing, 113–114, 234–235
keys for, 22–23
in piecewise-defined functions,
graphing, 113
Radian mode for graphing, 18
turning on and off, 10
two-variable statistical data
analyzing, 205–206, 207
plotting, 203–204
regression modeling, 208–210
tracing plots, 205
typing over characters, 14

• U •

undoing Zoom commands, 120
unions, shading in Inequality Graphing
application, 155–156
unit-to-unit link cable, 217–218
Update option, 175, 180, 183
upgrading the calculator OS, 216
user-named data lists, creating, 194–195

• V •

value command, 130–131
values
absolute, finding, 33
assigning to variables, 26–27, 41–42
of functions, finding, 129–131
minimum and maximum, finding,
32, 34
variables
assigning values to, 26–27, 41–42
for graphing functions, 106–108
for graphing transformations, 143,
145, 146
inserting numbers in arithmetic
expressions, 27
in one- and two-variable data
analysis, 206
set in Function mode Window editor,
106–108
X,T,Θ,*n*, 12
vector construction (GeoMaster), 59–60
vector sum construction
(GeoMaster), 90

vertical asymptotes in viewing window,
111–112
viewing. *See* displaying
viewing window. *See also* screen; Zoom
commands
adjusting in GeoMaster, 79
adjusting with ZSquare command, 110
graph accuracy and size of, 110–111
vertical asymptotes in, 111–112

• W •

Warning! icon, 5
Web sites. *See* Internet resources
weighting probability simulations
overview, 175–176
Pick Marbles simulator, 183
Roll Dice simulator, 181
Spin Spinner simulator, 186–187
Toss Coins simulator, 177
Wiley Web site, 5, 225–226
Window editor
ERR: WINDOW RANGE error, 235
GeoMaster viewing window
adjustment, 79
graphing functions and, 106–108
graphing inequalities and, 154
graphing transformations and, 144
plotting one-variable data and, 202
tracing a graph and, 122
user-generated tables and, 125
variables set in Function mode,
106–108
ZoomFit command and, 118
words, writing, 11–12

• X •

X= editor
evaluating definite integrals, 137
finding the slope of a curve, 136
Inequality Graphing application,
153–154
X,T,Θ,*n* key, 12
x-intercepts. *See* zeros of a function
Xmax variable, 106–107, 121, 122
Xmin variable, 106–107, 121, 122
Xres variable, 107–108
Xscl variable, 107
xth root function, 30, 32
xy-line plots, 203–204, 205

• Y •

Y= editor
  displaying functions in tables and, 122, 123, 125
  entering piecewise-defined functions, 112–113
  entering single functions, 104
  entering trig functions, 114
  finding value of a function and, 130
  graph styles, 108–109
  highlighting functions to graph, 110, 200
  highlighting Stat Plots to graph, 200
  Inequality Graphing application, 150, 151–153
  recalling settings, 116
  saving settings, 115–116
  tracing a graph and, 121
  Transformation Graphing application, 140, 141
  turning off Stat Plots, 105
  viewing with graph, 114–115
Ymax variable, 107, 121, 122
Ymin variable, 107, 121, 122
"Your batteries are low" message, 9–10
Yscl variable, 107

• Z •

ZBox command, 120
ZDecimal command, 118
zero command, 131–132
zeros of a function, 129, 131–132
ZInteger command, 119
Zoom commands. *See also specific commands*
  for finding appropriate viewing window for graph, 118
  for graphing functions in a preset viewing window, 117–118
  Inequality Graphing application and, 158
  for readjusting viewing window, 119
  undoing, 120
  for zooming in and out from graphed function, 119–120
Zoom In command, 119
Zoom Memory menu, 120
Zoom Out command, 119
ZoomFit command, 118, 234–235
ZoomStat command, 118, 201–202
ZSquare command, 110, 119
ZStandard command, 117–118
ZTrig command, 118, 144, 234–235

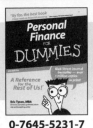

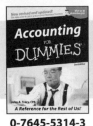

FOR DUMMIES®

A world of resources to help you grow

HOME, GARDEN & HOBBIES

Feng Shui
0-7645-5295-3

Gardening
0-7645-5130-2

Guitar
0-7645-5106-X

Also available:

Auto Repair For Dummies
(0-7645-5089-6)

Chess For Dummies
(0-7645-5003-9)

Home Maintenance For Dummies
(0-7645-5215-5)

Organizing For Dummies
(0-7645-5300-3)

Piano For Dummies
(0-7645-5105-1)

Poker For Dummies
(0-7645-5232-5)

Quilting For Dummies
(0-7645-5118-3)

Rock Guitar For Dummies
(0-7645-5356-9)

Roses For Dummies
(0-7645-5202-3)

Sewing For Dummies
(0-7645-5137-X)

FOOD & WINE

Cooking
0-7645-5250-3

Cookies
0-7645-5390-9

Wine
0-7645-5114-0

Also available:

Bartending For Dummies
(0-7645-5051-9)

Chinese Cooking For Dummies
(0-7645-5247-3)

Christmas Cooking For Dummies
(0-7645-5407-7)

Diabetes Cookbook For Dummies
(0-7645-5230-9)

Grilling For Dummies
(0-7645-5076-4)

Low-Fat Cooking For Dummies
(0-7645-5035-7)

Slow Cookers For Dummies
(0-7645-5240-6)

TRAVEL

Italy
0-7645-5453-0

Hawaii
0-7645-5438-7

Las Vegas
0-7645-5448-4

Also available:

America's National Parks For Dummies
(0-7645-6204-5)

Caribbean For Dummies
(0-7645-5445-X)

Cruise Vacations For Dummies 2003
(0-7645-5459-X)

Europe For Dummies
(0-7645-5456-5)

Ireland For Dummies
(0-7645-6199-5)

France For Dummies
(0-7645-6292-4)

London For Dummies
(0-7645-5416-6)

Mexico's Beach Resorts For Dummies
(0-7645-6262-2)

Paris For Dummies
(0-7645-5494-8)

RV Vacations For Dummies
(0-7645-5443-3)

Walt Disney World & Orlando For Dummies
(0-7645-5444-1)

Available wherever books are sold. Go to www.dummies.com or call 1-877-762-2974 to order direct.

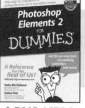

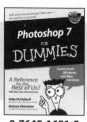

 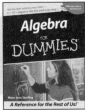 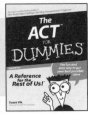